The Early Years Professional's
Complete Companion

The Early Years Professional's Complete Companion

Second Edition

Pam Jarvis, Jane George
and Wendy Holland

PEARSON

Harlow, England • London • New York • Boston • San Francisco • Toronto • Sydney
Auckland • Singapore • Hong Kong • Tokyo • Seoul • Taipei • New Delhi
Cape Town • São Paulo • Mexico City • Madrid • Amsterdam • Munich • Paris • Milan

Pearson Education Limited

Edinburgh Gate
Harlow CM20 2JE
United Kingdom
Tel: +44 (0)1279 623623
Fax: +44 (0)1279 431059
Web: www.pearson.com/uk

First published 2010 (print)
Second edition published 2013 (print and electronic)

© Pearson Education Limited 2010 (print)
© Pearson Education Limited 2013 (print and electronic)

ISBN: 978-0-273-77902-5 (print)
       978-0-273-77926-1 (PDF)
       978-0-273-77927-8 (ePub)
       978-0-273-77925-4 (eText)

British Library Cataloguing-in-Publication Data
A catalogue record for the print edition is available from the British Library

Library of Congress Cataloging-in-Publication Data
Jarvis, Pam.
The early years professional's complete companion / Pam Jarvis, Jane George and Wendy Holland.–2nd ed.
    p. cm.
  Includes bibliographical references and index.
  ISBN 978-0-273-77902-5
  1. Early childhood education–Handbooks, manuals, etc. 2. Early childhood teachers–Professional relationships–Handbooks, manuals, etc. I. George, Jane. II. Holland, Wendy. III. Title.
  LB1139.23.J37 2013
  371.21–dc23
                                                                              2012029878

10 9 8 7 6 5 4 3 2 1
16 15 14 13 12

Print edition typeset in 9.5/13pt Stone Serif by 73
Print edition printed and bound in Great Britain by Ashford Colour Press Ltd, Gosport

NOTE THAT ANY PAGE CROSS REFERENCES REFER TO THE PRINT EDITION

This book is dedicated to:

My mother, Norma Watts Crouch, who was born two days after British women finally achieved the franchise on the same basis as men: what a long way both you and we have travelled in your lifetime!

Pam Jarvis

To my parents, Mary and Leslie Robinson, who knew that a good childhood relies upon parents who freely give unconditional love and limitless time to their children. They invested their hopes in me and offered me many of the opportunities that they had been denied, I hope I have made good use of them.

Jane George

This book is dedicated to all those young children it has been my delight to know and share with the 'awe and wonder' that is early childhood. During my time in Early Years Education, the insight, honesty and imagination of young children have never ceased to amaze and encourage me. I would like to make this dedication especially to my grandchildren, Joseph, George and Alice, whose young lives continue to reinforce for me the richness in every child.

Wendy Holland

'... a thorough analysis of the contemporary new-era EYPS programme. ... The book presents a multi-disciplinary perspective and will add value to those studying across each of the new-era EYPS pathways.'

Denise Reardon, Department of Childhood Studies, Canterbury Christ Church University

'*The Early Years Professional's Complete Companion* is a valuable resource for any practitioner undertaking or considering Early Years Professional Status. It provides a wealth of support, ideas and guidance for anyone considering EYPS, as well as those who are already on the journey to achieving the award.'

Emma Slaughter, Regional Service Leader (EYPS), Eastern Leadership Centre

'This textbook will help students to build on their own knowledge and practice; it supports their thinking and encourages them to critically evaluate themselves via case studies, reflection and further reading. A very informative book which will help candidates on their EYPS journey.'

Nikki Fairchild, EYPS Programme Coordinator, University of Chichester

Contents

About the authors

Dr Pam Jarvis is a graduate psychologist, social scientist and educational researcher, with many years of experience of creating and teaching developmental, social science and social policy modules for Education/Child Development programmes for community, further and higher education; most recently within the area of Early Years Professional training. She has Qualified Teacher Status and has taught in school within her specialist subject areas of psychology, sociology and history. She is currently working as a Senior Lecturer in the McMillan School of Teaching, Health and Care, Bradford College, and as an Open University tutor, supporting education and child development students on a wide range of programmes at undergraduate and Masters level. She is also an active researcher, and has recently finished a piece of historical research on the life and work of Early Years pioneer Margaret McMillan. She was awarded a PhD by Leeds Metropolitan University in 2005 for her thesis 'The role of rough and tumble play in children's social and gender role development in the early years of primary school'. Her recent publications include:

Jarvis, P. (2010) '"Born to play": The biocultural roots of "rough and tumble" play, and its impact upon human development', pp.61–78 in P. Broadhead, J. Howard and E. Wood (eds) *Play and Learning in Early Years Settings: From research to practice.* London: Sage.

Brock, A., Dodds, S., Jarvis, P. and Olusoga, Y. (2009) *Perspectives on Play: Learning for life.* Harlow: Pearson Education.

Jarvis, P. (2009) 'Play, narrative and learning in education: a biocultural perspective', *Educational and Child Psychology*, 26 (2), pp.66–76.

Jane George (MEd) has extensive experience in the voluntary sector, in toddler groups and playgroups and managing and teaching for the Pre-School Learning Alliance. She has worked in Community Education developing and delivering Parent and Toddler at Play classes in areas of social deprivation and to various cultural groups. Working in colleges across West Yorkshire, she has developed and delivered a variety of Early Years programmes across the range of further and higher education. She was awarded an MEd in 2002. In her current role of Programme Manager for Early Years, Health and Care at Bradford College she manages the curriculum across the full range of Further and Higher Education programmes in Early Years and Health and Care, including the Foundation Degree in Early Years; the BA Hons Early Childhood Studies/Early Years Practice; the Masters in Early Years Practice and all four Early Years Professional Status Pathways. Her recent publications include:

Jarvis, P., Newman, S., Holland, W. and George, J. (2012) *Research in the Early Years Setting: A step by step guide*. Harlow: Pearson Longman.

Jarvis, P. and George, J. (2010) 'Thinking it through: rough and tumble play', pp. 164–78 in J. Moyles (ed.) *Thinking it Through: Reflecting on playful pedagogy in the early years*. Buckingham: Open University Press.

Wendy Holland (MA) has experience of teaching in mainstream nurseries, primary and special schools for over 30 years. From the 1970s onwards, her focus has been around inclusive provision and practice for childen 0 to 8 years. Through the establishment of mother and toddler groups and playgroups for children with particular needs, integrated mainstream provision for hearing and hearing impaired nursery and primary aged children, she has pursued her particular interests around the inclusion of parents/carers in the caring and educative process. The importance of the role of reflective practitioner as an agent for change is another of her interests, and she is presently involved in the training and assessing of Early Years Professionals at Bradford College. She is also currently working in the Teaching, Health and Care sector at Bradford College developing and producing modules for the BA (Hons) with Qualified Teacher Status degree and the BEd Studies degree, alongside supporting students engaged in a range of undergraduate and Masters level programmes. Her recent publications include:

Jarvis, P. and Holland, W. (2011) 'The early years professional and the children's centre: at the hub of the "Big Society"?', pp.79–92 in A. Brock and C. Rankin (eds) *Making it Work for the Child: Professionalism for the early years interdisciplinary team*. London: Continuum.

Holland, W. (2009) 'The patchwork quilt', pp.25–32 in G. Murphy and M. Power (eds) *A Story to Tell*. Stoke-on-Trent: Trentham Books.

Dr Clive Opie is the Dean of the McMillan School of Teaching, Health and Care, at Bradford College. He has been involved in the Early Years Professional Status initiative since its inception, taking on the role Chair of the EYPS Executive Committee while Deputy Director of the Institute of Education at Manchester Metropolitan University. His research interests have centred on the use of IT to support and enhance teaching and learning in a range of settings, e.g. schools, and undergraduate and postgraduate degree courses. He has had substantial experience of teaching at Masters level in the area of research procedures and data analysis. His current work revolves around developing an Enhanced Partnership with schools and his most recent paper 'Developing ITE without wholesale change to practice – an Enhanced Partnership' was presented at the conference on Re-Imagining Initial Teacher Education, Dublin (2011). Other relevant publications include a text jointly authored with Judith Bell *Learning from Research – Getting More from your Data*, Open University (2002) and acting as editor/author for *Doing Educational Research – A Guide for First Time Researchers*, Sage (2004).

Doreen Malcolm has over 19 years of working in local authority Early Years settings. She gained Early Years Professional Status in May 2008 and since 2009 has worked as the EYPS lead mentor at Bradford College. Her vast experience of practice, leadership and management has led her to work with diverse groups of practitioners, children, families and other professionals. She also teaches on higher and further education modules.

Poonam Cant gained Early Years Professional Status in June 2007 and now works as a trainer, mentor and assessor for Bradford College with EYPS candidates. She has worked as a volunteer with children since she was 15 years old and now owns and manages her own childcare business. Her experiences over the years have led her to work with children with English as a second language, children with special needs and children with unique family circumstances. This significant experience, coupled with leadership and managerial skills obtained from her previous career as a chartered accountant and training manager, has given her the appropriate skills to work with and understand EYP candidates.

Foreword

The fact that I am being asked to write the foreword to a second edition of this book in the space of three years reflects how well the first edition has sold and the publishers' confidence it will continue, with updates, to meet market needs. During the period of the initial programme delivery (2006–11), its success will no doubt have helped those wishing to attain Early Years Professional Status (EYPS) to achieve their goal of becoming future leaders of Early Years practice. It is rewarding to note that the present government has reaffirmed its commitment to graduate leadership of practice in English Early Years settings; this offers some personal satisfaction to those who care passionately about raising the status of Early Years leaders, in order to facilitate the healthy development of children from the earliest days of life.

The present policy for Early Years detailed in the document *Supporting Families in the Foundation Years* (DFE 2011) has led to the redesigned training programme for EYPS with a new set of standards (DFE 2012a) that have been slimmed down to match the newly streamlined *Early Years Foundation Stage* (DFE 2012b). After some lengthy and detailed negotiation, contracts for the delivery of EYPS were awarded in October 2011, and it was satisfying to learn that the McMillan School of Teaching, Health and Care, operating from Bradford College University Centre, will continue to support EYPS candidates as part of a larger regional consortium, with the authors of this book continuing to comprise the core EYPS team at the college.

This second edition sees *The EYP's Complete Companion* updated and also enhanced with input from Doreen Malcolm, who originally came to McMillan as an EYPS candidate. Doreen currently uses her considerable experience as a leader of Early Years practice in Bradford to contribute to the work of the McMillan's EYPS teaching and training team. The team as a whole continues to reflect a very high level of experience in a wide range of roles in Early Years related disciplines, while individual members continue to share their personal enthusiasm and commitment to Early Years, providing professional encouragement not only to their own candidates but also through the pages of this book, to candidates across the nation.

While the new national EYPS programme has jettisoned the past pathway names of 'short', 'long' and 'full' for the more meaningful ones of Graduate Practitioner Pathway, Undergraduate Practitioner Pathway and Graduate Entry Pathway, additionally introducing the new Undergraduate Entry Pathway, the key change resides in the review update and streamlining of the original 39 standards to eight standards with a range of sub-elements. This second edition incorporates these changes so that the positive attributes I noted in my foreword to the first edition are equally valid in the second. It is interesting to note that little has changed beyond relevant updating; the skills and knowledge needed to lead successfully in Early Years practice endure beyond the 'tinkering' of successive governments.

What if I want to attain EYPS? What do each of these pathways offer? I might possess high levels of practitioner competence and dedication but still harbour a range of qualms about the education and training I have to engage with at University level 6 (final year). So where might I find material to start to help me overcome my almost certain apprehension of academic study? Or material to help me engage with theoretical perspectives and thus help me to understand better my existing practice and help me to make it more effective? Or even material couched within a context that also explores theory and practice within many areas important to me in my day-to-day work as an Early Years practitioner, for example communicating and working in partnership with families and carers; teamwork and collaboration; and providing an environment for play and learning? Material, perhaps even more crucially, which could provide words of support from those who have achieved EYPS and who, through their stories, could help me to achieve my goal, both as writers and co-writers of chapters and as interviewees? That material is all in this book.

The authors start with an overview of EYPS standards and their supporting statements, then move on to an introduction to the EYPS framework, explaining the basis for its inception, the evolution of its structure and, critically, its implications for the range of learners who are seeking the status. They then move on to consider various theoretical perspectives, and at the beginning of each chapter helpfully identify which of the EYPS standards/sub-elements will be addressed within it. Throughout the book, chapters are structured to invite the learner to explore and reflect upon their own practice through the use of appropriate contextual material, concluding with the provision of a comprehensive set of references for further reading. While the latter chapters engage more specifically with the EYPS process, considering such aspects as working with your mentor and placement supervisor, and partnership and leadership in Early Years, it is perhaps the last chapter 'Early Years Professionals: in their own words', which will convince even the most reticent learner that they can achieve EYPS if they have the will, enthusiasm and fascination to seek the considerable responsibility of leading practice with young children in this most important stage of development.

This material recognises the base from which many seeking to achieve EYPS commence, and skilfully guides them through what must initially seem like a labyrinth of EYPS terminology and academic theory. This second edition brings the specific training requirements of EYPS referred to in the book up to date and thus, hopefully, will meet the needs of candidates to the end of the present contractual period in March 2015.

As I concluded in my foreword to the first edition: the material in this book typifies the enthusiasm and encouragement of its authors and will undoubtedly help those wishing to attain EYPS achieve their goal and, in so doing, help them to become positive, knowledgeable and inspiring leaders of Early Years practice.

Dr Clive Opie
Dean
School of Teaching, Health and Care
Bradford College
May 2012

References

DFE (2011) *Supporting Families in the Foundation Years*. London, DFE.

DFE (2012b) *The Early Years Foundation Stage*. Available at: http://media.education
.gov.uk/assets/files/pdf/e/eyfs%20statutory%20framework%20march%202012
.pdf. Accessed 26 April 2012.

The Teaching Agency (2012) EYPS Standards from September 2012. London: DFE

Acknowledgements

Pam Jarvis

As always, my first acknowledgements are for my family who put up with me while I write and edit! Many thanks are offered to all the people who have participated in my research over the years, various aspects of which are referred to throughout the chapters of this book. Thanks go to Maggie Smith who, alongside Jane Guilfoyle, initially set up the Early Years Professional Status programme at Bradford College that inspired us all to create the first edition of this book. A very big 'thank you' goes to Dr Clive Opie Assistant Director (Teaching, Health and Care) Bradford College University Centre for his ongoing encouragement and support, and (despite his modest comments in his foreword!) his very deep understanding of contemporary Early Years issues. Thanks also go to all of Clive's team in Teaching, Health and Care, many of whom have offered valuable professional support and encouragement over the period that this book was initially conceived and produced. We are housed in McMillan Building, named for Margaret McMillan, an early twentieth century pioneer of Early Years educare; her memory and her ethos continue to inspire us all. Especial thanks go to the Early Years Professionals without whose participation there would have been no chapter 11; I should also thank Chris Jarvis, Dr Simon George and Dr Sarah George for their patient proof reading, Michelle Megson who has given much valuable admin support to the team and last but definitely not least, every single one of the Early Years Professionals we have trained over the last five and a half years, who have taught me at least as much as I have taught them!

Jane George

To my husband Simon and children Sarah and Graham, their lives have been affected by my work, my study and my writing – from preparing and 'test-driving' activities to IT expertise and proof reading – you are always supportive towards my ideas even when you don't really understand them. To all the children and families I have worked with who have influenced my thinking and practice and allowed me to develop my skills and knowledge through them. To my colleagues at Bradford College and my former colleagues in other organisations, you have challenged me to challenge myself.

Wendy Holland

The very nature of Early Years Practice is founded on good team work, and I would like to acknowledge all the help and support and inspiration I've received from the dedicated Early Years teams I have worked with both in mainstream and special school settings here in Yorkshire and in Lancashire. I would also like to acknowledge the immense gratitude I feel for those parents and carers of young children, who have welcomed me into their homes and worked with me, sometimes in very difficult circumstances, to enhance the lives of children. To Barry Miller and Maggie Smith, a huge thank you for having the initial vision to see what a difference the Early Years Professional Status programme could mean for future Early Years Practice, and Jane Guilfoyle along with the tutors, mentors and assessors for turning that vision into the reality of a very effective EYPS programme at Bradford College. To Dr Clive Opie, my sincere thanks for his enthusiastic support and encouragement of a once fledgling programme that now commends wide recognition and respect. Finally, my thanks go to all my collaborators in this book for giving of their time, and sharing their knowledge and expertise to create something so uniquely knowledgeable and diverse for the Early Years Professionals of the future.

Guided tour

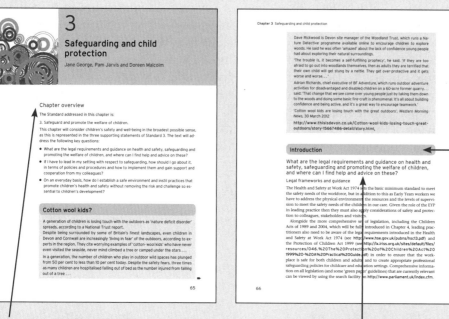

Chapter overviews begin by directing you to the standards that the chapter will address and highlighting some key questions that the chapter will cover.

Chapter introductions focus on the key themes and concepts that the chapter will build upon, often using mini-case studies.

The **subheadings** throughout the chapter highlight questions that you will need to consider as an Early Years leader.

The **Focus on practice** and **policy** features use real-life examples to help apply the theory of the chapter to a day-to-day context.

They typically close with a **Reflection** that will ask you to pause and engage in an activity and help you become a reflective practitioner.

Practical tasks throughout the book will help you to apply what you have learnt in each chapter.

5

Leading in children's learning and development
Wendy Holland

Chapter overview

The Standard addressed in this chapter is:

5. Make use of engagement, observation and assessment to meet the individual needs of every child.

Relating to the Standard we are focusing upon in this chapter, the following key questions will be addressed:

● What effective strategies can we develop for observing, assessing, planning, recording and reporting children's learning and development?

● How may we use such strategies to promote effective personalised provision based on a clear understanding of child development and possible next steps in children's learning?

● How can we achieve effective practice in supporting children's emergent language and communication skills, literacy and mathematics through sustained shared thinking and the provision of a language-rich environment?

Alice's progress

Alice, a twin aged 3 years, has been causing some concern. Her keyworker and Alice's mother have discussed how Paul, her twin brother, does all the talking for them. This practice seems to have increased since the arrival of their new baby brother. Alice's mother is particularly concerned about her language development and pronunciation. The twins are relatively new to the setting and Alice is still not separating well from her mother, despite her brother being there. Alice's keyworker has asked the Lead Professional, Jill, an EYP, to observe Alice for the afternoon.

At the beginning of the session, Alice settles after a tearful parting from her mother. She joins her brother at the water; filling containers seems to calm her and her sense of well-being appears to improve. Her levels of concentration and involvement

125

Theory is applied to practice in short stories or **vignettes** highlighting practical situations in a variety of Early Years settings.

Conclusion

Task
● Now think about your role as EYP and how you would respond to Wasim.
● Consider your role as an EYP in a multi-agency team and how your perspective might change.
● As EYP in a multi-disciplinary team how might you attempt to support Mary and her family?

I hope that from this reflection you will conclude that Wasim has one piece of a large jigsaw and how different his perspective is to the perspective of a member of a multi-agency team who recognises and appreciates the difficulties Mary and her family are in.

Armed with your knowledge of legislation, guidelines, policy and practice (see Chapter 4) and your knowledge of children gained from close working relationships with parents and carers (see Chapter 8) and your highly developed observation skills (see above), you should be in a good position to notice, observe and record changes in behaviour and demeanor which may indicate a child falling short of their potential, or a child/family experiencing difficulty. You may produce a vital piece of the safeguarding jigsaw relating to an individual child, or support one of your colleagues to do this; remember, if this had occurred within each of the cases cited in the frame of 'child protection tragedy', the problems leading up to the ultimate outcome may have been neutralised before the child came to serious harm. One thing is certain that you, like any other professional working with children and families, will produce only a part of the jigsaw and it is only when a number of pieces are put together through multi-agency working that a coherent picture is produced. We are a part of a multi-agency team – a team far wider than our workplace – who may build a picture which causes us to refer a child to the local safeguarding authority but, within the role of setting lead professional, to refer is the limit of our role.

Conclusion

This chapter has sought to answer the following questions:

What are the legal requirements and guidance on health and safety, safeguarding and promoting the welfare of children, and where can I find help and advice on these?

The complex issues of safety vs risk and what constitutes 'well-being' have been discussed above. If you have to cover a work-based learning module in the course of your training, it might be worth considering a project in this area of policy, which is currently high on the Early Years reform agenda, and a subject of discussion in many different arenas, both academic and practitioner oriented, see for example Tovey (2007) and Pen Green (2008).

83

Short **chapter conclusions** reflect on the topics the chapter has covered, and will help you to consolidate your learning. The conclusions summarise the key features of each chapter by looking back at the questions posed in the chapter overview.

Chapter 5 Leading in children's learning and development

The real acknowledgement of the diversity of languages within a setting, as well as the celebration of that diversity and difference, is important for establishing positive relationships and a confident sense of self in young children. The means to create music, dance and rhythm as ways of expression, both indoors and out, need to be resourced. **Listening** to children and taking their questions seriously, sharing their thinking as they engage in activities and experiences, both self- generated and adult-led, are important in encouraging the development of a language-rich environment.

Further reading

Bee, H. (1997) *The Developing Child*. Harlow: Longman.
Bruner, J. (1983) *Child's Talk: Learning to use language*. New York: Norton.
Cohen, D. (2002) *How the child's mind develops*. London: Routledge.
David, T., Gooch, K., Powell, S. and Abbott, L. (2003) Birth to three matters, a review of the literature. Available at: **http://www.standards.dfes.gov.uk/eyfs/resources/downloads/rr4444.pdf.**
Donaldson, M. (1978) *Children's Minds*. London: Fontana.
Lindon, J. (2008) *Understanding Child Development: Linking theory and practice* (2nd edn). London: Hodder Arnold.
Nutbrown, C. (2006) *Threads of Thinking: Young children learning and the role of early education*. London: Sage.
Piaget, J. and Inhelder, B. (1969) *The Psychology of the Child*. New York: Basic Books.
Smith, P., Cowie, H. and Blades, M. (2003) *Understanding Children's Development*. Oxford: Blackwell.
Vygotsky, L. (1978) *Mind in Society*. Cambridge, MA: Harvard University Press.

Websites

EPPE: **http://www.ioe.ac.uk/schools/ecpe/eppe/.**
EYFS (2012) **www.foundationyears.org.uk; www.education.gov.uk/publications.**
REPEY report: **http://www.dcsf.gov.uk/research/data/uploadfiles/RR356.pdf.**

References

Athey, C. (1990) *Extending Thought in Young Children: A parent-teacher partnership*. London: Paul Chapman.
Bernstein, B. (1976) *Class Codes and Control*. New York: International University Press.
Bronfenbrenner, U. (1979) *The Ecology of Human Development: Experiments by nature and design*. Cambridge, MA: Harvard University Press.
Callcentre (2008) Picture Exchange Communication System. Available at: http://callcentre .education.ed.ac.uk/SCN/Level_A_SCA/Using_Symbols_SCB/Hot_PECS_News_HTA/hot_pecs_ news_hta.html. Accessed on 18 February 2009.
Cryer, D. (1999) 'Defining and assessing early childhood program quality'. *Annuals of the American Academy of Political and Social Science*, 563.

152

At the end of each chapter, **further readings** and **relevant websites** are suggested to help you take your knowledge and understanding to the next level.

Publisher's acknowledgements

We are grateful to the following for permission to reproduce copyright material:

Cartoons
Figure 2.4 from Universal Uclick, CALVIN AND HOBBES © 1986 Watterson. Dist. by UNIVERSAL UCLICK. Reprinted with permission. All rights reserved; Cartoon on page 93, Beveridge's Five Giants, Solo Syndication/ Associated Newspapers Ltd.

Figures
Figure 2.1 from *Psychology: the science of mind and behaviour*, Hodder Arnold (Gross, R. 1996) p. 888, reproduced by permission of Hodder Education; Figure 2.2 from *Children's Language and Communication Difficulties: Understanding, Identification and Intervention*, (Dockrell, J. and Messer, D. 1999) p. 139, by permission of Continuum, an imprint of Bloomsbury Publishing Plc; Figure 4.1 adapted from A typology of youth participation and empowerment for child and adolescent health promotion, *American Journal of Community Psychology* (Wong, Naima T.); Figure 5.2 from *Thresholds of Need and Response: Child Concern Model*, North East Lincolnshire Council p. 5; Figure 8.1 from Opie, C. and Jarvis, P. 'Introduction to Methodology', in *Research in Early Years: a step by step guide*, Pearson Education Ltd (P. Jarvis, S. Newman, W. Holland and J. George (eds) 2012)

Photographs
(Key: b-bottom; c-centre; l-left; r-right; t-top)
Alamy Images: ClassicStock 206l, JUPITER IMAGES/BananaStock 206r; Corbis: Gary Houlder 206c; Creatas: 55; Milet Publishing Ltd: Laura Hambleton 199; Pearson Education Ltd: 188, Malcolm Harris 180, Jules Selmes 33, 34t, 34c, 34b, 35t, 35b, 45, 50, 61, 186, 190, 197; Courtesy of Persona Doll Training. www.persona-doll-training.org: 114; Alan Sprung 88; Courtesy of the Thackray Museum, Leeds: 90l, 90r

In some instances we have been unable to trace the owners of copyright material, and we would appreciate any information that would enable us to do so.

Introduction to
The Early Years Professional's Complete Companion, 2e

Pam Jarvis, Jane George and Wendy Holland

Welcome to the second edition of *The Early Years Professional's Complete Companion*. This book provides a companion handbook for candidates currently engaged in Early Years Professional Status (EYPS) training, their mentors, work placement trainers and tutors. It will also help Early Years Professionals (EYPs) and Early Years teachers to reflect upon and develop their practice and leadership skills and to consider potential routes for continuing professional development. The book will initially outline what is required in terms of entry to EYPS training, and the four pathways that candidates may take. Its central focus will be upon the Standards against which all Early Years Professional candidates are tested through the validation process. These Standards are conceptually grouped in chapters (see below) in which experienced EYPS tutors, mentors and trainers take the reader on a holistic journey through the skills and knowledge that the candidate needs to develop to meet the Standards required. Ideas for practical activities and further reading are suggested, and the text is interspersed with boxes outlining examples of practice, accompanied by reflection and advice.

The book is organised into four parts:

Part 1: Introducing Early Years Professional Status
Part 2: The Children's Agenda: principles in children's development, social policy and inclusion
Part 3: Leading practice in the Early Years setting
Part 4: Becoming an Early Years Professional: validation and beyond

The complex interface between EYPS training and the Early Years Foundation Stage, the Common Core Skills and the associated 'Lead Professional' role will be emphasised throughout the text. The text as a whole will also comprehensively reflect upon the role of the EYP in the range of childcare/education settings in the UK. It depicts the EYP as a graduate professional responsible for the leadership of practice in Early Years settings, through the Early Years Foundation Stage. From the basis of this approach, readers will be supported in their development of an organic, holistic perspective on childcare and education, where the EYPS Standards are achieved in a synthesis of practical skills and knowledge development, not on a mechanical Standard-by-Standard basis. As such, readers will find that the Standards are not always covered within the chapters in the exact order nor within the same groupings in which they appear in the Department for Education documents.

The Standards are as follows:

EYPS Standards from September 2012

An Early Years Professional must:

1. **Support the healthy growth and development of children from birth to the age of five.**
   1.1 Know and understand how children learn and develop and how this can be affected by individual circumstances.
   1.2 Support individual children through all areas of learning and development as outlined in the EYFS.
   1.3 Encourage and support children's learning in ways that are appropriate to their development.
   1.4 Support children through a range of transitions.
   1.5 Know when a child is in need of support and when to refer to other relevant services.

2. **Work directly with children and in partnership with their families to facilitate learning and support development.**
   2.1 Understand the important influence of parents/carers, engaging them effectively to support their child's wellbeing, learning and development.
   2.2 Communicate effectively with children from birth to age five, listening and responding sensitively.
   2.3 Promote positive social and emotional behaviour, attitudes and independence.
   2.4 Know and understand the significance of attachment and how effectively to promote it.
   2.5 Develop and sustain respectful relationships with children and their families.

3. **Safeguard and promote the welfare of children.**
   3.1 Know the legal requirements and guidance on health and safety, safeguarding and promoting the welfare of children and the implications for early years settings.
   3.2 Establish and sustain a safe environment and employ practices that promote children's health and safety.
   3.3 Know and understand child protection policies and procedures, recognise when a child is in danger or at risk of abuse, and know how to act to protect them.

4. **Set high expectations which inspire, motivate and challenge every child.**

   4.1 Establish and sustain a stimulating and inclusive environment where children feel confident and are able to learn and develop.

   4.2 Engage in sustained shared thinking with children.

   4.3 Give constructive feedback to help children evaluate their achievements and facilitate further learning.

   4.4 Demonstrate the positive values, attitudes and behaviours expected from children.

5. **Make use of observation and assessment to meet the individual needs of every child.**

   5.1 Observe, assess, record and report on progress in children's development and learning, using this to plan next steps.

   5.2 Engage effectively with parents/carers and wider professionals in the ongoing assessment and appropriate provision for each child.

   5.3 Differentiate provision to meet the individual needs of the child and provide opportunities to extend their learning and development.

6. **Plan provision taking account of the individual needs of every child.**

   6.1 Provide balanced and flexible daily and weekly routines that meet children's needs and interests and enable them to learn and develop.

   6.2 Plan and provide appropriate adult led and child initiated play and experiences that enable children to learn and develop.

   6.3 Select, prepare and use a range of resources suitable for children's ages, interests and abilities, which value diversity, and promote equality and inclusion.

7. **Fulfil wider professional responsibilities by promoting positive partnership working to support the child.**

   7.1 Understand the importance of and contribute to multi-agency team working.

   7.2 Take a lead in establishing and sustaining a culture of cooperative working between colleagues and wider professionals.

   7.3 Support colleagues to understand the part they play to enable every child to reach their full potential.

8. **Lead practice and foster a culture of continuous improvement.**

   8.1 Model and implement effective practice, and support and mentor other practitioners.

   8.2 Reflect on the effectiveness of provision, propose appropriate changes and influence, shape and support the implementation of policies and practices within the setting.

   8.3 Take responsibility for improving practice through appropriate professional development, for self and colleagues.

   8.4 Promote equality of opportunity through championing children's rights and anti-discriminatory practice.

8.5 Understand the implications of relevant legislation, statutory frameworks, including the EYFS, and policy for early years settings and apply in practice.

(The Teaching Agency 2012)

They are covered within the chapters as follows:

Part 1: Introducing Early Years Professional Status

Chapter 1: Introducing Early Years Professional Status

In this chapter, Pam Jarvis introduces the role of 'Early Years Professional', how and why it was created, and how these initial concepts were developed into a set of training programmes or 'pathways'. This chapter covers the following points:

- What is EYPS?
- Why was it developed?
- Who can enter training?
- What are the 'pathways'?
- Is Early Years Professional training for *me*?

Part 2: The Children's Agenda: principles in children's development, social policy and inclusion

Chapter 2: Principles in childcare and education

In this chapter, developmental researcher Pam Jarvis and Early Years practitioner Jane George encompass the partnership in which they have designed and delivered child development modules for many years, synthesising the theoretical and the practical, and how these meet within the current Early Years guidance documents. This chapter is also used as a source of theoretical reference by the practice-based chapters throughout the book. This chapter addresses:

Standard 1: Support the healthy growth and development of children from birth to the age of five.

Standard 2: Work directly with children and in partnership with their families to facilitate learning and support development.

Chapter 3: Safeguarding and child protection

In this chapter, Jane George and EYP Doreen Malcolm join forces to discuss safeguarding and child protection, bringing their varied setting management experience together to explore this challenging area, while Pam Jarvis provides support for the legal/policy aspects relating to this area. This chapter addresses:

Standard 3: Safeguard and promote the welfare of children.

Chapter 4: Children as citizens: rights and responsibilities in the twenty-first century

In this chapter, Pam Jarvis not only outlines the current social policy for children and families, but, from her academic background as both historian and educational researcher, considers the concept of 'social policy', rights and inclusion from both a historical and international perspective, to support students not only in building their knowledge in this area, but also their critical and analytical skills, with Jane George and Wendy Holland providing pertinent and illustrative examples. This chapter addresses:

Standard 8: Lead practice and foster a culture of continuous improvement.

Part 3: Leading practice in the Early Years setting

Chapter 5: Leading in children's learning and development

In this chapter, Wendy Holland reflects upon over 30 years of experience as a nursery teacher and teacher/EYP trainer and assessor to outline the core daily work of an EYP in supporting children's learning in the Early Years. This chapter addresses:

Standard 5: Make use of engagement, observation and assessment to meet the individual needs of every child.

Chapter 6: Promoting emotional security and positive behaviour

Moving directly on from Chapter 5, Wendy Holland now turns her attention to supporting children's emotional development, hence supporting positive behaviour within professional environments providing care and education for children from birth to age 5. This chapter addresses:

Standard 2: Work directly with children and in partnership with their families to facilitate learning and development.

Standard 4: Set high expectations which inspire, motivate and challenge every child.

Chapter 7: Transforming the environment for play and learning

Wendy Holland considers a range of positive environments in which to support children's learning, reflecting upon resources, routines and activities and the responsibility of lead professionals to provide high-quality experiences for the children in their care. This chapter addresses:

Standard 6: Plan provision taking account of the individual needs of every child.

Chapter 8: Partnership and leadership in Early Years

In this chapter, the editorial team reflect upon the broad range of partnerships required within the complex contemporary arena of Early Years education and care in the UK, encompassing nursery schools, children's centres and non-state sector settings. This chapter addresses:

Standard 2: Work directly with children and in partnership with their families to facilitate learning and development.

Standard 7: Fulfil wider professional responsibilities by promoting positive partnership working to support the child.

Standard 8: Lead practice and foster a culture of continuous improvement.

Part 4: Becoming an Early Years Professional: validation and beyond

Chapter 9: Managing your placement supervisor, mentor and your own continuing professional development

In this chapter, Early Years Professional and EYPS candidate mentor Poonam Cant focuses upon the workplace/work placement, considering how EYPS candidates can negotiate their way through the processes required to move successfully into validation, considering typical experiences of candidates on all four pathways. This chapter addresses:

Standard 8: Lead practice and foster a culture of continuous improvement.

Chapter 10: Surviving validation (Development Review and Assessment)

In this chapter, Pam Jarvis and Jane George guide candidates clearly and succinctly through the validation process, outlining:

- What to expect from the validation process
- Preparing for the Development Review
- A holistic approach to the Standards
- Some tips for the written tasks
- Preparing for the assessment visit.

Chapter 11: Early Years Professionals: in their own words

In this chapter, Pam Jarvis turns her research focus upon the experiences of Early Years Professionals. She interviews seven EYPs who approached their validation on a range of pathways, and who inhabit a range of professional roles in Early Years settings. They reflect upon their experience of validation, their current professional roles, how their training and achievement of EYP status have impacted upon their professional lives, and how they see their future careers in terms of challenges and opportunities.

Throughout the book, the reader is invited to engage in the carefully coordinated EYP training programme developed by this highly effective team, as the innovative programme that they deliver is communicated through the text. *The Early Years Professional's Complete Companion* is a text that is unquestionably produced specifically for Early Years Professionals, by a team who has a sole focus on teaching and assessing Early Years Professionals, and informed by the opinions of those who have already entered this new professional arena as Early Years Professionals as products of this training programme. It is presented in this second edition to maintain its status as a key text for early career EYPs and EYPS candidates, and for tutors, trainers, assessors and mentors contributing to EYPS training programmes across the UK. This is not to say that Early Years Practitioners on other related routes – for example, teacher training and foundation degrees – may not find its content useful; the holistic approach taken should render the text quite flexible in this way.

Reference

The Teaching Agency (2012) Early Years Professional Status Standards available at: http://media .education.gov.uk/assets/files/pdf/r/eyps%20standards%20from%20september%202012 .pdf. Accessed on 16 June 2012.

Part 1

Introducing Early Years Professional Status

1

Introducing Early Years Professional Status

Pam Jarvis

Chapter overview

This chapter will address the following key questions that you are likely to ask as you consider your entry to Early Years Professional Status training:

- What is Early Years Professional Status?
- Why was EYPS developed?
- Who can enter training?
- What are the pathways?
- What is involved in the EYPS validation process?
- Is EYP training for *me*?

Introduction: what is Early Years Professional Status?

Early Years Professional Status (EYPS) is a graduate leadership role for Early Years settings in England, initially developed by the Children's Workforce Development Council (CWDC). The training programme was successfully piloted in 2006, and its first full year of operation commenced in January 2007. The introduction of this role into all professional settings providing care and education for children aged from birth to age 5 was instigated by the New Labour Government with the intention that a graduate-led workforce would raise standards, skills, experience, commitment and effective leadership of practice across the range of Early Years provision.

The Coalition Government elected in 2010 has demonstrated its commitment to EYPS training by redesigning the programme. This has resulted in minor adjustments to the Standards and the process of validation, but in essence, the programme remains the same. Training providers have been grouped into consortia, eight of which cover the whole of England. Consortia have some freedom to adapt and enhance the basic training programme, recognising the previous expertise developed between 2007 and 2011.

Within an EYPS 'validation' process (see below), candidates must demonstrate their competence in areas covered by the EYPS Standards (see the Introduction to this book), which are both knowledge- and practice-based, and cover leading practice with babies and children from birth to the end of the Early Years Foundation Stage (EYFS). The EYFS concludes at the point that children enter Year 1 primary, which, in England, is the education stage for children who will have their sixth birthday between the September and August of the relevant education year.

EYPS Standards and requirements are *more* than the sum of their parts and the Standards are designed to be assessed holistically. It cannot be emphasised strongly enough that EYPS training *cannot* be undertaken in a shallow, outcome-by-outcome fashion; candidates should perceive the Standards as interlocking pieces of an integrated jigsaw of academic knowledge and practitioner skills. Candidates must remember that the supporting statements for each Standard are just that – not boxes to be ticked in a National Vocational Qualification style. The status is awarded to highly competent senior practitioners who can demonstrate, through a rigorous set of written and oral assessments, that they are capable of reflexively leading practice within the complex arena of the contemporary Early Years settings.

Why was EYPS developed?

In October 2005, the Early Education Advisory Group (EEAG) in England agreed that the organisation and management of Early Years care and education services needed to be reviewed and reshaped. Their focus was to produce a role which, while it retained many of the very positive features of the existing nursery teacher role, also encompassed the multi-agency practitioner leadership of a childcare and education team in the twenty-first century, which was increasingly offering services to children under the age of 3 and their families. The other aspect that the Advisory Group wished to address was that services for children under the age of 3 were, at that time, most frequently led by staff who, while typically possessing high levels of practitioner competence and dedication, had not received education and training at the university level (or Higher Education/HE). Many recent high-profile Early Years research projects, in particular, the British-based Effective Provision of Pre-School Education (EPPE) project (1997 ongoing, 2008 online), made a clear finding that outcomes for children, especially those from a background of disadvantage, were improved when the practice in the setting was led by a graduate. The role of the Early Years Professional was developed from this basis, representing an attempt to retain the best concepts and structures of Early Years practice in England, and developing it from this basis into a more flexible model for the twenty-first century, with some features drawn from the role of the 'pedagogue', which has a long record of success in Scandinavian countries.

The Early Years Professional is therefore a new role with the brief to lead practice within an increasingly complex Early Years Care and Education system. There are many challenges associated with entering such a new profession, but also many opportunities for EYPs to proactively mould their professional role and the Early Years settings in which they are becoming the leaders of practice.

Who can enter training?

Those applying to enter the Graduate Practitioner Pathway (GPP) must be graduates within disciplines relating directly to Early Years education and care. Applicants with the minimum of a Foundation Degree/HND in Early Childhood Studies or closely related subjects (e.g. Foundation Degree in Supporting and Managing Learning), and current professional experience in an Early Years care/education role are eligible to apply for EYPS training on the Undergraduate Practitioner Pathway (UPP). They will also be expected to study for a BA or BA (Hons) in a childcare/education-related subject during their EYPS pathway. Graduates who have no previous training or professional background in Early Years practice may also access training through the Graduate Entry Pathway (GEP). Finally, BA (Hons) Childhood Studies or BA (Hons) Early Years undergraduates may enter EYPS training during the final year of their degree; this is the Undergraduate Entry Pathway (UEP).

EYPS candidates must have achieved both English and Maths GCSEs at grade 'C' or above, and provide a suitable Criminal Records Bureau (CRB) enhanced clearance that indicates their fitness to work with young children. They also have to provide good references from previous employers/tutors, and those who have previous childcare and/or education experience will need to provide positive references from these specific employers. Finally, EYPS candidates wishing to apply for government-funded places must have the right to live and work in the UK; those who do not cannot be accepted on to the programme.

EYPS training is available to all graduates who work with, or have an ambition to work with children under the age of 5; however government-funded places are limited and will be offered to those who can best demonstrate that their skills will be used to work with children and families in areas of disadvantage, reflecting the Coalition Government's agenda.

What are the 'pathways'?

The pathways are:

- The 6-month part-time Graduate Practitioner Pathway (GPP);
- The 12-month part-time Undergraduate Practitioner Pathway (UPP);
- The 12-month full-time Graduate Entry Pathway (GEP);
- The 12-month full-time Undergraduate Entry Pathway (UEP).

Candidates on government-funded pathways do not pay tuition fees for their EYPS training. Those on the 'entry' pathways are eligible for a small bursary, and employers of those on the 'practitioner' pathways may be able to claim some reimbursement for cover costs (while the student is engaged in training). Undergraduate candidates may be able to claim some funding to help with payment of their degree tuition fees. For further information please refer to your training provider.

The Graduate Practitioner Pathway (six months part time) is probably for you if:

- You are currently employed in a senior role in a childcare/education setting that deals with at least part of the age range within the Early Years Foundation Stage age range (0–5); *and*

- You have a degree in a childcare/Early Years education-related discipline in which you have achieved at least 60 credits at level 6 (HE level 3).

GPP candidates will be provided with a range of training experiences tailored to their individual needs and availability. This may involve both college attendance and short placement experience; the programme will be spread over six months including the validation process.

Focus on practice

GPP candidate Sanjay initially trained as a nursery teacher. He spent five years teaching in a nursery school, then, three months ago, he was appointed to lead practice in a children's centre. As Sanjay worked only with children over the age of 3 in the nursery school he does not have any substantial knowledge of working with younger children. He has never worked professionally with children under the age of 3 in any capacity, although he does have his own young family, and has assured the training provider that he has plenty of practical experience in nappy changing and bottle feeding! He is bilingual and worked as the home-school coordinator for families with English as an Additional Language when he was in post at the nursery school. It is agreed that Sanjay will join the GPP, attending a programme of early evening sessions at college with other GPP candidates, covering developmental theory from birth to age 3, and the requirements of the Early Years Foundation Stage. Such sessions will also provide some opportunities for the candidates to 'network'. Sanjay will also undertake a one day a week placement over eight weeks in the baby room of a local private daycare centre, as his children's centre does not yet provide care for babies. His training provider has asked him to carry out a set of observations on the babies that he will be working with, and with the support of his mentor he will use these to develop some activities for them. As the children's centre is in a district that has been designated a 'super output area' by the government (that is an area experiencing multiple disadvantages) Sanjay's employer will receive funding to provide cover for him while he attends placement.

Reflection *Sanjay is clearly very experienced at enacting and leading practice in one area of the relevant age range, but has recognised that he needs to develop his experience of provision for children under age 3. He already has some basis for developing these skills in his experience as a parent, and his placement and study are arranged around a timetable that he can work with. He has a wealth of experience of working with parents and families. All of these are important indications that Sanjay is a strong candidate for the GPP.*

The Undergraduate Practitioner Pathway (12 months part time) is probably for you if:

- You are currently employed in a childcare/education setting that deals with at least part of the age range of the Early Years Foundation Stage (0–5); *and*
- You have an HND or Foundation Degree in a childcare/Early Years education-related discipline or an ordinary or honours degree in a non-childcare/early years education-related subject.

UPP candidates will study a range of HE childcare and development modules at level 6 (Stage 3 HE). To go forward to EYPS validation, non-graduate candidates must pass modules totalling a minimum of 60 credits, leading to the award of a BA in Early Childhood Studies/Early Years. Some candidates will opt to undertake the full 120 credit award of BA (Hons) in Early Childhood Studies/Early Years.

Focus on practice

UPP candidate Sean finished his Foundation Degree in Playwork five years ago. He initially worked in an adventure playground with children over the age of 7, but when that lost its funding and shut down three years ago, he opened a child-minding business with his partner Jamelia; this is currently doing very well. They received a particular commendation on their last Ofsted report for their excellent liaison with families; this was due to a recording and information sharing system that Sean designed.

Jamelia did not initially have any qualifications in childcare, but she is currently just completing a level 3 in Children's Care, Learning and Development (CCLD). Last year the business made enough money for the couple to employ an assistant, who Sean and Jamelia have encouraged to take a level 2 in CCLD. As they now have an extra member of staff, Sean can now spare the time to take the top-up year to convert his Foundation Degree into a BA in Early Childhood Studies, followed by EYPS validation. He can cover the leading practice standards as he leads the practice of Jamelia and the childcare assistant in his setting. At the moment the setting does not care for any children under the age of 2, but they have had some recent enquiries. Sean will keep his tutor informed about the progress of this situation, and, if a firm booking does not result, the college will arrange a short placement for him in the baby room of a local children's centre towards the end of his top-up programme, where he will carry out the same programme of observations and planning as Sanjay.

Reflection *Sean has organised his time to ensure that he can cope with the demands of the long pathway. He has recognised a possible pitfall in terms of covering the full age range and has made a contingency plan in case things do not work out as he might hope. Sean has a solid background in practice with children, and while 'lone' childminders sometimes struggle to demonstrate the leadership* *skills required for EYPS validation, Sean should not have a problem with this as he is clearly the leading practitioner in a setting with two other workers. He has shown particular aptitude for working with families, and this has been recognised and praised by an Ofsted inspector. All of these factors indicate that he is a strong candidate for the UPP.*

The Graduate Entry Pathway (12 months full time) is probably for you if:

- You have limited, or no experience of working with children aged 0–5;
- You have a strong ambition to develop or change your career in order to work in a leadership role in an Early Years setting, and you are in a position to undertake a year's unpaid intensive professional development in order to accomplish this;
- You have a degree in which you have achieved at least 60 credits at level 6 (HE level 3) in any subject or discipline.

GEP candidates attend college across one calendar year (which may run September–August or January–December), to undertake the academic study of child development, Early Years education and care. A substantial percentage of the year's programme will additionally be spent gaining work experience – the minimum time allocated for this is stipulated as 18 full weeks by the government, but many centres will judge that this needs to be substantially more for students to gain the necessary knowledge and skills, which must include leadership. Many centres will give students the opportunity to gain some credit for academic study undertaken during full pathway training, either at BA (Hons) or Masters level, depending upon the specific programme offered.

Focus on practice

GEP candidate Amelia always had an ambition to work with young children when she was at school, but her parents and teachers persuaded her that she could 'do better', particularly when she got very good GCSE and 'A' level grades, showing a particular aptitude in maths. Amelia eventually completed a BA (Hons) in Business Studies and went to work in a building society when she was 21, reaching the rank of deputy manager by the time she had her own two children, who are now 14 and 16. She returned to work in the building society part time as a section leader after her first maternity leave. Three months ago, she applied for voluntary redundancy as she calculated that this would give her enough money to take a year out from paid work. She plans to undertake the EYPS GEP and then purchase a private daycare setting. Her husband Rob will be her business partner, and he is very supportive of her plans to re-train. Amelia has undertaken some recent voluntary work in her friend's private daycare setting, which she enjoyed very much. She also feels that she will bring many transferable skills to her studies. For example, she is an experienced parent; she was one of the founder members and coordinators of a parent and toddler club in her local area when her children were young, and she has a wealth of experience of team leadership and management from her role at the building society. She also has an excellent grasp of accounts and financial planning, and is looking forward to using these skills to benefit her own business. Last but not least, she is very used to the self-organisation and time-management that is an essential feature of coping as a working parent. She is looking forward to the course as a whole, but most particularly to returning to college to study child development – the subject that she wanted to take when she was 18. Her training provider has constructed an academic programme for GEP candidates so that they can complete the first third of a Masters qualification alongside their EYPS training, so Amelia should finish the year with a postgraduate certificate in Early Years in addition to her EYPS. The children are intrigued that mum is 'going back to school' and both they and Amelia are looking forward to all sitting down to do their 'homework' together.

Reflection *Amelia has clearly thought very hard about why she wants to undertake the full pathway; this is based on a long-term ambition and a realistic business plan for the future. Her redundancy pay means that she is not likely to experience severe financial problems over the year's training if she is unable to earn money during this period. She has undertaken voluntary work within the Early Years sector to make sure that she has realistic expectations of the childcare environment. She has clear plans relating to how she wishes to use her new qualifications, and she possesses a large set of transferable skills and experience to take forward into her new role, including some voluntary experience of organising and coordinating a service for children and their parents. Her family are very supportive, and her children are old enough to cope relatively independently if she has to undertake placement during school holidays. Amelia also brings her strong time-management, self-organisation and academic aptitude forward into a very intensive programme where she will need to progress very quickly. All of these factors indicate that Amelia is a strong candidate for the GEP.*

The Undergraduate Entry Pathway (12 months full time) is probably for you if:

- You are in the final year of a BA (Hons) in Early Childhood Studies or Early Years;
- Your experience of working with children aged 0–5 is limited to placements in the first two years of your degree (plus possibly placement experience on pre-HE study for early years qualifications);
- You have a strong ambition to develop your career towards working in a leadership role in an Early Years setting.

Undergraduate Entry Pathway (UEP) candidates attend college across one calendar year (which may run September–August or January–December), to undertake the academic study of child development, Early Years education and care within the modules that they are studying on their degree. If they opt additionally to become UEP candidates, a substantial percentage of the year's programme will additionally be spent gaining work experience – the minimum time allocated for this is stipulated as 18 full weeks, but many centres will judge that this needs to be substantially more for students to gain the necessary knowledge and skills, which must include leadership, as is also the case for the GEP. UEPs will therefore have to study for the final year of their degree alongside their EYPS training. Some centres may choose to extend UEP training across the final *two* years of the Early Childhood Studies/Early Years degree.

Focus on practice

Undergraduate Entry Pathway candidate Jenny has had an ambition to work with young children since she was very young herself. She does not always find the academic aspects of her study very easy, but she worked hard to gain a good grade in a [level 3] Early Years qualification after leaving school with six GCSEs grades B-C, including English, Maths and Science, and then moved on to a BA (Hons) in Early Years at the same college where she took her pre-HE training. She has a good reputation in the varied set of placements she has been given, and has been in some settings more than once over the five-year period of her studies. She has been told that she has a very good 'way' with the children, and as she moved into the second year of her degree, one setting gave her the chance to support a younger level 3 student on her first placement, which Jenny really enjoyed. Her tutors have encouraged her to apply for the UEP, and after going through a series of interviews and aptitude tests, she was successful in her application.

Reflection *Jenny has demonstrated her suitability for the UEP pathway over a long period of time, and has already had some experience of supporting the work of others at the time of her application. She has always had a strong ambition to practice within Early Years, which has not waivered over the long period of training upon which she has embarked. She already has the GCSEs that she needs to become an EYP, and if she decides after receiving her degree and EYPS that she wants to move into Early Years teaching, she also has the required GCSE in Science. All of these factors indicate that Jenny is a strong candidate for the UEP. Students in the final year of a degree who have less practical experience, or who are less sure of the path they wish to take when they complete their degree might do better to wait and see, returning to take their EYPS via the GPP at a later point in their career. Those who are precluded from the UEP by lack of GCSE English and Maths also have this option open to them, once they have passed the GCSEs.*

Candidates for all pathways should carefully consider their individual needs and learning styles when choosing a training provider. There is a multitude of ways to provide EYPS training, and the candidate should choose wisely, considering which combination of face-to-face, open and blended learning offered by different training providers they feel would best develop their skills, and how flexible different training providers are able to be with regard to offering individual programmes. There is also great variation in the amount of individual tuition offered by different training providers; GEP candidates in particular should be wary of training programmes that rely almost exclusively on placement/workplace experience, with little time or tuition offered to develop Early Years-related theoretical skills, or for group reflection with fellow candidates, or for individual and small group interaction with tutors and mentors. Some training providers may also offer the chance to study for additional accreditation on conventional HE programmes, for example to study relevant postgraduate modules as part of the training programme, which obviously adds value to the training process.

What is involved in the EYPS validation process?

The validation process is described in detail in Chapter 10. Students on the early part of their EYPS training journey are advised to consider their training as a holistic process, engaging them in the development of both academic knowledge and practical skills, knitted together by engagement in reflection on practice, from which the EYP competencies will emerge. A highly summarised guide to validation is provided below, however, to give students a basic outline of what to expect.

Formal validation training will typically be provided over five days of college attendance which will be carefully staged over four months or possibly longer for entry pathway candidates. Each centre will make its own arrangements for this; as such there is some element of flexibility for days/times to be agreed with individual candidate groups. The input is structured as follows:

- **Day 1**: Introduction to the Standards.
- **Day 2**: Introduction to the written tasks.
- **Day 3**: Preparation for the development review.
- **Day 4**: The development review of skills. After participating in formative assessment exercise(s) designed by the relevant consortium, candidates will receive formal feedback from an assessor at the centre relating to their stage of readiness for validation. They will be given targets to meet, which will feed into a formal action plan.
- **Day 5**: Introduction to the setting visit.

Candidates produce a *set of written tasks*, which will be determined by the consortium within which they are studying. The written tasks are examined by an EYPS *assessor*, who will then subsequently undertake a *visit to the candidate's setting* over one working day where they will carry out a range of assessment activities for which the candidate must produce a *range of supporting evidence* (e.g. planning documents, centre policies developed by the candidate etc.). This must include written testimony relating to the candidate's skills from at least three independent witnesses.

This includes the candidate hosting a 'tour' of the setting where, based on the evidence they have presented in the set tasks and supporting evidence, they illustrate to the assessor how they lead practice, a short observation of practice and an in-depth interview with the assessor.

The assessor makes a judgement on the written evidence presented and the evidence collected during the setting visit, and subsequently makes a recommendation as to whether the candidate has satisfactorily met all the Standards. This decision is internally verified by a team of assessors representing the consortium. When this somewhat lengthy process is complete, candidates are advised of their result, either 'met' or 'not met'.

Is EYP training for *me*?

The first issues to explore are whether you have the relevant qualifications to access EYPS training (see above). For those who have pre-HE qualifications and significant experience of working in childcare/Early Years education, but do not yet have credits at the HE level, do not give up at this point. Make enquiries with your local Early Years HE provider, as you may qualify for some Accreditation of Prior Experience and Learning (APEL), based on previous experience/qualifications, and hence be eligible to undertake a truncated programme towards the award of a degree. Many training providers may also allow such experienced, mature students who are employed within the Early Years sector as senior practitioners to undertake some or all of their study via open, distance and/or blended learning, which helps students to balance their work commitments with study.

For those who are just starting out on their careers, you will need to start at the relevant level of the qualifications ladder – for those who are sure they want to work with children from birth to age 5, the most relevant qualification at the 'A' level standard currently (early 2012) is a level 3 Diploma in Childcare and Education. You can then move on to a degree programme in Early Childhood Studies, taking every chance to build practical experience via either placement or paid work as you go. The government is currently engaged in aligning the Standards across the full range of Early Years qualifications, so pre-HE qualifications in childcare and education are also currently undergoing change and development. Consequently, it is advisable to keep an eye on the DFE website to keep pace with ongoing changes – **www.dfe.gov.uk**.

For those with the relevant HE qualifications and experience, you need to make sure that you meet the CRB requirements (see above) and that you have the relevant GCSEs. If you do not have these GCSEs then you will need to obtain them before entry to an EYPS training programme. Those who have a degree in a different discipline from Childcare/Early Years/Early Years Education, and no previous work experience in Early Years childcare/education settings should seriously contemplate the following advice before undertaking EYPS training, based on my experience over five years of leading the EYPS full (now called 'Graduate Entry') pathway:

- The GEP is a 'fast track' training programme for graduates. It assumes that candidates will possess solid graduate-level skills in terms of academic aptitude, self-motivation, self-organisation, personal and academic maturity and the potential for leadership. It puts considerable demands upon students in terms of an expectation that they will take in information very quickly and develop both academic knowledge and practical skills at a very fast pace. For this reason it is very much a full-time course, and those who take it on should expect placement and study to be their full-time occupation throughout the full year of their training.

- Bearing in mind the level of commitment outlined above, it is extremely advisable that entry on to the GEP is undertaken only after consultation with people sharing the candidate's everyday life (e.g. partners, parents and children), particularly those who may be expected to provide financial support during the training year.

- The potential GEP candidate should also consider very carefully whether they are fully aware of the substantial physical and psychological demands of a leadership role in Early Years childcare and education, and if they do not have previous experience of the collective care of children aged 0–5 they are strongly advised to obtain at least two weeks' full-time experience as a volunteer in a children's centre or private daycare setting before confirming their registration to the EYPS training programme. They may find that most centres will insist that they have undertaken such experience before admitting them to the programme.

- As the only outcomes available for EYPS in the new assessment structure are 'met' and 'not met' it is crucial for candidates to ensure that they are ready for validation at the relevant time, and this is most important in the case of those signing on to a fast-track, novice entry programme.

With regard to candidates for the other pathways, they need to consider the following points:

- Do I work with children across the full EYFS age range (0–5)?
- Do I guide the work of other practitioners?
- Do I have a solid understanding of the requirements of the EYFS?
- Am I involved in leading/managing the delivery of the EYFS?
- Am I involved in monitoring/influencing the work of other practitioners, including giving them feedback/guidance?
- Do I interact with professionals inhabiting different roles from myself during the course of my regular duties?
- Am I involved in team working within my setting?
- Do I have a good understanding of how to assess children's progress, and do I/ could I support others in this endeavour?
- Do I work in partnership with parents/carers to support children's learning and development and do I/could I support other practitioners to do so?

Success at validation depends upon being able to answer 'yes' to all these points. Those joining the UPP are unlikely to enter with all these attributes fully developed, but they must be able to extend to this point over the time during which they undertake EYPS training. Again, as a tutor who has been involved in supporting the long pathway over the past two years, I would advise aspiring UPP candidates who do not have substantial work-based practitioner experience in Early Years setting(s) to make sure they can build this up to a sufficient level, and secure the opportunity to gain significant leadership experience over the period of the training programme. If this seems unlikely, consideration should be given to completing the academic programme of study and gaining additional work experience before enrolling on the EYPS programme, as at the time of writing (early 2012) there is an ongoing opportunity to access the GPP pathway when the practitioner feels they have attained the commensurate level and mixture of professional experience. What is not possible, however, is to receive a funded place on the GPP programme after receiving a 'not met' outcome on the UPP. Candidates should thus consider their options carefully. It is emphasised that EYPS is not awarded purely for practitioner competence; it requires the candidate to **show evidence that they have led others in practice.** This does not, however, mean that all EYPS candidates have to be line managers – it means that they need to be able to show that they are trusted by their setting's stakeholders to *model* good practice and therefore lead the work of others whose practice is not yet developed to such a high level.

Each potential candidate will need to decide **in partnership with their training provider** whether EYPS training is for them and, if so, which pathway. Whichever pathway is accessed, you should certainly expect to engage in a lot of hard work over the course of your training, which will also underpin some very rewarding professional and personal development.

The book is designed specifically to be a first port of call for those seeking advice on the basic knowledge and skills required by EYPs, and where to access further information with regard to both printed materials and online. We look forward to taking this journey with all of you. In the more distant future, we hope some of you will write your own books for the second generation of EYPs, creating a growing body of literature to more substantially underpin rich reflective practice within what will then be an increasingly mature profession.

Focus on practice

Starting a reflective journal and continuing professional development portfolio

Many of you will have kept reflective journals for previous qualifications. The EYP reflective journal is special, in that it is hoped that, once you start it, it will always be ongoing, acting as a cornerstone of your continuing professional development, long beyond your EYPS validation.

Initially, what you need to do is to produce a basic introduction to your setting and your role within it. This will need to be revised when inevitable changes occur (you move to a different role, move settings etc.). You should try to write an entry at least every three or four days, focusing on aspects of your work-based experience that caused you to reflect upon and develop your practice. Incidents that form the basis for your reflections may be positive, negative or neutral, and mundane, dramatic, funny or sad. You should not have to share your whole journal at any time (as this may inhibit the scope of your reflection), but it is useful from time to time to share edited extracts with fellow students, tutors and colleagues. *Do* make sure that your journal text is safely anonymised, particularly if you are storing it electronically – it is surprisingly easy to unwittingly stray outside the data protection legislation if you use full, real names for colleagues, children and locations!

Alongside your reflective journal, you should also maintain a continuing professional development (CPD) portfolio where you keep records of training courses attended, job reviews/appraisals, possibly some samples of children's work (with their permission) and associated planning from activities you designed that went particularly well, letters/cards expressing thanks from parents and carers (you could even keep communications of complaint with associated notes relating to how you rectified the relevant issues!) and any other materials that you feel serve to document your continuing development as a practitioner.

References

Early Education Advisory Group (EEAG) (2005) Annex 3, Paper 05/5/9, Item M. Available at: http://www.tda.gov.uk/upload/resources/doc/b/boardoct05_early_years_teachers_c.doc. Accessed on 2 April 2008.

The Effective Provision of Pre-School Education (EPPE) project (2008) 1997 ongoing, available at: http://k1.ioe.ac.uk/schools/ecpe/eppe. Accessed on 29 March 2008.

Part 2

The Children's Agenda: principles in children's development, social policy and inclusion

2

Principles in childcare and education

Pam Jarvis and Jane George

Chapter overview

The Standards addressed in this chapter are:

Standard 1 Support the healthy growth and development of children from birth to the age of five.

Standard 2 Work directly with children and in partnership with their families to facilitate learning and support development.

The text will address the following key questions:

- What are the main EYFS principles, and how do they relate to mainstream development theory and research?

- What are the main theoretical perspectives that describe how children develop and learn, particularly between birth and their sixth birthday?

- What influences and experiences in the setting and beyond including transitions can impact on children's well-being, development, learning and behaviour and how can we connect these to the theoretical perspectives introduced in the previous section?

The culture of childcare - 'then' and 'now'

Caroline, an Early Years Professional, was very surprised at the level of distress that her mother, Jean, exhibited on being told that her 3-year old granddaughter, Maisie, would have to undergo a series of treatments as a hospital in-patient. Jean had known that Maisie would need treatment since she was born; the situation was not life-threatening, and had a very positive prognosis: Maisie had a slight deformation of her feet, which would respond to a series of routine operations between the ages of 3 and 5. Caroline reassured her mother: 'She will be fine, Mum.'

'That's what my mum thought when I had my tonsils out in 1958', replied Jean, with tears in her eyes. 'I was only 3, too - she didn't see how much I cried when she wasn't there. I still remember a nurse who got very cross with me and told me to "pull myself

➡

together" – I didn't even know what that meant, so I asked my mum at visiting time. There was also the sister in charge of the ward – she wouldn't let your Auntie Sue come in because, your grandma told me later, she said "10-year-olds are crawling with germs". Even your grandma got upset the first time she visited me – I don't remember this, but she told me that I said "I don't live with you any more, mummy, do I?" She tried to explain, but she could only visit for an hour a day . . . apparently, I was only in for a week, too, but it seemed like a year to me . . .'

'Oh, mum', said Caroline, now feeling tears welling in her own eyes, 'don't be silly. This isn't the dark ages now. One of us will be with Maisie nearly all of the time when she is in hospital. She's also going to get a visit from one of the staff before she goes in, and she is going to visit the ward, so it won't seem so strange to her. There's a nursery nurse, an EYP and a teacher attached to the ward, so Maisie will be able to do nearly all the activities that she would be doing at nursery, and later at school if she ever needs to be in for longer periods of time. But they will only keep her in for the shortest time that they need to, hopefully not even a week after each operation, and her nursery have already discussed with the hospital how they are going to look after her while her feet are still in plaster.'

'She's going to nursery with her feet in plaster?' said Jean. 'They wouldn't have let you in my day . . .'

'But an awful lot of things have changed since your day, like treating children as individual human beings with their own set of needs, for a start', replied Caroline. 'Now . . . we need to discuss when you will be available to stay with Maisie when she is in hospital this time. I'm working out a rota, so all the people she is attached to can take a turn. Don't you remember, attachment theory? I did a project on it at college.'

'No', said Jean more cheerfully, 'I don't. But it sounds like an awful lot of things have changed for the better since I was 3 years old . . .'

Introduction

Jean is certainly right about one thing – an awful lot of things *have* changed in the field of Early Years practice since she was 3 years old, including our understanding of children's emotional development, and the capacity for practitioners to engage in multi-agency working, including ongoing liaison with parents, who are now seen as the most important 'experts' in the pursuit of defining their child's individual needs.

The underpinning principles of childcare and education require that leading practitioners have a solid, up-to-date working knowledge of the current national guidelines for Early Years practice, and of a range of theoretical principles that describe how children develop emotionally, socially and intellectually. This chapter will outline a summary of the principles of the current Early Years Foundation Stage (EYFS) guidance (DFE 2012), followed by a summary of the core theoretical perspectives that have underpinned the huge changes in Early Years practice that have occurred over the last 50 years. The recommended reading list will give you a range of texts to study further on these topics. It is hoped that you will use this chapter as a reference base for the key underpinning theories of child development and the key content and principles of the EYFS, returning when necessary from the later chapters in the book to check (for example) developmental stage information or references to theoretical concepts.

What are the main EYFS principles, and how do they relate to mainstream developmental theory and research?

The EYFS principles (DFE 2012) focus around three prime areas and four specific areas of learning. The prime areas are proposed to relate to the underpinning knowledge and skills for 'school readiness' and it is proposed that they should be developed through activities within the specific areas.

The prime areas are:

- Communication and language;
- Physical development;
- Personal, social and emotional development.

The four specific areas are:

- Literacy;
- Mathematics;
- Understanding the world;
- Expressive arts and design.

The EYFS also requires that practitioners additionally use '**four guiding principles**' to inform practice in Early Years settings. These are:

- That every child is a **unique child**, who is constantly learning and can be resilient, capable, confident and self-assured;
- That children learn to be strong and independent through **positive relationships**;
- That children learn and develop well in **enabling environments**, in which their experiences respond to their individual needs and there is a strong partnership between practitioners and parents and/or carers; and
- That **children develop and learn in different ways and at different rates**, including those children who have special educational needs and disabilities.

The EYFS proposes that to plan and guide children's activities, practitioners should reflect on the different ways that children learn and utilise these in their practice. It is proposed that the characteristics of effective teaching and learning are:

- **Playing and exploring** – children investigating, experiencing and 'having a go';
- **Active learning** – children should be encouraged to continue their concentration and to keep on trying if they encounter difficulties, enjoying the eventual achievement;

- **Creating and thinking critically** – children developing their own ideas, making links between ideas, and working out strategies for getting a specific result.

There is also a requirement for every child under 5 to be assigned a key person, who manages the child's learning to address their individual needs, and who interfaces with the child's parents and family. In order for this to be done effectively, the government propose that there is a clear need for highly skilled staff in Early Years settings, EYPs in particular.

By the time the child arrives at their sixth birthday, the expectation is that they will be able to do the following:

Communication and language

- Listen attentively, and respond with relevant comments, questions and actions;
- Speak effectively, showing awareness of listeners' needs, using past, present and future forms accurately. They should be able to create their own narratives and explanations, connecting ideas or events.

Physical development

- Show good control and coordination in large and small movements. They move confidently in a range of ways, safely negotiating space. Fine motor skills are in place, allowing them to handle equipment and tools effectively, including pencils for writing.

Health and self-care

- Know the importance for good health of physical exercise, and a healthy diet, and how to basically keep healthy and safe.
- Manage their own basic hygiene and personal needs, including dressing and going to the toilet independently.

Personal, social and emotional development

- Have the confidence to try new activities, and say why they like some activities more than others.
- Have the confidence to speak in a familiar group about their ideas, choosing the resources they need for their chosen activities.
- Have the confidence to say when they do or don't need help.

Managing feelings and behaviour:

- Have the ability to talk about how they and others show feelings.
- Be able to discuss their own and others' behaviour, and its consequences with the knowledge that some behaviour is unacceptable.
- Be able to work effectively as part of a group or class, understanding that they must obey certain rules.
- Be able to adjust their behaviour to fit particular situations.
- Cope with changes of routine.

Making relationships:

- Play cooperatively, taking turns with others, sharing ideas about how to organise an activity.

- Show sensitivity to others' needs and feelings, and form positive relationships with adults and other children.

The specific area targets for children leaving the Early Years Foundation Stage (in the school year that they become six) are summarised below:

Literacy: read and understand simple sentences, using phonic knowledge to decode regular words. There is growing knowledge about decoding common irregular words, and can comprehend what they have read and talk to others about it. They should also be able to use their phonic knowledge to write words in ways which match their spoken sounds. They can write simple sentences, additionally using some irregular common words which can be read by themselves and others.

Mathematics: count reliably with numbers from 1 to 20, place them in order and say which number is one more or one less than a given number. They can also add and subtract two single-digit numbers and count on or back to find the answer, and are able to double, halve and understand 'fair shares'. They have the ability to talk about issues relating to size, weight, capacity, position, distance, time and money, comparing quantities and objects to solve problems. There is recognition, creation and description of patterns. They explore characteristics of everyday objects and shapes and use basic mathematical language to describe them.

Understanding the world: children talk about past and present events in their own lives and in the lives of family members. They know about similarities and differences between themselves and others, and among families, communities and traditions, and are sensitive to the fact that people do not always enjoy the same things. They know about similarities and differences in relation to places, objects, materials and living things, talking about their immediate environment, making basic comparisons with other environments. They make observations of animals and plants and try to explain changes. They know that various technologies are used in homes and schools, and are able to select and use technology for particular purposes.

Expressive arts and design: children sing songs, make music and dance, and experiment with these. They safely use and explore a variety of materials, tools and techniques, experimenting with colour, design, texture, form and function, using what they have learnt about media and materials in original ways, thinking about uses and purposes. They are able to represent their own ideas, thoughts and feelings through design and technology, art, music, dance, role-play and stories.

(DFE 2012)

This will be re-visited in many of the chapters following, so do not worry if this all seems rather a lot to take in at first. To keep up with what is required in your work, particularly with respect to leadership, you will need to engage in continuing professional development activities once qualified; see Chapter 9 for further information on this point. Senior practitioners also need to lead and liaise with other professionals in cross-agency practice, based on the guidelines contained in the *Common Core of Skills and Knowledge for the Children's Workforce* (DCSF 2010). These are as follows:

- Communicating and engaging effectively with a wide range of colleagues, including those from other professional sectors that provide services for young children and their families;
- Understanding how children and young people develop and being clear about one's own professional role to support them in this process;
- Safeguarding and promoting the welfare of the child based on a core knowledge of current legal procedures and frameworks;
- Supporting transitions, being able to skilfully judge when and how to intervene in this process;
- Multi-agency working from the basis of an understanding of one's own role and the complementary roles of other professionals;
- Sharing information from the basis of an understanding of the complexities involved in this, balancing families' rights for confidential services with an understanding of when and how to share information and concerns with colleagues and professionals from other agencies, based on an underpinning knowledge of current policy guidance and legislation.

Focus on practice

Henry: a 'naughty boy' or a difficult situation? A multi-agency response

Henry, aged 2½, caused some amount of concern to the staff at the playgroup he began attending for four mornings a week. He did not seem to have any problems in separating from his mother, but his attitude towards the other children in the group was very aggressive, pushing and biting. Josie, a nursery nurse and Henry's keyworker, found that if she responded to this by sitting Henry on her lap and talking quietly and calmly to him he would calm down very quickly and go back to play – until the next time. After Henry had a tantrum where he 'swiped' a set of quite heavy wooden toys off a table where several children were playing (luckily not resulting in any injuries), Josie spoke to Sam, the centre EYP, about how they should proceed.

Identifying good practice
Sam suggested that the centre staff should carry out a series of **focal child observations** (see Chapter 3) on Henry, so they might be able to discern some kind of pattern that indicated what might be the cause of Henry's temper tantrums, then they could discuss how they might respond. He asked Josie to talk to Henry's mother, Jan, about this, and to let her know that both Josie and Sam were always available to discuss ongoing issues. After this was done, Josie reported back to Sam that Henry's mother was relieved – she had put Henry's problems down to the 'terrible twos' stage on the advice of her own mother, but was now beginning to think that there was more to it

than that, although she had been unsure. It had been agreed in this meeting that Jan would have full access to the observations and a regular weekly discussion with Josie.

Leading practice

Sam suggested that Josie share the task of carrying out the observations with Angie, the other nursery nurse in the setting, so that the collected data was not based only on the opinions of one person. After a fortnight, Josie, Sam and Angie met to discuss what had been observed. It emerged that Henry had no problems with other children if they approached him from the front, but both observers had recorded that if they came from the side, particularly the left, he would lash out. It was agreed that Sam and Josie would meet with Jan to discuss this. Sam's suggestion was that maybe Henry had some problem with his sight that meant he was being taken by surprise when children approached from the side, but he was unsure why this had not been picked up in Henry's two-year sight check. All was revealed when Jan informed him that Henry had not yet had his two-year sight check because the family had moved around this time, and been allocated to a different health visitor. She subsequently contacted her new health visitor, who carried out the test the following week. Henry was found to have some problems with the test, and was referred to an optician. The optician's diagnosis was a 'lazy' left eye.

Reflection *Sam's decision to investigate this situation properly created the positive result that, instead of becoming the setting's 'naughty boy', as might have happened in earlier times, Henry's underlying problems were diagnosed and treated. This illustrates one of the key purposes behind the two-year progress check introduced by the coalition government in 2012. However, diagnosis does not always mean instant improvement. In Henry's case, the treatment the optician advised involved patching the 'good' eye for a time, so Henry's experience was that, for a short time, his sight got worse instead of better, and consequently his behaviour deteriorated to some extent. But the centre staff now knew about the underlying problem and Sam suggested various ways that they could cope with this, which included consideration for the safety of the other children in the setting. Due to other children leaving the setting to move on to nursery during this time, Sam managed to reduce Josie's keyworker caseload temporarily so that she was consistently available to give Henry the emotional support he needed while his eye was patched. When his eye was unpatched, Henry was prescribed a pair of glasses which gave him relatively normal vision, and his behaviour improved dramatically.*

Early Years Education (2012) explores the EYFS using the six overlapping phases of child development initially used in the previous EYFS documents (2007):

Birth to eleven months

The initial stage where babies are focused principally upon physical and social development. They learn to control the basic movements of their bodies, understand in basic terms the information that is being filtered through their senses, and begin to communicate with the other people who inhabit their world.

Pearson Education Ltd/Jules Selmes.

Eight months to twenty months

From eight months infants begin to learn about locomotion, rolling, crawling and eventually walking. From the middle of the first year they begin to show attachment to familiar people in their world, and as they move towards the final third of their first year, the first words are uttered; these are often the names of people who represent the infants' closest bonded attachments, e.g. 'mama', 'dada', 'gan'.

Pearson Education Ltd/Jules Selmes.

Sixteen months to twenty-six months

Children moving from babyhood to toddler-hood are frequently full of energy, using their new skills of mobility to investigate every inch of their surroundings. Safety considerations within everyday environments now become paramount; children of this age will have little understanding of everyday dangers, so, for example, fireguards, electric socket shields and stair gates will be necessary in order to protect them from potentially harmful results of such investigations. Children will also usually enter the two-word utterance stage of language development during this stage (see below), and,

Pearson Education Ltd/Jules Selmes.

while they will become quite skilled at communicating meaning to familiar adults, there may be misunderstandings with people with whom they do not regularly interact. The will to do or communicate something may not always be matched by the necessary capacity at this stage, meaning that there may be frustration and temper tantrums that need skilful handling by carers.

Twenty-two to thirty-six months

Language continues to develop to the point that the child becomes more able to interact successfully with a wide range of others, including peers. If children have the opportunity to mix with a range of adults and peers during this stage they will become more socially competent, developing rudimentary skills of peer negotiation, although where difficult situations arise they will turn to bonded adults for help. Children in the later part of this stage will typically begin to deal with

Pearson Education Ltd/Jules Selmes.

simple intellectual challenges such as shape-matching, simple counting, naming colours and learning simple songs and rhymes. Fine motor skills develop rapidly, meaning that children in this stage will typically enjoy mark making and simple construction activities.

Thirty to fifty months

Children's abilities to engage in peer interactions increase; in particular they are able to engage in, and enjoy increasingly intricate collaborative make believe scenarios with their peers. Gender preferences in play styles and play companions begin to emerge, as does recognition of cultural differences and curiosity relating to this. There is a growing independence in 'self-care' activities such as toileting and dressing. Children will be happy to leave bonded adults for increasing periods of time, while still needing readily available help from familiar adults when confused, or comfort when distressed. The first literacy skills emerge, usually starting with the child's ability to recognise and then write their own name, moving on to recognise and copy other familiar words and phrases.

Pearson Education Ltd/Jules Selmes.

Forty to sixty months

The child is now beginning to build an increasingly independent role in the peer group, typically engaging in literacy and numeracy activities with enjoyment and increasing understanding. Independent problem-solving and reasoning skills are now developing quickly and children of this age are very capable of having a simple (albeit usually quite brief!) reasoned debate. They are also increasingly capable of controlling their own behaviour towards a projected end; this includes a developing ability to delay gratification for short periods of time.

These stages have been drawn from many years of developmental research. We have provided a brief overview of such research below; however, you (especially those who do not

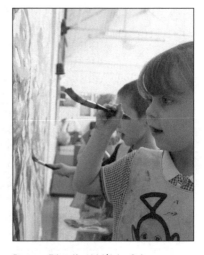

Pearson Education Ltd/Jules Selmes.

have significant child development education and training prior to undertaking their EYPS pathway) are advised to read more widely on this point, using the recommended reading list at the end of the chapter as your starting point.

What are the main theoretical perspectives that describe how children develop and learn, particularly between birth and their sixth birthday?

The first questions to be asked about human psychology were posed by the ancient Greek philosophers. They proposed that human beings expressed individually different temperaments, which they named as sanguine (easy-going), phlegmatic (sluggish), choleric (irritable) and melancholic (depressive) (Galen, second century BC in Thomas 1990). Modern theorists reject such early conclusions, but the study of personality – in its infant guise, temperament – is still ongoing today (see below), increasingly underpinned by the biological knowledge that is continually being developed by studies in the field of human genetics and brain biology.

Modern studies of human development have their roots in the 'Enlightenment', the beginnings of scientific study that began in the late seventeenth century in Europe, following the Renaissance. Some of this research was carried out in the field of pedagogy, and you will read about this in Chapters 5, 6 and 7, which deal with Early Years education practice. This chapter will introduce you to the principal theorists and theories in the field of developmental psychology.

1 Introduction to emotional development: attachment theory

Attachment theory was originated by the British psychologist John Bowlby (1969) over the period directly following the Second World War (1939–45). It was based on a mixture of Freudian ideas and extrapolation of concepts from studies that biologists had carried out on non-human animals and their offspring. Bowlby's central proposal was that human mothers and babies have a natural, evolved instinct to form a strong emotional bond. While this fixed focus on mothers was later found to be highly problematic, Bowlby's concept of the 'Internal Working Model' is still a central facet of modern attachment theory. He proposed that, based on the earliest relationship (nowadays relationships), infants construct an Internal Working Model (IWM) of what to expect from other people, and of their own level of 'lovability'. Bowlby proposed that a positive mother–child relationship creates an 'other people are nice and I am lovable' IWM, whereas a troubled mother–child relationship creates an 'other people are unkind and I am *not* lovable' IWM. This basic belief, he proposed, was the basis of all subsequent interactions and relationships for the child.

Bowlby also carried out studies with James Robertson, a social worker (Robertson and Bowlby 1952), on the problems that children experienced in the hospitals of the time, where visits by parents were extremely limited (see Jean's memories of being in hospital during the late 1950s above). This research indicated that children went through a process of initial distress, followed by despair, and, if contact with attachment figures was lost altogether, they finally detached from the adult concerned. If the detachment stage was reached, the relationship became very difficult to rebuild. The younger the child at the time the relationship was put under strain, the more quickly they went through the stages and the greater the negative effect the process had upon their psychological health and subsequent emotional development.

Schaffer and Emerson (1964) found, in a longitudinal study of babies aged 0–2 that *several* bonds with adults were formed in the first months. The babies tended to have one primary attachment and several secondary attachments, being perfectly content to be cared for by any of these 'bonded' adults. Only approximately 50 per cent of these babies had the primary attachment to the mother; the other 50 per cent had formed a primary attachment to another member of the family (most commonly the father or grandmother). The primary attachment tended to be the person in the family who showed the most sensitive responsiveness to the baby. The studies of Mary Ainsworth (e.g., Ainsworth and Bell 1970) also indicated that the quality of attachment that a child had to the main carer had a lasting effect on the IWM. However, later studies found her 'strange situation' methodology to be flawed, particularly in its tendency to diagnose problematic attachments in children from non-Western cultures, where, on examination of the child's life outside the laboratory situation that Ainsworth created for her tests, no such problems appeared to exist.

Modern studies of the attachments children build in daycare have produced complex and controversial findings, but the picture that emerges is that children in high-quality daycare do not suffer attachment problems, while those in low-quality daycare suffer a range of problems relating to both emotional and intellectual development. Such findings led directly to the New Labour Government's decision to fund dramatic improvements in daycare provision over the first decade of the twenty-first century; this included developing the role of the EYP. A summary of findings is presented in Table 2.1.

Table 2.1 Recommendations for daycare drawn from attachment theory

Developmental psychology	Recommendations for daycare
Children under 3 (and preferably under 5) need **regular care** from adults to whom they are **attached**, and can **rely upon**.	Daycare settings need to do everything in their power to **avoid high staff turnover**, e.g. good wages and working conditions; employment of well-qualified, dedicated staff.
Children need a lot of **individual attention** from adults, including one who sees the child as their 'especial' focus.	Daycare settings must have a **high number of adult staff** so that children can receive a lot of individual attention, much of which should be given by a **keyworker** whose role is to provide care for a small group of children.
. . . who show **sensitive responsiveness** to the child, showing a genuine interest in their communications, and an understanding of what they want/need at different times and in different situations (sustained shared thinking).	Staff in daycare settings need to be **specifically trained to work with children under 5**, and to have enough **professionalism, personal maturity and experience** to be able to 'decentre' from their own thoughts and needs to understand and show interest in the sometimes mundane communications of small children.
Children need **developmentally appropriate play resources** and **help/encouragement from adults** to progress in their learning.	Daycare settings should be **well-resourced** with toys and large indoor and outdoor play equipment and **adults should be specifically trained to understand how young children learn**, particularly what levels of understanding to expect in children throughout the 0-5 developmental period.

Note: Basic hygiene/health and safety practices etc. are not noted here, but are still obviously important!

Focus on practice

Antony, his brothers and 'sensitive responsiveness'

(Author's observation. Note: this observation was undertaken in a time when Reception was still part of Key Stage 1, before the instigation of the Foundation Stage.)

Antony, just 4, who is three weeks into his Reception year, is on the far side of the Key Stage 1 playground when I arrive, nearly into the older children's playground. He is in fits of giggles, being given a piggy-back by his oldest brother, while the next oldest one looks on. Antony has two older brothers, very close in age, one in Year 2 and another, the piggy-backer, who is in Year 4 and really should be in the older children's playground . . .

Later during the play session, the lunchtime supervisor rings the bell, which is the signal for 'stop play'. She gives the children a general reminder that they are not to push, or pull each others' coats, and tells them they are all to stand still for two minutes as a punishment for doing this . . . Antony remains standing quite still for a moment after play resumes. Kirsty, his friend from Reception, was individually told off by the lunchtime supervisor for jigging around when the children were standing still, and she cried. She is now holding the lunchtime supervisor's hand and several of the children in her class are around her, Antony being one of these. This is interesting because Antony is usually very active at playtimes . . . Some of the other Reception children also seem quite subdued, probably because they are not used to being punished in this way.

Antony's oldest brother comes over; he is well into the Key Stage 1 playground now. He twists Antony's shoulders, making him 'dance', then rubs his nose against Antony's and they stand forehead to forehead. Antony then goes around behind his brother, puts his arms around him, the brother walks forward and Antony follows, arms around him, and then the older boy turns around and rubs Antony's hair. This was not the only time I observed that, when some of the Reception children became upset, concerned or worried, an older sibling appeared to offer some comfort and reassurance. The staff generally seemed to turn a 'blind eye' to this . . . The lunchtime supervisor spotted Antony's brother, but she did not tell him to go back to his own playground in this instance.

Identifying good practice

I was a visitor in this school, carrying out observations of the children for a piece of extended research, so it took me a while to learn 'the rules', and even longer to learn that sometimes the staff allowed some rules to be stretched where they thought it would be of benefit to the children. While the formal rule in the school at that time was that the Key Stage 1 playground was for the children in Reception, Year 1 and Year 2, and the Key Stage 2 playground was for the children in Years 3, 4, 5 and 6, the unwritten rule seemed to be that staff did not reprimand or send an older child back to the Key Stage 2 playground if they were there to comfort a younger sibling, and the older children seemed to be fully aware of this. While all attempts were made by this school to ease the Reception children into mainstream school as was the practice at that time, the staff fully recognised that children who were only just 4, while they were moving into a stage of development where they can manage to function for a large part of their day without immediate access to people to whom they had bonded attachments, may still craved such support in times of unhappiness and uncertainty. In this way, the older siblings were neatly providing a 'sensitively responsive' interaction by filling such an 'attachment gap' and the school's flexible approach to this situation also indicated 'sensitive responsiveness' to practice with their youngest pupils.

Leading practice
As I got to know the setting better, I found out that there had been some instances where support staff (typically those who were new and untrained) had tried to enforce the playground allocation rules, regardless of the older child's purpose in the younger children's playground – usually to great protest from the older child in the situation. The Key Stage 1 and lunchtime coordinators dealt with such situations with great tact, finding somewhere else for the siblings to go together, and explaining to the adult concerned at a later time that this rule was 'made to be broken' in *some*, very specific instances. This is actually quite a difficult and dichotomous message to communicate to a member of staff – how do you think you might go about this?

Reflection *What do you think about the existence of 'rules that are made to be broken' (in some circumstances) in Early Years settings?*

Task Discuss this with your fellow EYPS candidates and colleagues. Where might you find a flexible rule like this in a non-school based setting? Do you think it would be easier to deal with, more difficult, or about the same?

2 Introduction to individual differences: temperament theory

The underpinning idea for a concept of 'temperament' came from a very famous psychologist called Hans Eysenck. He was concerned with adult psychology and is the originator of the modern concepts of an extravert/introvert, neurotic/stable personality. Eysenck (1981) proposed that there were very subtle differences in the brain biology of individuals, rather like the setting of a thermostatic mechanism. This, he proposed, would underlie our outwardly expressed personality. Developmental researchers soon proposed that the origins of adult personality could be discerned within infant styles of interacting with the external environment; this area of individual difference was termed 'temperament'.

Based on the New York Longitudinal Study of temperament, which began in the 1950s, Thomas and Chess (1977) proposed that they had discovered nine dimensions of infant temperament:

- Activity level
- Quality of mood
- Approach/withdrawal
- Rhythmicity

Figure 2.1 Dimensions of personality

Source: Gross, R. (1996) *Psychology: the science of mind and behaviour*, p.888. Reproduced by permission of Hodder Education

- Adaptability
- Threshold of responsiveness
- Intensity of reaction
- Distractibility
- Attention span.

Not surprisingly, these proved difficult to define reliably in more short-term studies. It was subsequently proposed that these dimensions were not all fully independent of each other, and could be collapsed into three basic 'types': the 'Easy', 'Difficult' and 'Slow to Warm Up' child. Other researchers and practitioners did not necessarily find potentially judgemental labels such as 'easy' and 'difficult' particularly helpful, however!

Buss and Plomin (1984) proposed that they could simplify Thomas and Chess's temperament dimensions to three, and that these could be related to Eysenck's theory of adult personality:

- Emotionality (relates to Neuroticism)
- Activity (relates to Extraversion/Introversion)
- Sociability (also relates to Extraversion/Introversion).

Buss and Plomin further proposed that impulsivity and shyness might also be independent dimensions from the three named, although they maintained that their 'EAS' system was an adequate model of temperamental differences between infants. Kagan (1988) suggested that there was a firm physiological basis for differences underlying temperament types, due to regulation of neuronal activity in the limbic system – again, similarly to Eysenck's theory. Kagan's theory was based on strength of emotional reaction, a continuum which he proposed was principally responsible for levels of personality traits such as sociability, shyness, adventurousness, talkativeness. Kagan proposed that people could consciously try to modify their behaviour and reactions, but that they could not change the biological activity that occurred in their bodies, e.g. increased heart rate and pupil dilation; hence, he proposed, the basic temperament 'type' was determined by genetic inheritance. More recent studies (see below) have suggested that cortisol levels may not be 'set' only by individual inheritance, but also by external events occurring during gestation and early childhood.

Dunn and Kendrick (1982) suggested that events that the child was exposed to in infancy and early childhood (particularly the birth of a sibling) could have a considerable effect on their behavioural style, and that, as time went on, transactions in the relationships between the carers and the siblings would have an important impact on all the children's temperaments and eventual adult personalities. Chess and Thomas (1984) suggested that 'goodness of fit' between a child's temperament and that of their regular carers has a huge effect on the child's self-confidence and resilience. This leads back to the concept of 'sensitive responsiveness' evoked in attachment theory, and how important this can be for a child during unsettling 'transition' phases in their life.

Focus on practice

Kayleigh and Sarah: 'sensitive responsiveness' to children *and* their parents during times of transition

Kayleigh was a premature baby who spent three weeks in an incubator before coming home for the first time. Her mother Sarah had always been rather anxious about her, and as she has grown older Kayleigh has shown many of the signs of being what Chess and Thomas might call a 'difficult' child. She shows high emotion and great sensitivity to environment; she does not like to mix with strangers, either adults or children. Sarah has identified that Kayleigh seems very sensitive to her emotional responses, and realises that this can create a 'vicious circle', in the sense that Sarah will worry that Kayleigh will respond poorly to a situation, and her concerns will seem to communicate themselves to Kayleigh, so Kayleigh's emotional responses are heightened. Kayleigh is now just 3, and in good health, and Sarah is five months pregnant. She wants to settle Kayleigh into a private nursery class for four mornings a week before the baby arrives. She has taken Kayleigh for an introductory session, during which Kayleigh cried and clung to her mother most of the time, apart from a short period of interest at the painting table. Kayleigh is to return next week, and Sarah is already dreading the experience. Jenny, the EYP in the setting, who manages the transitions, is aware of the situation.

Identifying good practice

Jenny talks to Barbara, the nursery teacher, and Jill, the nursery practitioner who is to be Kayleigh's keyworker, about how to proceed. They decide the following:

- Jill will undertake another home visit, and talk to Sarah about Kayleigh's normal activities and routines, and how these might be a little more closely aligned with the activities and routines of the nursery class, so that Kayleigh feels some familiarity within the nursery environment.

- Jill will also try to ensure that Sarah feels as much at ease with her, and with the situation, as possible, so that Kayleigh is not picking up so many negative emotions from her mother about the situation.

- Amber, who lives next door to Sarah and Kayleigh, is attending the nursery for one more term before moving on to the Reception class in the school in September. Kayleigh knows Amber a little, and they have sometimes 'visited' to play. Jill is going to suggest that, if possible, the parents take turns in bringing Kayleigh and Amber to nursery together (Sarah for the first couple of weeks if she prefers), so that Kayleigh does not come in alone.

- Jill will also find out if Kayleigh has a favourite toy that she would like to bring to nursery, one that can act as what attachment theorist Winnicott (1951) called a 'transitional object', providing some comfort when people to whom she has bonded attachments are not physically present.

- Sarah and Jill will agree a schedule via which Sarah will leave Kayleigh for longer and longer periods over the first few weeks of her attendance until she is attending the whole session without Sarah. Jenny explains to Jill that this will not only involve providing reassurance for Kayleigh, but also for Sarah.

Leading practice

When Kayleigh has been at nursery for three weeks, Jill and Barbara inform Jenny that, while Kayleigh seems to be making good progress, despite Jill's efforts at reassurance that Kayleigh is happy and settled, Sarah seems unable to leave her in the setting for more than an hour without popping back to 'see if she is OK'. Barbara and Jenny decide that it would be a good idea for Jenny to talk to Sarah about this. If you were Jenny, how do you think you would approach this situation?

Reflection *Such conversations with parents cannot be wholly planned, as the practitioner undertaking them needs to be able to respond to the situation as it unfolds, sometimes involving other staff on a 'need to know' basis. By this time Sarah will be nearly six months pregnant, and perhaps helping her to focus on how she will maintain Kayleigh's routine when the new baby arrives (which should include the three-hour session at nursery) might help Sarah to move on in the previously agreed schedule, leaving Kayleigh for progressively longer periods in the nursery. Jenny will try to help Sarah to consider that, if Kayleigh is used to spending the full session at nursery without her mother present by the time the baby arrives, the resulting changes will not unbalance Kayleigh's routine so dramatically, and thus minimise the unsettling events arising for her from the new arrival. If Jill (who is currently completing her Foundation Degree in Early Years, with a view to eventual EYPS validation) is informed and involved in this process, Jenny will also be able to model good practice in working with parents for her.*

3 Introduction to social development

Uri Bronfenbrenner (1979) did not deny that genetics was very important in determining what children become in later life. However, he proposed that crucial interactions with the child's 'nature' were created by the 'nurturing' environment. Many highly influential childhood intervention and enrichment projects eventually grew from the basis of Bronfenbrenner's ideas. He proposed that children inhabited a series of systems that were nested one within the other like a set of Russian dolls.

- The innermost system is the *Microsystem* which describes the child's everyday environments (e.g. home, school).
- The *Mesosystem* provides the contacts between the structures of the microsystem, e.g. a parent–teacher association or a local parent and toddler group.
- The middle system is the *Exosystem* which describes aspects that have a direct influence on the microsystem environment (e.g. parents' jobs, relationships with extended family and friends).
- The outer system is the *Macrosystem* which describes the cultural surroundings of these environments (e.g. language, culture, wealth and poverty, ethnicity and religion).

See Figure 2.2.

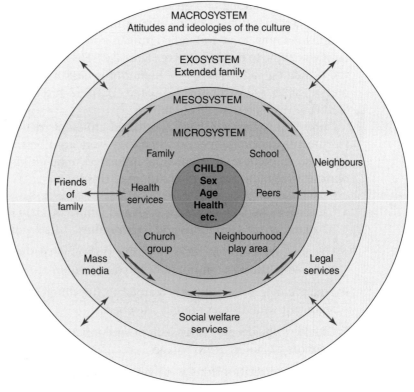

Figure 2.2 Bronfenbrenner's concept of 'systems'

Source: © Dockrell, J. and Messer, D. (1999) *Children's Language and Communication Difficulties: Understanding, Identification and Intervention*, p. 139, by permission of Continuum, an imprint of Bloomsbury Publishing Plc.

Figure 2.3 Extending children's development

At a time when many scientific discoveries were beginning to indicate that what we 'are' is determined to a great extent by genetics, Bronfenbrenner emphasised the still crucial influence of the environment. He made it clear that, while nature determined how 'long' individual human potential was, nurture determined how far it was going to be 'pulled' (see Figure 2.3). His theories have subsequently been the launching pad for two very high-profile childhood enrichment programmes on both sides of the Atlantic, HeadStart (US 1962–present, 2012 online) and Sure-Start (UK 1998–present, 2012 online).

Dunn and Kendrick (1982) considered children's development in family environments during the period when they were aged between 3 and 7 years. The following important environmental influences upon children's early social development were indicated by the findings of this study:

● Children's interactions with friends and family strongly impacted on their ability to understand emotions and 'other minds' ('theory of mind').

● Frequent discussion about why people do/feel what they do especially seemed to develop 'theory of mind' skills in young children.

● Young children very quickly learned to use different types of discussion and argument with different family members.

● Children who develop early skills of emotional understanding build on this and are more advanced at later stages.

● Child–child relationships were very important in their development of these skills, both with siblings and with friends.

Focus on practice

Five-year old football play and resulting peer relationship learning

(Author's observations)

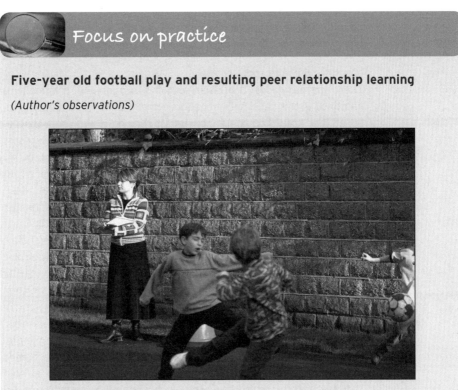

Pearson Education Ltd/Jules Selmes.

Over 2002–03, I carried out an ongoing series of observations in primary school, of which one of the aims was to study the relationships developed by the children through their outdoor free play. Some of the observations undertaken were of the 5- and 6-year-old boys in the group when they engaged in football play. Here is an extract from one of the transcripts. At this time, Antony had just had the plaster removed from a recently broken arm, and was not really supposed to engage in football play at all:

'Antony gets the ball. The other boys are very careful not to tackle Antony and they let him have his turn with the ball . . . He kicks it, and all the other boys run after it. I hear Leo's voice: "Tom, it's my turn". Tom kicks at goal, and Antony saves it in front of Benji. We seem to have three goalkeepers now, Aiden also standing by the goal post. Benji takes the ball from Antony and kicks it out. It hits Ashley on the hand and a cry goes up: "hand ball". Antony picks up the ball and takes it out of play. He says "I'm taking it, hand ball." (Chanting "score, score, score".) He puts it down, takes a kick at goal and scores. He says "like Beckham".

'The ball rolls out of play down to the tarmac. Tom brings it back up. He is standing on the hill looking like he is going to throw in, but he kicks it instead. It goes behind the goal. Antony takes the next throw in. They seem very sure about the boundaries of their football pitch, but it is not clear to an adult observer . . . He puts the ball down and kicks it through the goal sideways and then jumps up and down (children cheer). Benji says "no goal" as he was not in the goal at the time . . . But they are not counting the goals anyway. Benji is saying "no, no" and holding on to the ball. They all chant at him: "time waster". So he kicks the ball back out into play again.'

Identifying good practice

There are many aspects of social learning through peer relationships that can be identified in this short set of observation extracts. Though only 5, these children re-alised that Antony could not play unless they gave him some special consideration, and it is clear that they effectively managed to do this. This indicates some amount of ability to decentre from their own situations to understand the situation of an-other, currently recovering from injury. The children show some rudimentary knowl-edge of the rules underlying football in their invocation of 'hand ball', 'time wasting' and 'goal scoring', and their understanding that there is a designated area outside which the ball is no longer in play, but it is clear that this is still at a very basic level, indicated (for example) by the presence of three goalkeepers and a complete lack of team-based play. Benji indicates that, while he can evoke the rules as he under-stands them, he is also willing to acquiesce to majority opinion and send the ball back into play – a highly flexible response to social pressure, which also indicates some underlying 'Theory of Mind'. As these children play, they co-create rules and practices. My analysis, after several observations of this nature, was that their learn-ing about the rules of the game was very much secondary to their learning about the social interactions that they had with each other, all underpinned by the impetus to achieve the continuation of a play situation that they were all enjoying. There is little that is required from adults in such a situation, apart from a discreet vigilance to ensure that physically dangerous or 'bullying' situations do not develop.

Leading practice

During my time on this piece of research, I occasionally saw adults intervening in the children's play in attempts to completely change the meanings that the children had created between themselves, with the inevitable result that such play broke down. For example, when a group of boys were playing a chasing game which involved Benji dragging a skipping rope while the other boys chased him, the female teacher on playground duty stopped their game, and gathered the group together to talk to them. She showed them how to turn the rope, with one child at each end. All the boys tried to skip, but none seemed to have any idea of when to jump as the rope swung around. The teacher then called to Miranda to demonstrate . . . she was very good at skipping, but the boys lost interest and wandered off. The chasing game soon began again, with Benji at the front, this time with a 'push wheel'. When the bell went, I asked him what they were playing. 'Fire engines', he replied. I wondered if that was also the game ongoing with the skipping rope. If so, the play narratives used by the boys and the adult were not at all compatible. It could also be theorised that some of these differences were underpinned by a cross-gender misunderstand-ing, something that all female Early Years Practitioners (who massively outnumber men within the profession) need to consciously consider.

As a leading practitioner, how would you explain to your staff how to judge when and how to intervene in children's play, to protect and enhance, without imposing a potentially destructive adult agenda?

Reflection *The only real 'rule' here is that each situation must be approached on its own merits, underpinned by an adult's aim to build on and extend the children's ideas, rather than attempting to impose their own agenda on top of them. There are many instances where building shared understandings with other children is the most important aspect of a play event, whether or not those understandings are judged as 'correct' by an adult. The key point here is to focus on the activity's processes rather than its outcomes. You need to consider this point deeply during the observations that you undertake in the early part of your training (see Chapter 3). Such a focus will develop your knowledge and sensitivity in this area, which will in turn help you to support other staff towards a greater understanding of the benefits of child-led play, as part of your evidence for the leadership standards as you move towards validation.*

4 Introduction to cognitive developmental theory

Jean Piaget was the first theorist to produce a comprehensive theory of human intellectual development. In *The Psychology of the Child* (Piaget and Inhelder 1969) he outlined his theory that children learn in interaction with the *concrete* world (i.e. world of objects), with experiential learning underpinning the child's construction of a cognitive network of schemas, assimilating and accommodating new knowledge. A schema is, in Piaget's context, a set of mental connections. At the time of Piaget's research there was little evidence of how the living brain worked, but now we know that infants and children do indeed rapidly build up connections between brain cells called neurons over the developmental period. Piaget proposed that the child either assimilates a new experience (taking it into thought without creating a new concept, e.g. you lick an ice cream and you also lick an ice lolly) or accommodates it (creating a new concept in thought, e.g. you can't pick up spaghetti with just a spoon, or a knife and fork; you have to learn a new action with a spoon and a fork). The child moves towards accommodation by a process of 'equilibration', which means needing to balance all related schemas against one's current picture of reality.

Piaget proposed that building thought processes to adult competence continued until the child was 12. Nowadays, we know it takes much longer than this, and that there is a wealth of individual and cultural difference in such construction. However, Piaget's concept of stages is still useful as a rough guide to children's intellectual competence in the early years of life. He carried out an extensive series of experiments that indicated babies under about six months do not even realise that objects that they cannot immediately see still exist within the world; hence he proposed that such young infants have no concept of 'object permanence'. This, he proposed, relates to lack of mental connections within such an immature mind. Babies do not yet have the available symbols within their mind to 'hang' such concepts and memories upon. Achieving the concept of object permanence is one of the major goals of the sensori-motor stage (birth to 18 months), alongside organising information coming from the senses, and the achievement of basic motor skills (walking, holding objects etc.). Children aged approximately 18 months move on to the 'pre-operational' stage, where they will spend approximately 4½ years

Figure 2.4 An example of 'centration'

Source: CALVIN AND HOBBES © 1986 Watterson. Dist. by UNIVERSAL PRESS SYNDICATE. Reprinted with permission. All rights reserved.

building schemas relating to developing linguistic and social competence and reducing egocentricity (a focus solely on the self and one's own point of view). Children in the earlier periods of this stage are unable to hypothesise logically with respect to social or intellectual situations, frequently showing 'centration' (a focus on only one simple, surface-based aspect of a situation). Margaret Donaldson (1978) outlined a series of experiments undertaken by her research team that indicated that, once a child understood the social situation in which a problem was embedded, they were much more likely to be able to work towards a successful solution. It is therefore common, but not inevitable, that children will show more sophistication in dealing with social situations than intellectual situations as they move through this stage. A Piagetian concept that can be used to describe this inconsistency is 'décalage' (literally 'gap' or 'interval'). Once children reach the next stage, that of 'Concrete Operations' (7–12 years), their ability to think logically about both social and intellectual situations becomes more flexible and mature.

The Russian developmental psychologist, Lev Vygotsky, was also a theorist in the constructivist tradition, like Piaget, proposing that children built their understanding of the world on the basis of their interactions within it. However, Vygotsky (1978) placed more emphasis upon the role of interaction with other people, proposing that language was crucially important in learning, in that it was the principal medium through which a child would begin to 'internalise the external'. While Piaget proposed that cognition precedes language, Vygotsky proposed that language precedes cognition. While Piaget proposed that a child had to be 'ready' to grasp a particular skill or idea, Vygotsky proposed that interaction, particularly with an adult or a more able peer, could take a child one step further in their learning than they were able to move alone. He referred to the area into which a child could be 'coached' as a 'Zone of Proximal Development' (ZPD). Jerome Bruner, who brought Vygotsky's work to the attention of the West, proposed that the adult's ongoing role in a teaching and learning process is to progressively *scaffold* the child's learning at an appropriate level, i.e. within the ever-progressing ZPD (Wood, Bruner and Ross 1976). Building on this point, Wood and Middleton (1975) proposed that the best way adults can help children learn is by creating a contingency, by consciously and carefully tailoring adult input on a minute-to-minute basis so it is always contingent to the child's learning (i.e. supporting the child into the constantly moving zone of proximal development). This leads us back to the concept of 'sustained shared thinking' that is advocated in the EYFS.

Focus on practice

On a Bear Hunt with Pinky: developing sustained shared thinking

Three-year-old Anastasia is constructing a picture based on a story that her teacher has read the group called *Bear Hunt*. There is a box of pre-cut card bear shapes on the table, and a basket of brown furry material. Anastasia has spread glue on her bear shape, but she is looking around for some pink furry material, because she wants the bear to look like Pinky, her favourite teddy who sits on her bed at home. She goes to the trainee nursery practitioner, Vanessa, who has designed the activity and is working with the children at the table. Anastasia holds out a piece of brown material to Vanessa and says 'Where's the pink?' 'Can't you stick it on, Anastasia?', says Vanessa, 'Here you are.' She sticks the material on to the middle of Anastasia's bear shape and says, 'There. Can you do the next one?' Anastasia shakes her head, and wanders off to the painting table, where she finds some pink paint. She is soon in conversation with Brenda, the centre EYP, about the picture she is painting of Pinky, her teddy bear. Vanessa finds the abandoned bear shape on the table at the end of the session when the children have gone home. She shrugs, and then puts it into the waste paper bin.

Identifying good practice

In order to access Anastasia's zone of proximal development, Vanessa needed to *listen* to what Anastasia was saying to her and respond appropriately, i.e. to consider what the child was thinking rather than seeing the situation from her own adult point of view. Anastasia was presenting her with a problem that she needed help to solve, but Vanessa provided her with a solution that Anastasia had already considered and rejected. In doing so, Vanessa has missed the opportunity to help the child to solve the problem in a way that she would comprehend as useful and effective. If Vanessa remembered that the abandoned bear shape belonged to Anastasia after the session, she might wrongly conclude that the task was 'too difficult' for the child; this is what frequently happens when adults do not try to consider the situation from the child's point of view. If Vanessa had responded to the situation with more insight, she might have moved on to consider that the activity itself was very limited, given the materials available to the children, and then towards some ideas on how to improve the activity next time by providing a wider range of materials for the children to use.

Leading practice

Brenda sees Vanessa put the unfinished bear picture into the bin. She has picked up from her conversation with Anastasia that the child had abandoned the activity; she also knows that Anastasia was not the only child in the setting to do so during that session. She has allowed Vanessa to design and run the activity in this way so that she can learn from the experience, but Vanessa's response to this indicates that she has not intuited that there is anything wrong with the activity; in fact, Brenda heard her telling another member of staff during the session that the children 'are not very good at sticking activities'. What would you say to Vanessa, if you were in Brenda's position?

➡

Reflection *It can sometimes help with very young trainees to give them a very limited set of paints and ask them to paint a picture of themselves – they will very quickly comment that they haven't got the right colour for their hair/eyes etc. and from that personal, practical experience they can more easily move on to consider how every craft activity should offer children a choice and a chance to personalise their work. From there they can then move on to understand why the perennial Early Years prompt to 'tell me about your picture' is such a crucial interaction between young children and their carers, and why forcing children of this age into the 'Blue Peter' situation (where they are required to make a copy of something an adult has made earlier!) is not particularly helpful at this stage of their development.*

5 Introduction to language development

Words are *symbols*. Each word that we utter 'stands for' something, in our own minds, and (hopefully!) in the minds of the person we are talking to. Usually these meanings match – if they do not, there can be misunderstandings, which may be quite amusing. For example, in a very old joke:

'I say, I say, I say – my dog has no nose.'
'Your dog has no nose? How does he smell?'
'Terrible!'

Some words will stand for simple concrete objects, e.g. 'dog', 'cat', 'table'. Other words stand for complex abstract ideas, e.g. 'love', 'peace', 'justice'. However, the average 10-year-old child will have a working (if not exact) idea of what all these words mean.

When we converse with someone we match the symbols in our heads with the symbols in theirs. This is usually possible when we use the same sounds (and squiggles, if we include written language) to stand for the same ideas and objects, although we may not always communicate exactly what we intend. If people use different sounds and squiggles from us to stand for the same ideas and objects (i.e. they speak a different language), translation is often possible, but this inserts an extra 'step' which makes communication even more imperfect.

The basic stages of language development proceed as follows:

Protoconversation

The 'protoconversation' was first described by Mary Bateson in the 1970s. She described 7-to-15 week old infants responding to their mothers' talk with appropriately timed smiles and coos in a give-and-take, dialogue-like pattern, hence 'proto' (stands for) conversation (Bateson 1975). The adult will often act as though the baby's 'responses' are intentional. In this way, Bateson proposed, the baby learns the turn-taking conventions of adult conversation.

Pearson Education Ltd/Jules Selmes.

Stage 1

This is the one-word stage; the child develops a small repertoire of single words, usually the names of familiar people and objects, e.g. 'mum', 'dad', 'cup' [around 1 year to 18 months].

Stage 2

Two-word sentences which tend to be simple descriptions of actions and possessions now emerge, e.g. 'my ball', 'throw ball'. This stage was referred to as **telegraphic speech** (Oates and Grayson 2004); nowadays we might be more likely to call it 'text speech'; the point is that the child usually manages to convey a surprising amount of information in very few words (alongside gestures and facial expressions) [around 18 months to 2½ years].

Stage 3

Simple grammatical sentences are now beginning to be uttered, and towards the middle of this phase their content begins to encompass past tenses, reflecting a growing understanding of past and future. Children start to use grammatical constructions, e.g. 'I walked', but in doing this they sometimes inadvertently 'regularise' irregular verbs, e.g. 'that tree growed' instead of the grammatically correct 'that tree grew'. This indicates that they are not just simply repeating adult speech but learning (and sometimes stumbling on) grammatical rules to underpin their own original utterances. They also begin to learn to play with language in songs and rhymes [around 2½–3½ years].

Stage 4

The 'where, what, why' stage. The child becomes a competent language user, and begins to use this new skill to ask adults everything the child wants to know about the world. As any parent knows, some of these questions will be impossible to answer; for example, at this age my son once asked his father 'Why elephants?' On further investigation this did not refer to *what* elephants were, or what they *did*, but simply *why* they 'were'. Children of this age sometimes appear to use their new linguistic competence to engage in a developmental stage of what could be termed basic philosophical enquiry! [around 3½–4½ years].

Stage 5

Children may now use more complex sentences involving more than one clause. For example, they will begin to use the more grammatical 'Who is playing with that ball?' structure, rather than the more babyish 'Who play ball?' [around 4–5 years].

Stage 6

Children now join sentences smoothly together with conjunctions like 'and' and 'but', e.g. 'John and Asif came with me' and 'I used to like Samantha, but I don't like her now.' They can also turn the meanings of sentences around, e.g. 'Is that your coat?' and 'That is your coat', and enjoy playing with language in this way; for example, see the joke at the beginning of this section! [around 4½–5½ years].

Children who have had other developmental problems also tend to have delayed development of linguistic competence. This may be particularly in evidence if hearing loss has been a problem. Children who have been diagnosed with, or are in the process of being investigated for, conditions within the autism spectrum disorder category also typically have a range of difficulties with language development.

The day-to-day adult role in assisting children with their language development is very important. As outlined above, carers and small babies show turn-taking behaviour in interactions that psychologists have labelled 'proto-conversation' (Dougherty 1999). Later on, when children begin to speak, adults and older children automatically simplify their speech when talking to small children, emphasising key words and often repeating key phrases. This has been referred to as 'parentese' or the 'baby talk register', but adults who are not parents, and even older children will usually instinctively do this when conversing with children under 2. Another instinctive adult technique is to introduce a 'frame', e.g. 'What is this? It's a frog. What is this? It's a fish.' A lot of toddler books are constructed in this fashion; a favourite with my children was 'Where's Spot?' (Hill 1980), which repeats 'Where's Spot? He's not in the . . .' over a few pages until Spot is found.

Traditional songs and rhymes that small children are taught to sing are also frequently constructed in this fashion as well, e.g. 'The Wheels on the Bus' and 'Ten Green Bottles'. This format presents a nugget of information in a familiar 'frame', so the child pays attention to and learns the new information without the pressure and confusion of a continually changing 'frame'. Such games can be very useful in extending children's language competency.

6 Introduction to biological perspectives of child development

The human central nervous system begins developing at two weeks gestation. The human brain weighs around 350 grams at birth; by the end of the first year it weighs 1000 grams. An adult brain weighs between 1200 and 1400 grams. This illustrates the huge importance of the first year of life for brain development. When we are born we have many more neurons (brain cells) than we actually need. Over the first few years of life, the human brain undergoes a huge neuronal connection programme. Those neurons that are not connected to others shrivel and eventually die. Most children have a 'good enough' environment, but if they experience extreme neglect their brains do not develop as they should; in particular, there is a fixed 'window' for some skills to be triggered (e.g. language). If this window is missed, the child may not be able to make up the lost ground at a later point in their life. A well-documented case of this type is that of 'Genie', a 13-year-old American girl who was found locked in her bedroom in the early 1970s (Rymer 1994). The evidence that could be put together suggested that she had been locked away from other people since she was a very small child. Although she was unable to speak when she was discovered, she initially made good progress in learning individual words; however, she never progressed to putting these words together to form grammatical sentences. The researchers concluded that the developmental window for learning grammar and syntax had passed for 'Genie', that the neurons that should have been dedicated to this task had died away, and were not able to be reactivated. Modern research increasingly indicates that much early brain development, while underpinned by genetic programmes, is shaped by a child's early environments. A good example of this is how easily small children learn to be bi- or even multi-lingual, developing native competence in all languages learned in infanthood, while adults struggle to learn subsequent languages and seldom become accomplished enough to speak them without a foreign accent.

Recent biological research also suggests that the amount of stress that children are placed under in infancy has a crucial 'thermostat setting' effect on the biological mechanisms relating to the stress response, commonly known as 'fight or flight'. Children who have a lot of stress in infancy, in particular that created by experiences of being passed from carer to carer with little or no attention paid to the time to form bonded relationships, are vulnerable to developing abnormalities in the levels of the hormone cortisol, which mobilises the 'fight or flight' mechanisms in all mammals. Children experiencing ongoing stress typically have abnormally high resting levels of cortisol and these take longer to return to baseline after individual stressful experiences.

Initial studies of children in Western daycare suggested that, across the board, they appeared to show cortisol levels that rose steadily throughout the day, a very worrying finding. However, Antipodean researchers Sims, Guilfoyle and Parry (2006) compared the cortisol levels of children in daycare settings judged as 'high quality' against the cortisol levels of children in daycare settings judged as 'satisfactory'. They found that, while the children's cortisol levels rose throughout the day in the satisfactory settings, they fell throughout the day in the high-quality settings. These researchers went on to outline what features defined a 'high-quality setting':

- **Staff relationships:** happy engaging atmosphere, with staff guiding children's behaviour positively.
- **Respect:** staff initiate and maintain communication with children, accommodating their individual needs, including the recognition of social and cultural differences.
- **Partnership:** staff and families exchange effectively both verbal and written information about the children, and about the centre's routines and expectations.
- **Staff interaction:** staff communicate effectively and function as a team.
- **Planning and evaluation:** the centre programmes reflect a clear centre philosophy and shared goals, which cater for the needs, interests and abilities of all the children, and all the children are helped towards successful learning.
- **Learning and evaluation:** the centre programmes encourage children to make confident choices and take on new challenges.
- **Protective care:** staff supervise children at all times, and individual needs for safety, rest and comfort are met. Children are appropriately dressed for indoor and outdoor play. Toileting and nappy procedures are positive experiences.
- **Managing to support quality:** staffing policies and practices facilitate continuity of care for each child.

(Sims *et al.* 2006)

53

These features lead us back to the beginning of the chapter, where similar aspirations can be found in the content of the EYFS.

> ## Focus on practice
>
> ### Providing a calm environment in a stressful world
>
> It is a Monday morning, 9.20 a.m. Four-year-olds Jenna, Shaun and Olivia are hanging up their coats at the children's centre that they regularly attend. Jenna's father has just been made redundant, and her mother has just finished her nursing degree. Jenna's mother is currently working on a series of part-time temporary contracts, still looking for a permanent job. This morning, Jenna heard her parents arguing because her mother wanted her father to take Jenna to the setting, but he was still in bed. Both of Shaun's parents work long hours, and his father, who brought him to the centre, was running late today. He made a business call on his mobile phone as soon as he got out of the car outside the centre, and forgot to kiss Shaun, or to say goodbye. Shaun looks out of the window, watching his father pull quickly out of the car park. Olivia lives with her single mother and her 11-year-old sister Amy. Amy has some important tests at school today and, when Olivia started to sing at the breakfast table this morning, Amy (who can be quite nice sometimes) screamed at her to 'shut up'.
>
> The children all have their own pegs in the cloakroom, and they recognise the pictures that have been there since they started at the centre over a year ago. Although all their families were running a little late this morning, there is no pressure for the children to be exactly 'on time'; the morning starts with the children's self-registration, which is accomplished by their removing a name tag that hangs on their coat pegs so they can hang their coats up, and then putting the tag in a basket by the playroom door. The children are not called together as a group until 11.30 a.m., although it is standard practice for their keyworkers to greet them on arrival, and speak briefly to their parents.
>
> As they hang up their coats and put their tags in the basket, the children can see their keyworkers interacting with other children playing with the activities on the tables in the playroom. The children know that they can ask any of the adults in the setting for help at any point, and that their request will meet with a calm and helpful response. A snack will be available shortly, and the children will be able to have this any time between 9.30 and 11.00 a.m. Lunch, afternoon snack and tea will also be served at regular intervals in the day, and there will be regular activities that punctuate the day, for example a story before lunch and a song with actions just before the afternoon snack is available.
>
> The setting is light and roomy, and the staff try to ensure that no one pushes or shouts, although the children are allowed to be a little noisy when they are running around and laughing outside. The equipment is well maintained and the centre policy is to maintain a slightly higher adult-child ratio than the minimum required by law.
>
> The adults work well as a team; all of them are fully aware of the centre practices and policies, and the children's parents are encouraged to engage with the

children's activities in the centre; this is more often successful at the end of the day rather than at the beginning, when the parents' schedules may be very tight.

Shaun runs in and joins in a game with the 'matchbox' toy cars that has already begun between his friends Jon and Andrew. Olivia makes her way to the painting table, dips a brush into the red paint and begins spreading the paint across the paper. 'That's very bright, Olivia', says Rob, her keyworker. 'It's Amy, she's cross about her SATs', says Olivia. 'Oh dear', says Rob, 'I was cross when I had SATs, too. What other colours are sort of "cross" do you think?' Olivia thinks for a moment, and then dips her brush into the yellow paint. She applies it to the paper so that it drips into the red, creating a bright orange. 'That's great, Olivia', says Rob, 'all really sort of "cross" colours, look at that orange you've made with the red and the yellow.' Jenna goes into the Home Corner and picks up a doll. When Dominic follows her in she says, 'why can't you take her to school, Daddy? I'm busy'. 'OK', says Dominic. They begin to put the doll into the little buggy, which Jenna then takes outside.

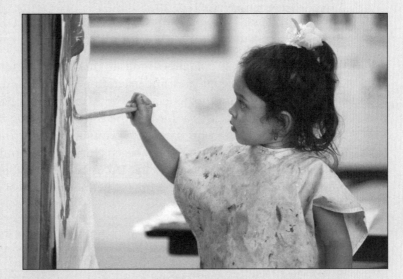

Creatas.

Identifying good practice

What stresses have the children been exposed to in their home lives, and how has the practice in the setting helped them to settle down more calmly to their day after a rather fraught start at home? Go through the description above, producing your own bullet-points relating to the relevant practices.

Leading practice

Task A new placement student in the setting runs after Jenna, intending to tell her not to take the doll and the pushchair outside. How would you respond to this situation? How would you explain to the student that it is important for the child to move through her narrative with the doll and the pushchair, even if it does end with the toys abandoned in the corner of the playground, when Jenna decides she would prefer riding around on a tricycle? Discuss this with your fellow EYPS candidates and colleagues.

Reflection *In common with many other examples outlined in the activity boxes above, the key issues here focus around the adult decentring to the child's position, and sometimes offering the type of 'sustained shared thinking' response that Rob demonstrates, 'tapping in' to the art activity in which Olivia has engaged. In doing so, he manages to extend Olivia's understanding of colour mixing, while validating her feelings and those of her sister, and not interfering in a self-defined activity which appears to be offering Olivia some amount of emotional catharsis.*

What influences and experiences in the setting and beyond can impact on children's well-being, development, learning and behaviour, and how can we connect these to the theoretical perspectives introduced in the previous section?

We have seen from the information above that the underpinning theory and the current early years guidelines indicate that young children need to gradually develop their knowledge and understanding of the world principally through self-selected play-based experiences. These should involve active learning, in calm, well-resourced environments where they are supported cognitively and emotionally by adults who have a sound underpinning knowledge of child development, and an understanding of each child's unique individual needs. While no setting is perfect, this chapter has led us to the consideration of what 'good practice' may actually entail, and how to define this against practice which is not so enlightened.

Focus on practice

Developing the independent learners of the future

We are going to provide you with an example of two different (fictional and highly stereotyped) settings to consider:

Brilliant Babies	Jolly Jumpers
Has a fixed start time	Has a flexible start time
Has very fixed routines which serve the convenience of the adults	Has flexible routines which serve the needs of the children
Has set tasks that the children must complete	Has a range of activities from which the children can choose freely
Has a set routine that the adult staff must follow, whether or not this fits in with the needs of the children in their care	Expects adults to self-regulate their duties in partnership with others (including parents) and encourages them to be as flexible as possible

Brilliant Babies	Jolly Jumpers
Has a set regime for recording that the adults must follow, even where the procedures do not 'fit' with the information they wish to record	Allows the adults to record how and what they judge to be useful, as long as enough information on every child is collected via the processes undertaken
Adults tell the children what to do	Adults are emotionally and cognitively available to the children
Adults feel that their role is to direct and instruct	Adults feel that their role is to support the children's development and learning
The practice is driven by targets and 'box-ticking'	The practice views the current Early Years Framework as a set of useful guidelines
The leaders in the setting 'direct practice' and 'manage learning'	The leaders in the setting 'lead practice' and 'support learning'
The child is dependent upon the adults and learns to blindly obey	The child becomes an independent learner, building their knowledge and understanding of the world principally through a range of self-selected, play-based activities with sensitive adult support
The child enters later years of schooling unable to evaluate a situation in order to make judgements and choices	The child enters later years of schooling able to evaluate and make choices on the basis of their own judgements

Identifying good practice

Of course, you are unlikely to find a 'pure' example of 'Brilliant Babies' or 'Jolly Jumpers' in your own practice environment – most settings have features of both, although they may have more features of one than the other! By this point in the chapter, you should be very clear about which setting is exhibiting the best practice; however, the challenge remains as to how to achieve this in a 'real world' environment, where highly directive regimes in the later stages of education may have a 'top-down' pressure that Early Years settings may sometimes find hard to completely resist.

Leading practice

At some stages of your career, you will be expected to defend your setting's practice in the face of some criticism, not least with regard to inspection.

Task How would you defend child-centred, play-based learning, even if it does not generate the 'correct' mechanical responses to fixed assessment measures that more structured practice may produce in very young children? Discuss this with your fellow EYPS candidates and colleagues.

Reflection *Even experienced professionals are likely to experience some qualms when considering the question above. Early Years practitioners must remain firm in their core understanding that an emotionally secure, reflective, independent learner is not quickly produced within the process of development and learning. We can look for inspiration to the Scandinavian countries and their measured 'educare' approach to Early Years education for support in this respect, particularly with regard to the excellent outcomes their children achieve in the later years of development (see Chapter 3).*

Developmentally appropriate practice

We have been discussing 'developmentally appropriate practice' all through this chapter, but as we come to the end we would just like you to take a moment to reflect on this as a concept. It may seem obvious that one would not expect to teach and care for 16-year-olds in the same way as one would teach and care for 6-year-olds. However, development is so rapid over the first five years, it can be difficult to keep up with ongoing changes, sometimes over a period of weeks rather than months and years.

The American National Association for the Education of Young Children (NAEYC) propose that developmentally appropriate practice can be achieved if practitioners focus on the following aspects:

1. What is known about child development and learning – referring to knowledge of age-related characteristics that permits general predictions about what experiences are likely to best promote children's learning and development.

2. What is known about each child as an individual – referring to what practitioners learn about each child that has implications for how best to adapt and be responsive to that individual variation.

3. What is known about the social and cultural contexts in which children live – referring to the values, expectations, and behavioral and linguistic conventions that shape children's lives at home and in their communities that practitioners must strive to understand in order to ensure that learning experiences in the program or school are meaningful, relevant, and respectful for each child and family.

(NAEYC 2009, pp.9–10)

You will see a lot here that you can relate to the theories above, particularly Bronfenbrenner, Piaget and Vygotsky. However, it is easy to be lulled into a false sense of security in collective settings, in the sense that just because you have a comprehensive approach to continuous provision that you are engaging in developmentally appropriate practice. This was at the heart of a debate that raged for over 20 years in primary education, as a response to the Plowden report (1967). Eventually, it was suggested that some teachers had misunderstood Piagetian theory and its representation in the Plowden report to the extent they had the idea that children could be almost entirely left alone to structure their own learning within an environment of developmentally appropriate resources (see for e.g. Gillard 2004, online).

Leading developmentally appropriate practice within a collective care and education environment is by contrast a much more difficult prospect than 'teaching from the front'. The adult has to educate the child from the basis of the child's own agenda, being fully aware of the zones of proximal development of all the children under their care, and carefully working within these to scaffold learning, which requires much 'decentring' from the adult position in order to engage in authentic sustained shared thinking with each individual child.

Reflection *If 4-year-old Zac (who is clearly deeply involved in his play with a train set) tells you that a train track that he is currently playing with 'has broken so the trains can't go any further', how might you respond to this? How might you deal with a less experienced practitioner who immediately says 'well then you need to put in a signal' and continues with a barrage of questions to find out what Zac knows about signals (What does red mean? What does green mean? . . .). Think back to Anastasia's pink teddy, and then consider how you might interact with Zac to find out why he proposes the track is broken, and what he thinks should be done about it.*

Coping with transitions

Children undergo a range of transitions in their first five years, some more than others. While some may be a feature of simply 'growing up' (e.g., from nursery to school) others may be unplanned and less easy to control (e.g. from living with mother and father to mother and grandmother if parents separate). It is the role of the key worker to help children cope with transitions in their lives and to work through these with the least amount of upset possible.

Allingham (2011) suggests that adults need to promote the following aspects:

- Positive attitudes
- Diversity and difference
- Safety
- Valuing individuals
- Listening
- Respect
- Cultural identity
- Physical and emotional well-being
- Building relationships
- Confidence
- Feeling safe to take risks
- Positive sense of self and others
- Secure relationships
- Autonomy
- Independence
- Positively affirming environments.

Reflection *Think about how you felt when you made a recent transition in your life – for example moving house, moving to a new job or starting your current training programme. Apply the above bullet points to this, reflecting in your journal what may have gone well and what may not have gone quite so well.*

Identifying good practice

If you can also remember a situation where one of the children you were working with had to cope with a transition, it would be useful to apply this list to their situation, again considering what may have gone well and not quite so well, and what you did to try and help them through the relevant event.

Leading practice

If you could develop a reflective training session for the staff in your setting on this topic, using the prompts above, you might be able to include reference to this in your validation tasks, particularly if you are on one of the entry pathways and in need of some evidence for your knowledge and leadership of working with parents and families (as this will undoubtedly come into your reflections). You should see plenty of opportunities to use the developmental theory you have read about, in this chapter and in the recommended reading in an activity of this nature.

Conclusion

What are the main EYFS principles, and how do they relate to mainstream developmental theory and research?

Summaries of the EYFS principles and the mainstream developmental theories/research are detailed above, and we hope you will view this first chapter as a key source of reference as you move through the following chapters, returning to its pages where authors raise related points. You are also directed to the DFE website, where you will find regular updates on the EYFS.If you are on the three longer pathways, you should also find that the child development content of your college programme will give you a range of opportunities to relate theory and research to the EYFS and your day-to-day practice. Those on the GPP may also be offered 'refreshers' and online resources to address this aspect of EYPS training. If you want to supplement your reading, you will find some ideas for recommended texts at the end of this chapter. You may also find the Open University 'Open Learn' pages relating to child development to be of interest in this respect: www.open.edu/open/learn and follow the link to 'Childhood and Youth'.

What are the main theoretical perspectives that describe how children develop and learn, particularly between birth and their sixth birthday?

While it was impossible to cover all theoretical perspectives that might be useful in this respect, this chapter has been designed to get you off to a good start, by introducing central theories and theorists in the areas of emotional, cognitive, social, language and biological development, and theories of individual difference underpinned by temperament. We hope that you will use the directions to further reading below to increase your knowledge in these areas, and engage in discussions with your fellow EYPS candidates and colleagues relating to the more controversial aspects of each area of theory. The more widely you read, the more

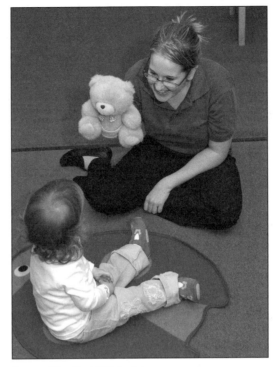

Pearson Education Ltd/Jules Selmes.

confident you will become in such debates. You should also become a regular reader of at least one of the journals listed below, so you can keep up with theoretical, policy and practice developments in your chosen professional field. Leaders in any field must be, by definition, independent learners.

What influences and experiences in the setting and beyond can impact on children's well-being, development, learning and behaviour, and how can we connect these to the theoretical perspectives introduced in the previous section?

You should now be beginning to make such connections, for example:

- Attachment theory with the keyworker system
- Zone of Proximal Development, scaffolding and contingency with sustained shared thinking
- Biological theory relating to the initial calibration of the arousal mechanisms within the infant brain with calm, flexible routines within childcare and education settings.

The wide range of concepts introduced within this chapter should serve as a platform from which to access the following chapters within this book; so please feel free to return to this base as many times as you wish to reflect upon the later ideas with which you are presented. You have now launched your journey towards becoming an expert and leader in child development, hence the hub around which the practice of a childcare and education setting will revolve: that is, an Early Years Professional.

Further reading

Bee, H. (1997) *The Developing Child*. Harlow: Longman.

Brock, A., Dodds, S., Jarvis, P. and Olusoga, Y. (2009) *Perspectives on Play*. Harlow: Pearson.

Cohen, D. (2002) *How the Child's Mind Develops*. London: Routledge.

David, T., Gooch, K., Powell, S. and Abbott, L. (2003) Birth to three matters, a review of the literature, available at:
http://www.standards.dfes.gov.uk/eyfs/resources/downloads/rr444.pdf.

Donaldson, M. (1978) *Children's Minds*. London: Fontana.

Flanagan, C. (1996) *Applying Psychology to Early Child Development*. London: Hodder & Stoughton.

Gerhardt, S. (2004) *Why Love Matters: How affection shapes a baby's brain*. London: Routledge.

Gopnik, A., Kuhl, P. and Meltzoff, A. (2001) *How Babies Think: The science of childhood*. London: Phoenix.

Johnson, J. and Nahmad-Williams, L. (2009) *Early Childhood Studies*. Harlow: Pearson.

Kehily, M.J. (ed.) (2004) *An Introduction to Childhood Studies*. Maidenhead: Open University Press.

Lindon, J. (2008) *Understanding Child Development: Linking theory and practice* (2nd edn). London: Hodder Arnold.

MacLeod-Brudenell, I. (ed.) (2008) *Advanced Early Years Care and Education* (2nd edn). Oxford: Heinemann.

Nutbrown, C. (2006) *Threads of Thinking: Young children learning and the role of early education*. London: Sage.

O' Hagan, M. and Smith, M. (2002) *Early Years Child Care and Education: Key issues*. London: Bailliere Tindall.

Smith, P.K., Cowie, H. and Blades, M. (2003) *Understanding Children's Development*. Oxford: Blackwell.

Some useful websites

The Department of Education:
www.education.gov.uk/childrenandyoungpeople/earlylearningandchildcare.

Early Education: www.early-education.org.uk.

The Early Years Foundation Stage framework:
http://www.education.gov.uk/schools/teachingandlearning/curriculum/a0068102/early-years-foundation-stage-eyfs.

The Effective Provision of Pre-School Education (EPPE) project (1998–ongoing), available at:
http://k1.ioe.ac.uk/schools/ecpe/eppe/.

The Teaching Agency:
http://www.education.gov.uk/aboutdfe/armslengthbodies/b0077806/the-teaching-agency.

Journals

Child Development

Children Now

Early Years – an International Journal of Research and Development

Early Years Educator

Educational Researcher

Nursery World

Psychological Review

References

Ainsworth, M.D.S. and Bell, S.M. (1970) 'Attachment, exploration, and separation: Illustrated by the behavior of one-year-olds in a strange situation'. *Child Development*, 41, pp.49-67.

Allingham, S. (2011) 'Transitions in the Early Years'. London: MA Education.

Bateson, M.C. (1975) 'Mother–infant exchanges: The epigenesis of conversational interaction', in D. Aaronson and R.W. Rieber (eds) *Developmental Psycholinguistics and Communication Disorders: Annals of the New York Academy of Sciences*, Vol. 263. New York: New York Academy of Sciences.

Bowlby, J. (1969) *Attachment and Loss: Volume, attachment*. New York: Basic Books.

Bronfenbrenner, U. (1979) *The Ecology of Human Development: Experiments by nature and design*. Cambridge, MA: Harvard University Press.

Browne, A. (2010) *Bear Hunt*. London: Penguin Books.

Buss, A. and Plomin, R. (1984) *Temperament and Early Developing Personality Traits*. Hillside, NJ: Lawrence Erlbaum.

Chess, S. and Thomas, A. (1984) *Origins and Evolution of Behaviour Disorders*. New York: Brunner Mazel.

DCSF (2010) *The Common Core of Skills and Knowledge for the Children's Workforce*. Leeds: CWDC.

DFE (2012) The Early Years Foundation Stage. Available at: http://media.education.gov.uk/assets/files/pdf/e/eyfs%20statutory%20framework%20march%202012.pdf. Accessed on 26 April 2012.

Dockrell, J. and Messer, D. (1999) *Children's Language and Communication Difficulties: Understanding, identification and intervention*. London: Continuum.

Donaldson, M. (1978) *Children's Minds*. London: Fontana.

Dougherty, D. (1999) *How to Talk to Your Baby*. New York: Perigree.

Dunn, J. and Kendrick, C. (1982) *Siblings: Love, envy and understanding*. London: Grant McIntyre Ltd.

Early Education (2012) Development Matters in the EYFS, available at: http://www.ncma.org.uk/pdf/development-matters-in-the-eearly-years-foundation-stage.pdf. Accessed 5 April 2012.

Eysenck, H. (1981) *A Model for Personality*. Berlin: Springer Verlag.

Gross, R. (1996) *Psychology: The science of mind and behaviour*. London: Hodder Arnold.

Gillard, D. (2004) The Plowden Report, available at: http://www.infed.org/schooling/plowden_report.htm.

Hill, E. (1980) *Where's Spot?* London: Heinemann Young Books.

Kagan, J. (1988) 'Temperamental contributions to social behaviour'. *American Psychologist*, 44, pp.668-74.

National Association for the Education of Young Children (2009) Developmentally Appropriate Practice in Early Childhood Programs serving children from Birth through Age 8, available at: http://www.naeyc.org/fileposihais/psdap.pdf. Accessed 5 April 2012.

National Head Start Association (US) (2008) About the National Head Start Association, available at: http://www.nhsa.org/about/index.htm. Accessed on 24 March 2008.

Oates, J. and Grayson, A. (2004) *Cognitive and Language Development in Children*. Oxford: Blackwell.

Piaget, J. and Inhelder, B. (1969) *The Psychology of the Child*. New York: Basic Books.

Robertson, J. and Bowlby, J. (1952) 'Responses of young children to separation from their mothers'. *Courrier of the International Children's Centre,* Paris, II, pp.131-40.

Rymer, R. (1994) *Genie, a Scientific Tragedy*. London: HarperPerennial.

Schaffer, H.R. and Emerson, P.F. (1964) 'The development of social attachments in infancy'. *Monographs of the Society for Research in Child Development,* 29 (Serial No. 94).

Sims, M., Guilfoyle, A. and Parry, T. (2006) 'Child care for infants and toddlers: where in the world are we going? The First Years - Nga Tau Tuatahi'. *New Zealand Journal of Infant and Toddler Education,* 8(1), pp.12-19.

Sure Start (UK) (2008) Sure Start: About us, available at: http://www.surestart.gov.uk/aboutsurestart/. Accessed on 24 March 2008.

Thomas, A. and Chess, S. (1977) *Temperament and Development*. New York: Brunner/Mazel.

Thomas, K. (1990) 'Dimensions of personality', in I. Roth (ed.) *Introduction to Psychology,* pp.373-416. Hove: Lawrence Erlbaum.

Vygotsky, L. (1978) *Mind in Society*. Cambridge, MA: Harvard.

Watterson, B. (1995) Calvin and Hobbes, available at: http://www.calvinandhobbes.co.uk/. Accessed on 24 March 2008.

Winnicott, D.W. (1951) 'Transitional objects and transitional phenomena. A study of the first not-me possession'. *International Journal of Psycho-Analysis,* 34, pp.89-97.

Wood, D., Bruner, J. and Ross, G. (1976) 'The role of tutoring in problem solving'. *Journal of Child Psychology and Psychiatry,* 17, pp.89-100.

Wood, D.J. and Middleton, D.J. (1975) 'A study of assisted problem solving'. *British Journal of Psychology,* 66, pp.181-91.

3

Safeguarding and child protection

Jane George, Pam Jarvis and Doreen Malcolm

Chapter overview

The Standard addressed in this chapter is:

3. Safeguard and promote the welfare of children.

This chapter will consider children's safety and well-being in the broadest possible sense, as this is represented in the three supporting statements of Standard 3. The text will address the following key questions:

- What are the legal requirements and guidance on health and safety, safeguarding and promoting the welfare of children, and where can I find help and advice on these?
- If I have to lead in my setting with respect to safeguarding, how should I go about it, in terms of policies and procedures and how to implement them and gain support and cooperation from my colleagues?
- On an everyday basis, how do I establish a safe environment and instil practices that promote children's health and safety without removing the risk and challenge so essential to children's development?

Cotton wool kids?

A generation of children is losing touch with the outdoors as 'nature deficit disorder' spreads, according to a National Trust report.

Despite being surrounded by some of Britain's finest landscapes, even children in Devon and Cornwall are increasingly 'living in fear' of the outdoors, according to experts in the region. They cite worrying examples of 'cotton- wool kids' who have never even visited the seaside, never mind climbed a tree or camped under the stars . . .

In a generation, the number of children who play in outdoor wild spaces has plunged from 50 per cent to less than 10 per cent today. Despite the safety fears, three times as many children are hospitalised falling out of bed as the number injured from falling out of a tree . . .

➡

Dave Rickwood is Devon site manager of the Woodland Trust, which runs a Nature Detective programme available online to encourage children to explore woods. He said he was often 'amazed' about the lack of confidence young people had about exploring their natural surroundings.

'The trouble is, it becomes a self-fulfilling prophecy', he said. 'If they are too afraid to go out into woodlands themselves, then as adults they are terrified that their own child will get stung by a nettle. They get over-protective and it gets worse and worse...'

Adrian Richards, chief executive of BF Adventure, which runs outdoor adventure activities for disadvantaged and disabled children on a 60-acre former quarry... said: 'That change that we see come over young people just by taking them down to the woods and doing some basic fire-craft is phenomenal. It's all about building confidence and being active, and it's a great way to encourage teamwork.'

'Cotton wool kids are losing touch with the great outdoors', *Western Morning News*, 30 March 2012

http://www.thisisdevon.co.uk/Cotton-wool-kids-losing-touch-great-outdoors/story-15667486-detail/story.html.

Introduction

What are the legal requirements and guidance on health and safety, safeguarding and promoting the welfare of children, and where can I find help and advice on these?

Legal frameworks and guidance

The Health and Safety at Work Act 1974 sets the basic minimum standard to meet the safety needs of the workforce, but in addition to this as Early Years workers we have to address the physical environment, the resources and the levels of supervision to meet the safety needs of the children in our care. Given the role of the EYP in leading practice then they must also apply considerations of safety and protection to colleagues, stakeholders and visitors.

Alongside the more comprehensive set of legislation, including the Children Acts of 1989 and 2004, which will be fully introduced in Chapter 4, leading practitioners also need to be aware of the legal requirements introduced in the Health and Safety at Work Act 1974 (see http://www.hse.gov.uk/pubns/hsc13.pdf) and the Protection of Children Act 1999 (see http://lx.iriss.org.uk/sites/default/files/resources/046.%20The%20Protection%20of%20Children%20Act%201999%20-%20A%20Practical%20Guide.pdf) in order to ensure that the workplace is safe for both children and adults, and to create appropriate professional safeguarding policies for childcare and education settings. Comprehensive information on all legislation (and some 'green paper' guidelines) that are currently relevant can be viewed by using the search facility on http://www.parliament.uk/index.cfm.

The National Standards for Daycare (2001)

In 2001 Ofsted published a set of National Standards for Daycare when they were given the responsibility of inspecting daycare settings by the government of the day. These standards are still valid, and concepts within them have informed the Early Years Foundation Stage (2007 and 2012). They are spelled out in detail below as they are key to basic safety in Early Years settings and underpin current practice.

The National Standards for Daycare are as follows:

Standard 1 – Suitable Person: Adults providing daycare, looking after children or having unsupervised access to them should be suitable to do so.

Standard 2 – Organisation: The setting meets required adult:child ratios, ensures that training and qualifications requirements are met and organises space and resources to meet the children's needs effectively.

Standard 3 – Care, Learning and Play: The setting meets children's individual needs and promotes their welfare. Activities and play opportunities are planned and provided to develop children's emotional, physical, social and intellectual capabilities.

Standard 4 – Physical Environment: The premises are safe, secure and suitable for their purpose. They provide adequate space in an appropriate location, are welcoming to children and offer access to the necessary facilities for a range of activities which promote their development.

Standard 5 – Equipment: Furniture, equipment and toys are provided which are appropriate for their purpose and help to create an accessible and stimulating environment. They are of suitable design and condition, well maintained and conform to safety standards.

Standard 6 – Safety: The setting takes positive steps to promote safety within their premises and on outings, and ensures proper precautions are taken to prevent accidents.

Standard 7 – Health: The setting promotes the good health of children and takes positive steps to prevent the spread of infection and appropriate measures when they are ill.

Standard 8 – Food and Drink: Children are provided with regular drinks and food in adequate quantities for their needs. Food and drink is properly prepared, nutritious and complies with dietary and religious requirements.

Standard 9 – Equal Opportunities: The setting and its staff actively promote equality of opportunity and anti-discriminatory practice for all children.

Standard 10 – Special Needs (including special education needs and disabilities): The setting staff are aware that some children may have special needs and are proactive in ensuring that appropriate action can be taken when such a child is identified or admitted to the provision. Steps are taken to promote the welfare and development of the child within the setting in partnership with the parents and other relevant parties.

Standard 11 – Behaviour: Adults caring for children in the provision are able to manage a wide range of children's behaviour in a way which promotes their welfare and development.

Standard 12 – Working in Partnership with Parents and Carers: The setting and its staff work in partnership with parents to meet the needs of the children, both individually and as a group. Information is shared.

Standard 13 – Child Protection: The setting complies with local child protection procedures approved by the Area Child Protection Committee (now 'Safeguarding Boards') and ensures that all adults working and looking after children in the provision are able to put the procedures into practice.

Standard 14 – Documentation: Records, policies and procedures which are required for the efficient and safe management of the provision and to promote the welfare, care and learning of children, are maintained. Records about individual children are shared with the child's parent.

(DFES 2003, pp. 6-8: **http://www3.imperial.ac.uk/pls/portallive/ docs/1/46973696.PDF**)

Reflection *For EYP candidates with extensive work experience, it would be helpful at this point to reflect on your own responses to the changes that the Early Years workforce has experienced during your working life. For GEP candidates, the further reading recommended at the end of Chapters 3 and 4, added to discussion with more experienced others, either within your workplace or with EYP candidates on the GPP pathway would be beneficial.*

As noted earlier, settings have to be safe as workplaces under the Health and Safety at Work Act 1974. Until September 2008 we all relied upon the National Standards for different settings to ensure we met basic health and safety needs of the children in our care. Many settings opted to exceed the basic levels outlined in the National Standards and may have applied for and achieved national and/ or local recognition for their good practice through a variety of quality measures. Since September 2008 the basic standards for health and safety in childcare and education settings have been subsumed within the Early Years Foundation Stage (EYFS) documents of 2008 and 2012.

The introduction of the EYFS in September 2008 prompted a review of all setting policies related to health, safety and child welfare to ensure that they were compliant with the most recent guidelines. The updated EYFS (2012) should again prompt a review, but in settings with high standards of practice reviews of policies and procedures are done at least yearly and also following incidents to evaluate their effectiveness. Dates of completed policy review and planned future review should be noted on the policy itself. These documents give us clear guidance on minimum acceptable standards for health, safety and welfare including detail on staffing and suitable persons, risk assessments which should be carried out and essential first aid skills. Legislation, guidance and related policies will go some way to creating a healthy and safe environment for both children and staff, but it is often the individual actions of children and adults which compromise health and safety in the setting! As such, it would be a good idea to find out if/when health, safety and child protection policy reviews take place in your setting and how the dates of such reviews are recorded.

An EYP, as leading practitioner in the setting must consider:

- The resources they offer to the children, which should meet both UK and European safety standards.

- The appropriateness of the selection of resources and activities for children at different ages/stages of development, as a developmentally inappropriate toy which is perfectly safe for the stipulated age group may still pose a significant danger to a younger child (for example toys with small parts for infants who are still using their mouths to explore the properties of objects).

- The 'ground rules' for activities, and how it will be ensured that both staff and children understand and comply with these.

- The basic levels of supervision required for different activities.

- How to prevent children putting themselves or others in danger without undermining their judgement and self-confidence.

- How to support children to take increasing responsibility for their own health and safety.

- How to be a good role model and demonstrate best practice in health and safety to children and adults.

Reflect on these points yourself, as an EYP candidate, with your candidate cohort and (if possible) with the staff team in your setting.

Focus on practice

Zac's day out

On a recent visit to a local country park I was lucky to observe a family at play. The two older boys aged (approximately) 4 and 6 years were playing a game of 'tig', running around the open grassy space. Zac, a younger brother aged (approximately) 2 years, ran after them trying to share their play. He ran quickly and confidently until he tried to change direction when he wobbled and leaned to one side but steadied himself and set off again following his brothers. He really struggled to slow down and stop, often relying on his brothers and parents to act as his brakes! He was temporarily distracted from the game by a small stream which he studied carefully then he walked alongside the stream in the direction of flow for a few moments. He watched the flow intently but never stumbled or tripped as he walked along the edge of the low bank. His parents observed him from a discrete distance but did not distract him from his task. He stopped when he reached a small bridge and re-engaged his family when he turned to them and shouted 'pooh-sticks'!

The family then moved towards a 'living playground', an area of yew and rhododendron with paths and tunnels and dens. Zac followed his brothers through a gateway onto a narrow path, his parents again at a discrete distance. When he saw his brothers through the shrubs Zac turned off the path and headed directly towards them through the undergrowth. He displayed great skill as he picked his way between the low branches, finding firm footings and using the higher branches as handrails. He climbed a muddy bank using similar skills – finding footholds and supporting and balancing himself by holding onto branches. His parents and siblings watched on but left him to concentrate and work out his own path, they did not distract him by calling his name or offering a 'helping hand', help which could so easily have been his downfall. When he reached the top of the bank he glowed with pride, he stood up tall and looked back over his 'Everest' and smiled. His achievement earned him lots of praise, in the form of attention and hugs, from his family.

Identifying good practice

I felt very privileged to observe Zac's play and reflected on what I had seen on the drive home. I considered that Zac had made extremely creative use of the resources offered to him, and he was supported in his play by people with whom he shared bonded attachments, who gave him confidence in his ability to explore and his judgement to keep himself safe as he challenged the limits of his skills. These factors made the afternoon's play an excellent child-led activity for Zac. Jarvis (2007) describes how important approval from slightly older males within the peer group is for the development of self-esteem of boys in the Early Years, and as such Zac's skills, confidence and self-esteem would not only have been boosted by the successes in his play, but also because his achievements had been noted by his older brothers.

Leading practice

When I began reflecting upon the contemporary early care and education environment I compiled a list of questions:

- Would Zac have been offered this (or a similar) opportunity within an Early Years setting?

- Would he be spending time with more skilful, adventurous, older children within an Early Years setting?

- Would an Early Years worker have stopped this play as unsuitable for such a young child, or on the grounds of accident prevention?

- Would an Early Years worker have tried to help – calling his name or offering a hand – which may have been counterproductive, reducing the scale of his achievement and/or possibly inducing a fall?

- Would I, as a leading practitioner, have let this play reach its natural conclusion, and/or expect my staff to have done so? Would there have been any element of 'blame' attached to an adult observer, if the child had met with an accident?

Reflection *In reflecting on Zac's play on a family outing, we can consider how adults' reactions to children's play may vary, depending upon whether the setting is an informal environment where the caring adults are from the child's own family, and or whether the setting is a formal, professional environment where the caring adults are paid professionals. In this case, the professional setting appears to struggle with problems that do not arise within the family environment. This is a complex issue, to which there are no easy answers, within the post-industrial culture of contemporary England, where practices are moving towards collective care during the working day for the majority of children under the age of 5. Discuss this issue with your colleagues, particularly with respect to how children's rights to exploration and 'limit testing' can be enhanced within your setting. I hope that this description of Zac's play has prompted you to reflect and question what your own practice might have been in this situation where both safety and inclusion should be equally important considerations.*

Brown (2008, p.222) neatly encapsulates the practitioners' 'safety versus independence' dilemma:

Once, when my wife was away in France, I collected my 5-year-old grandson from school. As a special treat we went to Rowntrees Park where there is a variety of brightly coloured adventurous play equipment. He went straight to the top of the 'spider's web' (about 10 metres off the ground). Admiring his agility, I sent a text message to my wife telling her of our grandson's feat. Almost immediately I received a reply saying, 'Are you mad? Get him down!' In an instant my whole perspective on the situation changed, and I began to encourage him to come down. . . reaching through the ropes he placed his hands on the central pole, but on surveying the scene, he pulled back and climbed back down the net (much to my relief).

Brown's grandson, like Zac, had a clear sense of his own abilities and was able to explore this to its limits, without taking over-ambitious risks. Logically, such a sense is likely to have been firmly inculcated by evolution within a successful species (a species that routinely takes risks well beyond its ability to cope is unlikely to survive for very long!). However, it is the balance between allowing children to take 'safe risks' and protecting them against accidents that we currently find very difficult. There is presently a lively ongoing debate about the curtailment of risk-taking in the management of the current generation of Western children (Stephenson 2003), and the increasing adult management of their play activities, largely due to fears relating to health and safety. Corsaro (1997, p.38) described this process as 'the institutionalisation of more and more children's leisure activities'. Adult fears relating to the injury of children in collective settings, particularly with regard to fears relating to the potential for parental litigation following even minor accidental injuries too often leads to the over-swift intervention of adults where they perceive the smallest potential danger. It is very difficult within our current cultural climate to get such a balance 'just right' in practice, hence the many ongoing, complex debates around this issue:

> Risky play is difficult to theorise but essential for well-being; children need opportunities to push themselves beyond boundaries in familiar environments; schools and classrooms have become risk-averse places and this is detrimental to children's development and well-being.
>
> (Tovey *et al.* 2008, online)

Well-being

Chapter 2, 'Principles in childcare and education', is a good summary of basic child development and the factors which influence development, it may be useful to refresh your thinking on social and emotional development and attachment before you explore the concept of 'well-being'. Well-being is not a new term, but recently the term has taken on great significance in the world of Early Years. John Bowlby established the link between bonded relationships and a child's emotional well-being in the early 1950s (see Chapter 2). Since then others have contributed to this area of research (a summary can be found in David *et al.* 2003, the research report which underpinned the Birth to Three Matters framework). Over time the emphasis has shifted from the mother as all-important to the quality of the pattern of care and attachments the child has within its daily environments. The EPPE project (1997 ongoing) identified that quality and consistency of personnel working with children was key to their well-being and development. The principle way that we measure children's well-being and development in Early Years practice is by careful observation of their behaviour within the setting.

Focus on practice

Observation

Those of you who have studied childcare and education on previous training programmes may already be accomplished at child observation, particularly if you are already a leading practitioner within your setting. However, if you are an entry pathway candidate (particularly a GEP) with little or no previous experience in childcare/education, it is absolutely crucial that you develop good observational skills while you are on your EYPS training pathway, as not only will you need to carry out professional observations of children in your day-to-day practice, but one of your key roles will also be to support the development of observational skills in more junior staff. There are many good texts about child observation, some of which are listed in the further reading below.

Task Based on your reading of such texts, ensure that you understand the following basic observation techniques:

Diagrammatic: including tracking and sociogram, and that you are able to present your results on simple charts (e.g., bar chart, pie chart).

Sampling: including target child, focal child, time sampling, snapshot, event sampling.

Observations using checklists: High/scope technique (Hobart and Frankel 2004, p.139) and see the Leuven Child Involvement Scale for Young Children in the Focus on practice box below.

Observations using photograph and video records: this must crucially include an understanding of conventional ethical practice when handling data generated in this way.

Participant observation: where you observe children while taking part in their activities (useful for understanding the event from the perspective of your own engagement).

Non-participant observation: where you observe children without participating in their activities (useful when you want to adopt a more objective orientation to the information gathered).

Collecting objective data

It is important to ensure that an acceptable level of objectivity is present in the observation records of the setting, relating to both individual children and specific areas. This is ensured by:

- Carrying out regular non-participant observations;
- Making sure that the child/area is observed by two or more members of staff within a two-to-three week period;
- Carrying out 'paired' observations where two people observe the same area or child simultaneously;
- Discussing any concerns that may arise from your observations with other practitioners on a 'need to know' basis (e.g., with the leading practitioner or key person).

Enacting more than one measure of the same person or area is called **triangulation** and ensures that some level of **validity** (if observation notes/evaluations agree you can be more confident that you are observing what you initially thought you were observing, for example that a particular child really is quick to anger, or a particular outside area always becomes very slippery after even a light fall of rain) and **reliability** (if more than one person observes the same individual/area and arrives at the same conclusion, this increases the possibility that the points raised are going to arise again in subsequent observations).

Having grasped the basic techniques you must ensure that you can select and enact a suitable observation method to gather information relating to:

- Children's individual personalities and 'styles';
- Children's individual and collective needs;
- How children learn;
- How children interact with peers and adults;
- Behaviour changes that might indicate illness or other underlying problems;
- How to plan future practice and activities;
- How children use resources;
- How to pursue your own professional development.

And to gather information about individual children's:

- Physical and sensory development;
- Intellectual/cognitive development;
- Language development;
- Emotional development;
- Social development;
- Aesthetic/spiritual development.

In early 2007, UNICEF produced the report *An Overview of Child Well-being in Rich Countries*. While many European countries (particularly those on the Scandinavian peninsulas) were high in the rankings, the UK was close to the bottom of the table along with the United States. The methodology of the survey has been questioned, but any evidence that our children may be experiencing a 'less than best' childhood should be unacceptable to any member of the children's workforce. Recent reports on a similar theme from Layard and Dunn (2009) and The Good Childhood Report (2012) from The Children's Society concur with these findings. In 2008 a review by the Child and Adolescent Mental Health Services 'Improving the mental health and psychological well-being of children and young people' identified continuity of staff and professionals as important to children and their families and workforce development as one of the challenges for the future. Work on well-being has been carried out in Belgium by Laevers (1997 and 2005) and this has been incorporated into the Pen Green Framework for Engaging Parents (2008), using the Leuven Child Involvement Scale for Young Children, initiated by Laevers and his colleagues. In essence Laevers created a 5-point scale from 1 – very low to 5 – very high for well-being (where level 1 behaviour includes signs of discomfort, crying, anger, withdrawal and self-harm and level 5 behaviour includes smiling, self-expression, humming, being relaxed, being open and approachable, being energetic and self-confident) which can be applied to the behaviour a child exhibits during an observation.

Focus on practice

Example of an observation evaluation method: The Leuven Child Involvement Scale for Young Children (LIC-YC)

Bertram and Pascal (2004) used this as the observation method in their Effective Early Learning Study (EELS). A summarised description of their method is outlined below.

The child involvement scale consists of two components:

- a list of 'involvement signals'; and
- the levels of Involvement in a 5-point scale.

The child involvement signals

Concentration: the level of attention the child directs towards the activity.

Energy: the effort the child invests in the activity.

Complexity and creativity: the level of competence the child shows in the activity, as measured against their previous best efforts; the consideration of whether the child is moving into their 'zone of proximal development' in engagement with this activity.

Facial expression and posture: the intensity of the child's posture and facial expression. Do they appear to be completely absorbed in the activity?

Persistence: the duration of concentration that the child gives to the activity, and the ease/difficulty of distraction.

Precision: the attention to detail within the activity.

Reaction time: how quickly a child reacts to further stimuli within the activity, showing motivation and keenness.

Language: how does a child talk about a particular activity, e.g., do they ask to do it again, or state that they enjoyed it?

Satisfaction: how proud is a child of their achievements within the activity? (NB: this does not have to relate to satisfaction with a specific product - it could be satisfaction with an experience).

Child involvement scale

The child involvement scale is to be used with reference to the involvement signals:

Level 1 Low Activity Stereotypic, repetitive and passive, with little effort or indication that the child feels that much is demanded. They are easily distracted, after which the activity is forgotten.

Level 2 A Frequently Interrupted Activity The child is engaged in an activity for part of the time, but spends approximately half of the observed period not paying direct attention. They are relatively easily distracted, after which the activity is forgotten.

Level 3 Mainly Continuous Activity The child seems busy at an activity but there is the feeling that 'something' is lacking and that the task is routine. They are relatively easily distracted, and may not return to the activity.

Level 4 Continuous Activity with Intense Moments There are some signs of intensity in the child's engagement. They can be interrupted, but not wholly distracted, seeking out and resuming the activity again following the interruption. They may resist interruption in some cases. Attention may fluctuate a little, but in general, there is high concentration and focus.

Level 5 Sustained Intense Activity The child shows concentration, creativity, energy and persistence for almost all the observation period. They show little response to interruptions, and have clear motivation to continue the activity.

The authors suggest that such observations are carried out via the time sampling method, observing a child for two minutes, and three times during a two sessions during a given week, resulting in 12 observations.

> **Task** Design a sheet for recording child involvement scale data with your col-
> leagues/peers and practise using this in your setting. (NB Bertram and Pascal
> include a sample sheet in their report, on page 8. You can use this method to
> assess individual children or to assess the general success of specific activities/
> areas of the setting. Keep this in mind as you move on to Chapters 5, 6 and 7.)

Clearly, using this scale would come with all the warnings you would expect to
be attached to the highly subjective process of observing children and allocating
a number to the behaviour can be subjective. However, an unhappy child who is
unhappy within its environment is unlikely to be learning from their experiences
in the way that a child who is comfortable, secure and happy is likely to enjoy
and benefit from their day-to-day experiences (see Chapters 6 and 7 for more
information on this topic).

What are the implications of the rise to prominence of 'well-being' for Early
Years practice and specifically for EYPs? What can EYPs do to ensure that children
are supported by adults who can give the quality and consistency of care so necessary to support well-being? After you have read Chapters 5 and 6, reflect on the
following points and consider your personal practice as well as your role as an
actual or potential lead practitioner.

- Your state of well-being and your ability to relate to and support others and the impact your personal well-being has on the quality of your interactions with others.
- Your ability and willingness to model desirable behaviour in regard to building
  positive working relationships with children and their families.
- Your skills as a key worker working closely with specific children and families to
  optimise their experience in your setting.
- Your ability to work with a team to create and operate an effective key worker
  system in your setting.

> **Reflection** *Think about your own state of mind when you are later than you have
> planned to be for the start of the day. Maybe you are generally OK if people leave
> you alone, but what if, directly you get to work, five different people immediately
> 'jump on you', demanding your attention? Your feeling of well-being (or not!) will
> probably influence your response!*

Safeguarding

In January 2003 David Batty wrote an article entitled 'Catalogue of cruelty' for
the *Guardian*, in which he outlined some of the 'most shocking' child kill-
ings in England since 1945. The majority were from the 1980s. He gives a brief
overview of more than 10 cases, in all of which he identifies poor communication,

breakdown in communication or a complete lack of communication between agencies tasked with protecting children as contributing to their demise. While these cases make harrowing reading, they have all critically informed the child protection frameworks that we work with now. The case of Tyra Henry in 1984 is noted as the stimulus for the production of new guidelines on child protection for social workers. Almost 20 years after this, the case of Victoria Climbié directly preceded a review of children's services, which was initialised by the Every Child Matters Green Paper 2003 (see Chapter 4) and an emphasis on multi-agency approaches to safeguarding children. More recent cases such as that of 'Baby P' in 2009 continue to create waves of concern in the media which ripple through the entire population and impact upon national concepts of the children's workforce:

> An analysis of press reporting of social work in national daily and Sunday newspapers in England between 1 July 1997 and 30 June 1998, showed that nearly two thousand articles were devoted exclusively to discussions of social work and social services. The 15 most common messages, accounting for 80 per cent of the total, were negative with regard to social work and included: 'incompetent', 'negligent', 'failed', 'ineffective', 'misguided' and 'bungling'.
>
> (Munro 2010, p.122)

The BBC news service reported a sharp increase in numbers of children being taken into the care of local authorities since the publication of the details of the 'Baby P' case, and the subsequent enquiry which culminated in the dismissal of all the leading professionals who had been expected to manage the case (BBC 2012b, online). The case of Vanessa George, a childcare worker who exploited her position to indecently assault very young children, and to take and subsequently distribute photographs of these incidents on her mobile phone (Savill and Bunyan 2009, online) has additionally brought practitioner conduct into sharp relief; for example the EYFS 2012 states: 'The safeguarding policy and procedures must include an explanation of the action to be taken in the event of an allegation being made against a member of staff, and cover the use of mobile phones and cameras in the setting' (DFE 2012, p.13). This serves to remind leaders of practice that they must extend safeguarding vigilance with respect to the conduct of individuals working within the setting, even if they have presented with clear Criminal Record Bureau checks.

If I have to lead in my setting with respect to safeguarding, how should I go about it, in terms of policies and procedures and how to implement them?

Armed with all this information and working with your colleagues the next step in the process is to review/create your setting's policies with regard to safety, inclusion and protection. We all have a duty to the children and families that we work with to be up-to-date in our practice. Keeping up-to-date has never been easier, there is so much information available to us via the internet as well as more traditional sources, the difficulty is finding the time to read it all or just to sift through it for anything relevant to you and your setting. Subscriptions to on-line information services are a simple way of getting the 'headlines' which should leave you time to read in more detail articles of specific interest to you and your setting, for example *Nursery World* and other publications, as well as government departments offer this service and it is free. If there are a number of you in your setting you could share out the reading and have weekly discussion groups to cascade ideas through your team. This would be a really good way of engaging all staff in planning and decision making.

It is vital to understand that policies are working documents; they are plans for action which all colleagues should follow under specific circumstances, they ensure a minimum quality of experience and consistency in practice. To be effective, all staff need to feel ownership of the policies; they need to be consulted when policies are being written, they need to be committed to act within the policy and they need to be involved in the review (see the Focus on practice box above). Each setting should have a plan for regular review of all policies, but should be flexible and prepared to amend policies which are no longer effective as and when the need arises. This is an activity that many successful EYP candidates identify within their validation tasks. The cycle of policy amendment should proceed as follows:

Figure 3.1 Cycle of policy amendment

Extended task

First, make an inventory of the policies in your setting and reflect on:

- What policies the setting has.
- Are there other policies that you feel they should have?
- How are staff, children and families and the wider community informed about these policies and how effective is this communication?
- When were the policies last reviewed?
- How are staff inducted into working with these policies?
- How do the staff feel about the policies?

Now consider, with your fellow candidates, the role the leading practitioner in a setting might play in ensuring that the policies serve the needs of all involved with the setting and that they are carried out effectively and consistently.

For the second part of this task we are going to ask you to go through an exercise where you consider how you might go about writing a safeguarding policy for your setting. Writing a policy can be a very challenging task and writing the safeguarding policy with the welfare of vulnerable children at stake can carry huge responsibility. Even carrying this out as an exercise may cause some qualms in Entry pathway candidates! Remember that one person should never be solely responsible for the protection of all children, but that leading practitioners must be key members of this particular team.

The checklist below may help you to frame your thoughts.

A safeguarding policy should:

- Outline clearly what the policy is for and how it links to the health and safety policy
- Ensure the vetting of staff required by law, and incorporate any changes to procedures that come along 'as and when'; for example in the Protection of Freedoms Bill 2011 (not yet fully operational at time of writing in spring 2012)
- Confirm understanding of types of abuse and signs and symptoms of abuse
- Detail the reporting procedure and how to respond to disclosure
- State who the designated person is and name a deputy
- Give clear guidance on staff supervision
- Give contact details for relevant local agencies such as police, local safeguarding board, social care team
- Include guidance on staff conduct
- Identify potential barriers to disclosure
- Identify potential barriers to reporting
- Outline 'whistleblowing' procedures
- Outline what processes should be followed if there are allegations against a member of staff
- State the review date.

Now that you have some ideas on what you should include try to create a first draft of a safeguarding policy and ask other candidate EYPs to review and evaluate your draft; then possibly work on a further draft together. It is vital that the policy is 'fit for purpose' and the key point here is writing a policy which is robust but is written in language that all staff can understand and commit to.

Reflection *While this may seem a lengthy exercise, you may be glad you carried it out if (or most likely when) you are asked to do this task 'in earnest' as a setting EYP!*

On an everyday basis, how do I establish a safe environment and instil practices that promote children's health and safety?

In 2003 the Every Child Matters Green Paper identified five outcomes for children (0–18 years) that we should all be working to meet. While these are no longer a set of 'stand alone' principles for action (see Chapter 4) the ideas have informed recent development in the EYFS. In particular, the aims noted in the outcome 'stay safe' are useful here. They propose that children should be safe from:

- maltreatment, neglect, violence and sexual exploitation;
- accidental injury and death;
- bullying and discrimination;
- crime and anti-social behaviour.

Also that children have security, stability and are cared for by adults to whom they have bonded attachments (see Chapter 2).

The New Labour Government reinforced this advice in their practice *The Common Core of Skills and Knowledge for the Children's Workforce* (DCSF 2010) under the heading 'Safeguarding and promoting the welfare of the child':

> People who work with children and young people have responsibilities to safeguard and promote their welfare. This is an important responsibility and requires careful attention. It means being able to recognise when a child or young person is not achieving their developmental potential or when their physical or health is impaired. It means recognising when a child is displaying risky or harmful behaviour, or is being neglected or abused. It also means being able to identify appropriate sources of help for them and their families. Sometimes more than one risk factor may be affecting a child or young person and it may be necessary to work with others to address them.

(DCSF 2010, p.13)

Distressing cases such as those of Victoria Climbié and Baby P are still thankfully very rare (which is of course, why they make the national headlines). Most safeguarding activities that Early Years Practitioners undertake on a day-to-day basis involve supporting children from troubled families who lack understanding of children and childhood, rather than life threatening abuse. A BBC news article suggested that one of the major problems with respect for safeguarding is that:

> . . .many parents are unclear about their legal responsibilities to children . . . more than 1,000 parents showed two-thirds felt the law on parenting was confusing. Three-quarters agreed there was no common understanding of what was meant by 'good enough' parenting [and] two-thirds would like to see a clear law defining parental responsibilities.

(BBC 2012a, online)

The role of referral and multi-agency working is also crucially important within safeguarding procedures (also see Chapter 8). Unless you are employed within a local authority or other agency team with specific responsibility to deal with child protection issues, you will not be called upon to *diagnose* safeguarding issues relating to individual children, but to *communicate* any suspicions to the agencies responsible for investigating them. Again for the EYP, this aspect of practice is also about your own actions and your role in modelling and leading best practice in others.

Under the heading multi-agency and integrated working the *Common Core* states that:

To work successfully on a multi-agency basis you need to be clear about your role and aware of and respectful of, the roles of other workers and agencies. You should actively seek and respect other people's knowledge and input to deliver the best outcomes for children and young people. These behaviours should apply across the public, private and voluntary sectors.

(DCSF 2010, p.18)

In terms of your own skills, the essentials are your ability to build good working relationships with parents and carers, your ability to communicate with a range of different professionals, your awareness of confidentiality and your 'trump card' – your observation skills (see above). Time spent developing and honing observation skills will generate huge rewards for:

- you – you will learn so much from observing children and reflecting on your practice;
- children – the better you know the children you are supporting, the better able you will be to meet their individual needs and the more likely you are to identify development and change; and
- families – demonstrating detailed knowledge and understanding of their children will support development of working relationships with parents/carers which can only benefit children in the long term.

Hobart and Frankel (2004) is a valuable text which you can use to further develop your observation skills; you may also find the more recent text, *Childhood Observation* (Palaiologou 2008), one of the 'Achieving EYPS' series, useful in this respect. Many years ago the idea that 'practice makes perfect' was lost to me when someone explained that 'practice did not make perfect – but it did make permanent'. The point that was being made was that unless your practice method was correct, you would be embedding the wrong way to do the task, which would be counterproductive and could take a long time to correct. It is important to the development of your observation skills that you have a critical friend to give fair and honest feedback to help you develop your skills or at least prevent you from developing too many bad habits! You must also develop skills in dealing with constructive criticism with respect to both taking this from and providing this to colleagues, if you are to support and lead best practice in others. Regular entries in your reflective journal should help you in this endeavour.

Focus on practice

Mary and her family lived in local authority housing. During a period of regeneration all of the houses on her road were being renovated and many of the families had been moved to alternative accommodation but Mary and her family were still waiting.

➡

Work on the empty houses started and Mary's family were finding life difficult as they experienced frequent breaks in water, gas and power supplies and the area was, according to her mum, 'like a building site'. The area was such a mess that a couple of weeks ago Mary had fallen over some wood the builders had left and hit her head on a wall and been taken to the hospital where she had had five stitches in a head wound and an overnight stay. The local health centre wrote to Mary's mum asking her to bring Mary in for a follow-up appointment, just to check on the head wound, but the letter was never delivered. The delivery driver had looked at the houses in the road and decided that no one would still be living there and eventually the letter was returned to the health centre. At the health centre the maternity cover health visitor eventually picked up on this missed appointment when she had 'got to grips' with her new job, but by this time is was almost 10 weeks since the original injury.

Identifying good practice

Mary started in an Early Years setting four months ago, her key worker Wasim told the leading practitioner Sarah that he is struggling to establish a good working relationship with Mary and her family. He tells her that the offer of a home visit before Mary started at the setting was politely but firmly refused. Mary's attendance is not good and she is often late. The explanations given for lateness and absence also seemed rather strange, for example the need to accompany her mother on regular shopping and launderette visits. He is also concerned about Mary's appearance and demeanour, as she appears dirty, sometimes smells unwashed, and she is always hungry, rushing to grab any food offered. He also shows Sarah a record he has kept of Mary's cuts and bruises and a head injury requiring stitches. She did not sustain any of these injuries in the setting. Her mother is frequently vague about how these were acquired, repeatedly offering the 'home is a building site' explanation.

Leading practice

Sarah reassures Wasim that he has acted appropriately. She thanks him for taking such an interest in Mary and her family and applauds the very professional efforts that he has made towards building a good working relationship in a difficult situation. She advises him to take care to remain objective when recording, and not to jump to any swift conclusions. She commends his use of the setting's policies and procedures in guiding his actions to date. As she is the setting safeguarding coordinator, she asks him to continue his observations and recording and to continue working positively with the child and her family. She suggests that they meet again the following week to review the situation, reminding Wasim of the confidentiality of their discussions.

Reflection *Put yourself in Wasim's shoes. He has seen:*

- *home visit declined;*
- *poor attendance and some lateness;*
- *signs of neglect, e.g., hunger, dirty, smelly;*
- *signs of injury.*

What would you do?

> **Task**
>
> - Now think about your role as EYP and how you would respond to Wasim.
> - Consider your role as an EYP in a multi-agency team and how your perspective might change.
> - As EYP in a multi-disciplinary team how might you attempt to support Mary and her family?
>
> I hope that from this reflection you will conclude that Wasim has one piece of a large jigsaw and how different his perspective is to the perspective of a member of a multi-agency team who recognises and appreciates the difficulties Mary and her family are in.

Armed with your knowledge of legislation, guidelines, policy and practice (see Chapter 4) and your knowledge of children gained from close working relationships with parents and carers (see Chapter 8) and your highly developed observation skills (see above), you should be in a good position to notice, observe and record changes in behaviour and demeanour which may indicate a child falling short of their potential, or a child/family experiencing difficulty. You may produce a vital piece of the safeguarding jigsaw relating to an individual child, or support one of your colleagues to do this; remember, if this had occurred within each of the cases cited in the frame of 'child protection tragedy', the problems leading up to the ultimate outcome may have been neutralised before the child came to serious harm. One thing is certain that you, like any other professional working with children and families, will produce only a part of the jigsaw and it is only when a number of pieces are put together through multi-agency working that a coherent picture is produced. We are a part of a multi-agency team – a team far wider than our workplace – who may build a picture which causes us to refer a child to the local safeguarding authority but, within the role of setting lead professional, to refer is the limit of our role.

Conclusion

This chapter has sought to answer the following questions:

What are the legal requirements and guidance on health and safety, safeguarding and promoting the welfare of children, and where can I find help and advice on these?

The complex issues of safety *vs* risk and what constitutes 'well-being' have been discussed above. If you have to cover a work-based learning module in the course of your training, it might be worth considering a project in this area of policy, which is currently high on the Early Years reform agenda, and a subject of discussion in many different arenas, both academic and practitioner oriented, see for example Tovey (2007) and Pen Green (2008).

If I have to lead in my setting with respect to safeguarding, how should I go about it, in terms of policies and procedures and how to implement them?

If you undertake the tasks in the chapter relating to constructing a draft safeguarding policy, you will begin to see that this does not have to be an impossible task, particularly if you involve your fellow candidates in this exercise. We would urge you to carry these processes out for the first time as an exercise rather than in earnest; the 'real thing' will then seem less daunting when it arises for the first time in the future – as it inevitably will for a leading practitioner within a childcare setting! You should also find Chapter 4 of use in terms of reviewing the legal/policy background, and Chapter 8 in terms of dealing with leadership issues.

On an everyday basis, how do I establish a safe environment and instil practices that promote children's health and safety?

In order to answer this question for yourself, we will end this chapter with a task that will help you to review all that we have covered, and allow you to seek wider information to help you answer this question for yourself. You will find that different practitioners, parents and other caring adults will have different viewpoints on this issue (for example, see Brown's comments on this on p.71). As long as you have considered your duties under the law, and taken a 'common sense' approach you will find your own way on this as your experience of leadership grows. Again, we would urge you to engage in this task in order to experience a simulation prior to being asked to undertake this process in earnest on being appointed to a setting as a leader or manager.

> **Task** Re-read the article in the box that opens this chapter. Then, systematically using the range of information in this chapter, produce a set of bullet points relating to how you would go about creating a holistic safe environment (i.e. paying attention to health and safety and safeguarding aspects) which you think should not attract the criticism of producing 'cotton wool kids'. You should pay close attention to section 3 of the EYFS document (DFE 2012); you may also find the box about Zac's outing especially useful here. If you can persuade some fellow candidates to do the same, discuss your points and try to come to some collective agreement about how you might revise your plans to come up with an agreed collective set of bullet points relating to acceptably safe settings that do not, on the other hand, attempt to 'wrap children in cotton wool'. This will no doubt create a basis for some very lively – and thought-provoking – discussion.

Further reading

Griffin, S. (2008) *Inclusion, Equality and Diversity in Working with Children.* Harlow: Heinemann.

Lindon, J. (2006) *Equality in Early Childhood Linking Theory and Practice.* London: Hodder Arnold.

Palaiologou, I. (2012) *Child Observation in the Early Years* (2nd edn), London: Learning Matters.

Tassoni, P. (2008) *Practical EYFS Handbook*. Harlow: Heinemann.

Whalley, M. (2008) *Leading Practice in Early Years Settings*. Exeter: Learning Matters.

Websites

http://www.barnardos.org.uk/.

http://www.11million.org.uk/?CFID=38069106&CFTOKEN=94998647
(The Children's Commissioner for England).

http://www.nspcc.org.uk/.

References

Alderson, P. (2008) *Young Children's Rights* (2nd edn), London: Jessica Kingsley Publishing.

Batty, D. (2003) Catalogue of cruelty. Available at http://www.guardian.co.uk/uk/2001/jan/13/childprotection.society4. Accessed on 26 April 2012.

BBC (2012a) Charity calls for reform of the law on child neglect. Available at: http://www.bbc.co.uk/news/education-17790086. Accessed on 27 April 2012.

BBC (2012b) Councils refer record numbers of children into care. Available at: http://www.bbc.co.uk/news/uk-16958373. Accessed on 26 April 2012.

Bertram, T. and Pascal, C. (2004) Effective early learning programme child involvement scale. Available at: http://www.decs.sa.gov.au/northerncountry/files/links/link_84047.pdf. Accessed on 16 February 2009.

Brown, F. (2008) 'Playwork', in A. Brock, S. Dodds, P. Jarvis and Y. Olusoga (eds) *Perspectives on Play: Learning for life*. Harlow: Pearson Longman.

CAMHS Review (2008) *Improving the mental health and psychological well-being of children and young people*. Available at: www.dcfs.gov.uk/CAMHSreview.

The Children's Society (2012) The Good Childhood Report. Available at: www.childrenssociety.org.uk. Accessed on 20 March 2012.

Children's Workforce Development Council (2010) *The Common Core of Skills and Knowlededge*. London: CWDC.

Corsaro, W. (1997) *The Sociology of Childhood*, Thousand Oaks, CA: Pine Forge Press.

Council of Europe (1996) The European Social charter. Available at: http://conventions.coe.int/treaty/en/Treaties/Html/163.htm. Accessed on 3 January 2009.

David, T., Gooch, K., Powell, S. and Abbott, L. (2003) *Birth to Three Matters: A review of the literature*. Research Report 444. London: The Stationery Office.

DCSF (2010) *The Common Core of Skills and Knowledge for the Children's Workforce*. Leeds: CDWC.

DFE (2012) The Early Years Foundation Stage. Available at: http://media.education.gov.uk/assets/files/pdf/e/eyfs%20statutory%20framework%20march%202012.pdf. Accessed on 26 April 2012.

DFES (2003) *Every Child Matters*, Green Paper. London: The Stationary Office.

DFES (2003) National Standards for Daycare. Available at: http://www3.imperial.ac.uk/pls/portal-live/docs/1/46973696.PDF. Accessed on 26 April 2012.

Griffin, S. (2008) *Inclusion, Equality & Diversity in Working with Children*. Harlow: Heinemann.

HM Government (2005) *Common Core of Skills and Knowledge for the Children's Workforce*. Available at: www.everychildmatters.gov.uk ref DfES/1189/2005.

HM Government (2006) *Working Together to Safeguard Children*. Available at: www.everychildmatters.gov.uk/socialcare/safeguarding.

Hobart, C. and Frankel, J. (2004) *A Practical Guide to Child Observations and Assessments* (3rd edn). Cheltenham: Stanley Thornes.

Jarvis, P. (2007) Dangerous activities within an invisible playground: a study of emergent male football play and teachers' perspectives of outdoor free play in the early years of primary school. *International Journal of Early Years Education*, 15(3) pp.245–59.

Jarvis, P. and George, J. (2008) 'Play, Learning for Life: the vital role of play in human development', in A. Brock, S. Dodds, P. Jarvis and Y. Olusoga (eds) *Perspectives on Play: Learning for life*. Harlow: Pearson Longman.

Laevers, F. (1997) Forward to basics! Deep-level-learning and the experiential approach, *Early Childhood Research Quarterly*, 12(2), pp.117–43.

Laevers, F. (2005) The curriculum as means to raise the quality of ECE. Implications for policy. *European Early Childhood Education Research Journal*, 13(1), pp.17–30.

Layard, R. and Dunn, J. (2009) *A Good Childhood: Searching for Values in a Competitive Age*. London: Penguin/The Children's Society.

Lindon, J. (2006) *Equality in Early Childhood Linking Theory and Practice*. London: Hodder Arnold.

Munro, E. (2010) The Munro Review of Child Protection. Available at: http://www.education.gov.uk/munroreview/downloads/8875_DfE_Munro_Report_TAGGED.pdf. Accessed on 26 April 2012.

Palaiologou, I. (2008) *Childhood Observation*. Exeter: Learning Matters.

Pen Green (2008) *The Pen Green Framework for Engaging Parents*. Corby: Pen Green.

Savill, R. and Bunyan, N. (2009) Nursery worker child sex abuse case; Vanessa George profile. Available at: http://www.telegraph.co.uk/news/uknews/crime/6249672/Nursery-worker-child-sex-abuse-case-Vanessa-George-profile.html. Accessed on 26 April 2012.

Stephenson, A. (2003) 'Physical risk taking: Dangerous or endangered?' *Early Years*, 23(1), pp.35–43.

TACTYC (2008) Summary from play research seminar, 2008. Available at: http://www.tactyc.org.uk/pdfs/2008_Colloquium_summary.pdf. Accessed on 2 January 2008.

Tovey, H. (2007) *Playing Outdoors: Spaces and places, risk and challenge (debating play)*. Buckingham: Open University Press.

Tovey, H. *et al.* (2008) Summary of finding from play research seminar, 2008. Available at: www.tactyc.org.uk/pdfs/2008. Accessed on 20 June 2012.

UNICEF (2007) Child poverty in perspective: An overview of child well-being in rich countries, *Innocenti Report Card 7, 2007*. Florence: UNICEF Innocenti Research Centre.

4

Children as citizens: rights and responsibilities in the twenty-first century

Pam Jarvis, Jane George and Wendy Holland

Chapter overview

The Standard addressed in this chapter is:

8. Lead practice and foster a culture of continuous improvement.

This chapter will outline a brief history of social policy for children and families in England, and then turn to the rise of the rights, inclusion and equality agendas, both nationally and internationally. It will address the following questions:

● How and why did legislation for children and families develop in England?

● What are the key aspects of social policy and legislation that underpin the work of contemporary Early Years Professionals, and how can they keep up with ongoing changes?

● What are 'human rights' and 'children's rights'; how are these protected through legislation, and what is the relationship between rights, equality and inclusion?

The recommended reading list at the end of this chapter will introduce readers to a range of texts and online resources in which to read further on these topics.

When I was 12 years old, I was thinking about growing up. Until that moment, I think I had somehow believed that when I grew up I would become 'normal', i.e., without a disability. 'Normal' then meant to me 'like my big sister: pretty, rebellious, going out with boys, doing wonderful, naughty things with them, leaving school, getting a job, leaving home, getting married and having children...I suddenly realised that my life was not going to be like that at all. I was going to be just the same as I always had been – very small, funnily shaped, unable to walk. It seemed at that moment that the sky cracked...The next two years seemed like a dark roller-coaster ride...My main preoccupation seemed to be desperately trying to deny the awareness of my difference, which had started on that day.

Micheline Mason in Campling (1981, pp.23–4)

Micheline Mason
Photo: Alan Sprung.

Introduction

The underpinning principles of childcare and education require that senior practitioners not only have a grasp of contemporary social policy and legislation relating to children's issues, but also the sociological grounding and flexibility to understand the reasoning behind policy making, particularly that relating to equality and inclusion policy. It is also a requirement that individuals invested with the responsibility for leading practice continually keep up to date with new legislation, and become able to engage in debate relating to ongoing changes, developing the potential to become one of those leading practice development both locally and nationally, as their career unfolds.

How and why did social legislation and children's legislation develop in England?

The first formal poor law in England was established in 1598 by Queen Elizabeth I, who decreed that 'parish relief' would be distributed to the 'destitute'. A medieval parish covered an area served by a specific church, and it was proposed that 'parish relief' should be collected, managed and distributed by the church in every district. Sunday schools subsequently arose (particularly under the Cromwells' Puritan rule, between 1653 and 1660) and took a role in the education of the poor, teaching children 'moral' behaviour and, sometimes, basic reading and counting skills. Elizabeth initially created the parish relief legislation to deal with aggressive roving beggars who were causing concern, as illustrated by the following rhyme:

Hark, hark the dogs do bark
The Beggars are coming to town
Some in rags and some in jags
And one in a velvet gown.

(Traditional)

(The Tudor meaning of 'jag' was a fashionable slit in a garment exposing a material of a different colour underneath.) The underlying reason for the law was to encourage each parish to 'look after its own' and avoid the violence that ensued when people in a particular town or village (with no formal law enforcement mechanisms beyond the village squire and priest) decided to run potentially undeserving strangers out of their territory! This mixture of compassion and practical governance can still be discerned in today's social legislation, as we will see later in this chapter.

The parish system operated for over three centuries, until industrialisation changed the ways that people were employed, creating a huge expansion in city-based living as people moved into the rapidly expanding towns to work in the new factories and mills. The parish relief was no longer practical in such large and impersonal communities, and in 1834 it was replaced by the unpopular workhouse system. 'Pauper' families were split up and sent to segregated male, female and children's sections in large institutions where they lived like prisoners, carrying out menial work for a place to stay and basic sustenance. Most families did everything they could to remain out of the workhouse system, even if it meant living in extreme poverty.

Reflection *There are a lot of old Victorian workhouse buildings still in existence in Britain, many of which have been converted to a wide variety of purposes. The picture below shows one of the old workhouses in Leeds, which is today used as a medical museum. Why not see if you can find an old workhouse building in the city nearest to where you live, and learn something about its history.*

Trade unions, created by working men, subsequently started 'friendly societies' where members donated a small percentage of their income to a collective insurance fund so that their families would be able to continue to receive an income (hence avoid the workhouse) for some length of time if they became unemployed, ill or died prematurely.

Some inmates of the workhouse to the east of Leeds city centre and the building today, which now serves as the Thackray Medical Museum
Courtesy of the Thackray Museum, Leeds.

The impersonal nature of life in the new cities underpinned many fundamental societal changes, including the creation of a statutory policing system, which began with the London 'Bow Street Runners' in 1829, who were the original Metropolitan Police force. Over the mid-nineteenth century, successive Victorian governments became increasingly concerned about the poverty and squalor in the new cities. In 1870 a Public Health Act made it compulsory for local authorities to provide clean water and sewerage systems paid for by a new local tax on householders called 'the rates'. Fired by the example of charitable education institutions such as Thomas Barnardo's 'ragged school' for pauper boys in Stepney, East London, which opened its doors in 1867 (BBC 2001, online), the government passed the first Education Act in 1870, which set up publicly funded school boards to ensure that all children aged 5 to 12 were allocated a free school place and maintained their attendance to ensure that they received a basic primary education, principally inculcating basic literacy, numeracy, practical skills and moral understanding. Mid-Victorian Britain was fast developing a cultural understanding of children as 'special' vulnerable human beings who needed care, education and protection under the law. By 1870, Barnardo had extended his charitable efforts to a home for orphaned and 'pauper' children (Barnardo's 2008, online).

As children from very poor backgrounds began to come into regular contact with middle-class professionals such as teachers and charity workers, concerns began to be raised with respect to their health and physical condition, and publicly aired in discussions relating to the prevention of neglect and physical ill-treatment. Leading Early Years education pioneer Margaret McMillan proposed: 'The state compels the children to work [in school] – it makes the demand for sustenance urgent, intolerable. But it does not compel parents to feed their children. Hence it is certain to some of these hungry little ones, free education is less of a boon than an outrage' (Mansbridge 1932, pp.41–2). McMillan went on to campaign for a range of public services for poor children such as medical inspections and free school meals, on the grounds that it was impossible to educate a tired, dirty, infested, diseased and hungry child, and the height of adult cruelty to insist against such odds that poor children entered a public education system that did not concern itself with their holistic welfare.

In 1884, the London Society for the Prevention of Cruelty to Children was created (BBC 2001, online). In 1889, the government passed the first Children Act to instigate legal procedures to protect children from physically abusive adults, and the London Society for the Prevention of Cruelty to Children became a national charitable institution, the NSPCC, which, alongside Barnardo's, still continues to provide help for disadvantaged children and their families today.

The Children Act 1889

This act was the first to impose criminal penalties on those who mistreated children. It enabled the state to intervene, for the first time, in relations between parents and children. Police could arrest anyone found ill-treating a child, and enter a home if a child was thought to be in danger. The act included guidelines on the employment of children and outlawed begging, which frequently involved children.

(DoH 1889)

Throughout the nineteenth century, the British government gradually extended the right to vote to working-class men (women had to wait until 1928 to get the vote on the same terms), which changed the political landscape, as politicians scrambled for working-class votes. This eventually resulted in the birth of the Labour party (emerging from the Trade Unions Congress as the political party for working men) in 1900, although it had to wait until 1924 for its first very short (nine-month) term of government. For most of the twentieth century, the Labour movement would bring a *collectivist* approach to government, raising taxation to fund services that acted to equalise the population, while the Conservative movement would bring an opposing *individualistic* orientation, cutting taxation on the basis that individuals and families had the right to decide upon the services that they required, and pay for them on a private basis.

The Children's Charter 1908

- Established juvenile courts.
- Introduced the registration of foster parents, which had the effect of regulating 'baby-farming' and wet-nursing, which in turn had the emergent effect of reducing infanticide (people secretly 'doing away' with unwanted children!).
- Prevented children working in dangerous trades and prevented them from purchasing cigarettes and alcohol.

- Local authorities were granted powers to keep poor children out of the work-house and protect them from abuse; this led to many councils setting up social services departments and county orphanages.
- Raised the minimum age for execution to 16, later raised to 18 in the Children and Young Persons Act 1933 (see below).

(DoH 1908)

Over the early years of the twentieth century, the Liberal party's popularity began to fall behind that of the new Labour party. This revelation in the political landscape gathered pace in Britain once the First World War ended (1918), as all men over 21 and all women over 30 were given the right to vote. However, one of the last Liberal administrations set up the very first national insurance system in 1906, based upon the model created over the previous century by the Trade Unions. At this time, national insurance was only for men, who paid a compulsory small amount that was taken at source from their wages. The resulting fund was used to pay old age pensions, and to insure those who paid into the fund against sickness, unemployment and disability. Some money was also put aside to fund school health checks, free school meals for poor children and the setting up of 'labour exchanges' (early job centres). Unfortunately, an international economic slump during the early 1930s exposed the inadequacy of this initiative. Men were laid off work for long periods of time, and as their unemployment pay ran out, several child deaths due to starvation occurred in families who refused to endure the misery, separation and degradation of the workhouse. Full employment was only finally achieved in the late 1930s due to the armament production and military service opportunities that directly preceded and endured throughout the Second World War.

The Children and Young Person's Act 1932/1933

- The Children and Young Persons Act 1932 broadened the powers of juvenile courts and introduced supervision orders for children at risk.
- In 1933, a further Children and Young Persons Act collated all existing child protection legislation into one act.

(DoH 1932/1933)

As the Blitz raged over London in the mid-1940s, the war government, a coalition of all political parties, asked William Beveridge (1879–1963), who was an economist and social reformer, to create a plan for rebuilding British society after the war. Beveridge (1942) proposed that there were 'five giants' of deprivation to slay:

- Want
- Ignorance
- Disease
- Squalor
- Idleness.

Beveridge's five giants

Source: Solo Syndication/Associated Newspapers Ltd.

As the war ended in 1945, the Labour party was voted into government by a landslide. The franchise now extended to all Britons, male and female, aged over 21. Over their first three years in office, this government set up the **British Welfare State**, based on the recommendations of the Beveridge Report (1942). This comprised:

- The **National Health Service** to tackle **disease**
- A comprehensive, nationally funded **benefits and pensions** system to tackle **want**
- Free high-quality **education** from 5–15 (16 from 1972) to tackle **ignorance**
- A national **housing** initiative to tackle **squalor**
- A national **employment** initiative to tackle **idleness**.

Many major industries were also permanently **nationalised** (for example the mines, the Post Offices and the railways) so that the national administration procedures that had been created in the war years could continue to operate. At the time, it was the most ambitious set of collectivist national projects in the Western world, which shocked some political commentators in the United States into comparing the new British regime to those that operated in the communist nations of Eastern Europe (Glennerster 2006).

1940s Social Legislation

- The Education Act 1944 was passed by the coalition Second World War government, a year before the post-war Labour Government was voted into power. This Act set up a system of state schooling from age 5-11 (primary) and 11-18 (secondary). The minimum school leaving age rose to 15 (DFES 1944). This basic structure remains, although the leaving age became 16 in 1972 and will become 17 in 2013, and 18 in 2015. It is currently proposed that apprenticeships should be available to those 14-18 year olds who would benefit more from this pathway than they would from academic study.

Main legislative measures of the post-war Labour Government:

- 1945 Family Allowances Act
- 1946 National Insurance Act
- 1946 National Insurance (Industrial Injuries) Act
- 1946 National Health Service Act (implemented July 1948)
- 1947 Town and Country Planning Act
- 1947 New Towns Act
- 1948 National Assistance Act
- 1948 Children Act
- 1949 Housing Act.

(BBC 2008, online)

- The Children Act 1948 established a children's committee and a children's officer in each local authority. It followed the creation of the parliamentary care of children committee in 1945 following the death of 13-year-old Dennis O'Neill at the hands of his abusive foster parents.

(DoH 1948)

These health, benefits and education systems, although much 'worked upon' by subsequent administrations, still form the bedrock of all the UK nations' social policy today. They remained pretty much unsullied throughout the 1950s and 1960s, but by the early 1970s, rising international oil prices sent the whole Western world into economic recession. Throughout the 1970s in Britain, a succession of both Conservative and Labour administrations battled with the Trade Unions, as inflation rapidly raised the cost of living and the unions called strike after strike in an attempt to force employers to raise wages to keep pace with prices. In 1978,

Britain entered what was to thereafter be known as 'the winter of discontent' where nearly all workers in the public and nationalised industries went on strike. Dead bodies remained unburied and piles of rubbish lay uncollected in the streets, attracting swarms of rats (Marr 2007).

In 1979, Britons voted in the Conservative administration lead by Margaret Thatcher, who subsequently became Britain's first woman Prime Minister. She undertook a comprehensive programme of de-nationalisation, and, while the welfare state remained materially intact, the value of benefits was slashed, and there were cuts and economies applied to nationally funded services including education and health. In The Housing Act of 1980, the Thatcher government gave tenants the 'right to buy' public housing stock that had largely been built in the period directly after the Second World War; in areas where this venture did not succeed, the management of public housing was subsequently largely removed from local authorities and sold on to private housing trusts. This government also denied subsidies to unprofitable manufacturing industries, allowing them to close down altogether. By the early 1980s Britain experienced a 10 per cent unemployment level, which disproportionately hit manufacturing industries, raising the unemployment levels in areas which housed factories, mines and mills proportionally well beyond those that had been experienced in the 1930s, particularly among male workers (Marr 2007). Subsequent urban regeneration projects undertaken over the late 1980s and early 1990s eventually achieved some amount of re-employment by encouraging 'service' and financial industries to set up their offices within the old industrial areas. The resulting new jobs were frequently temporary, part time and low paid, and disproportionately filled by women.

Meanwhile, despite the government's efforts to cut public spending in education and health, the advance of medical science hugely increased the costs of the NHS, as the range of treatments available increased, and in addition, technological advances began to create a requirement for a more technically competent workforce, hence a longer mass education for young people became necessary. The government increasingly began to contemplate how they could create a public education and social welfare support system that inculcated the 'correct' skills and attitudes within children to create a steady supply of 'useful citizens'. This eventually resulted in the Education Act 1988, which introduced the National Curriculum, swiftly followed by the Children Act 1989 as the government's response to a string of high-profile, controversial national and international debates about children's rights and holistic protection, including the recognition of more insidious areas of child maltreatment including neglect, emotional and sexual abuse.

While the age for voting was dropped to 18 in 1970, the school leaving age was raised to 16 in 1972, and, as the 1970s drew to a close, increasing numbers of young people remained in education until they were 18. Numbers attending university also increased over the 1970s and 1980s; such individuals remained in education until they were 21. However, at the other end of education provision, pre-school opportunities remained largely within the private sector. The Conservative administration remained in governance until 1997.

Reflection *Were you a child in Britain during the 1980s? What do you remember of the culture and society that formed the background to your childhood? For example what do you remember about adult employment roles and experiences of unemployment, and its effects upon the family? Do you remember taking SATs at school? Did you attend pre-school education? I remember that my young twins were only able to attend pre-school for two days a week before they entered primary school in 1991, because the private fees were so high, and pre-school children had no guaranteed right to a nursery place, whether or not they were 'multiples'! Share your memories of 'Thatcher's Britain' with your fellow students and tutors. How do you think life was different (and/or similar) to life today for young children and their families?*

Conservative Government 1979-97: Legislation for Children and Families
The Children Act 1989

Part one
Outlines the Paramountcy Principle (the child's welfare is paramount) and the concept of Significant Harm.

Part two
Sets out measures which may be used by social services departments who are in dispute with parents of children within their designated area.

Part three
Sets out the principle responsibilities of local authorities regarding children in their area.

Part four
Sets out the grounds under which courts may make an order, which, in simplified form, relates to evidence that a child has been suffering significant harm, or that a court feels that there is a strong possibility that s/he may be likely to do so in the future in his/her current situation.

Part five
Outlines the introduction of a new Emergency Protection Order to replace the old Place of Safety Order, and stipulates how the new Order may be used, and by whom.

Parts six to twelve cover:

● Guidelines regarding residential care

● Guidelines regarding fostering

● Standards concerning nursery and childcare arrangements for under 5s

● Court arrangements for dealing with children's issues.

(DoH 1989)

The New Labour years

In 1997, the British population elected a Labour government, which remained in power for the next 13 years. Labour politics had moved on considerably during their nearly two decades in opposition, and while the new 'New Labour' Government had promised to re-energise the Welfare State, it did very little to reverse the cutbacks instigated by the previous Conservative administration. This heralded a more sophisticated orientation to collectivism, ideologically separating 'New' Labour from the traditional 'one nation' Labour policies of the past. New Labour instead frequently sought 'deals' between the government and private sources of funding to manage health and education. Public funding was, however, steadily pumped into education initiatives, still driven by the (originally Thatcherite) focus upon producing an educated workforce to make Britain more internationally competitive. However, New Labour had an additional impetus to try and create a level playing field for all British children, embodied in an ambitious attempt to dramatically reduce the numbers of children living in poverty. To this end, they created the Sure Start initiative, initially based upon the Head Start initiative (2012, online) in the United States. Sure Start centres were initially set up across disadvantaged urban areas in England. Many of these became children's centres, which aimed to provide a 'one-stop shop' for health, education and care services for young children and their families. The initial focus was upon supporting low income families (including single parents) to find their own way out of poverty through paid work. Such a philosophy was clearly embodied in the Ten Year Plan for Childcare (2004, see below).

Over the final years of the New Labour administration, the number of children's centres grew rapidly. Many provided daycare for the young children of working parents, and the government's plans for the future of children's centres began to expand towards a universal offer of daycare and services to families across the country. This was therefore now moving away from the 'Head Start Project' model towards the universal eligibility for Early Years Care and Education that is found within the Scardinavian nations.

Sure Start Children's Centres Expansion 1998-2010

- Sure Start was introduced in the 1998 Comprehensive Spending Review, with the New Labour Government's announcement that it would set up 250 Sure Start local programmes in disadvantaged areas around the country.

- In 2000, the number of Sure Start projects expanded to 524.

- In what was designated 'Phase One' of the children's centres programme (2004-06), 800 existing settings were given the status of 'children's centres'.

- In 'Phase Two' (2006-08), funding was made available to open many more children's centres, taking the overall numbers to 2,500. Most of these additional settings were newly created.

➡

- By late 2008, there were 2916 children's centres in operation throughout the UK.
- By 2010, at the end of 'Phase Three', the target was for 3,500 centres nationwide (Children, Schools and Families Committee 2010, online). This was achieved by May 2010, the month that governance by New Labour ceased, due to a general election that gave the Conservatives a very small majority.

Having covered 500 years of social policy at some speed above, readers may now be asking what relevance this has to their work within the contemporary Early Years sector. The answer initially relates to the place of history in everyday life – it allows us to find our own point on an unfolding timeline where continually changing social and political perspectives can otherwise seem very confusing. It also allows us to reflect upon the fact that governments and populations frequently have to respond in the best way they can to situations that have not been thoroughly planned and may not be entirely of their own making.

Those who work in the Early Years sector should be very aware that children are particularly vulnerable to the problems and uncertainties created by the constantly shifting social and economic forces that underpin their parents' lives within modern societies. Physical deprivation and familial stress can have more devastating results upon developing bodies and minds than upon those of adults, and the individualistic mantra to 'fend for oneself' cannot be sensibly applied to those who are not yet old enough to do so. Governments of all political persuasions are often particularly interested in the fate of their nation's children, and not always for the most charitable reasons, being inclined to view them as 'projects' for a collective national future rather than as individuals. For the British government, the late-nineteenth-century discovery that city-raised men from poor families had frequently been so poorly nourished and cared for in childhood that they were unfit to be soldiers created a national imperative to provide free health services for poor children at the beginning of the twentieth century; at the beginning of the twenty-first century, Alderson (2008, p.53) similarly proposed that the Every Child Matters Charter (2003, see below) 'appears to be more concerned with the national economy than with the welfare and protection of young children'. This echoes the mixture of compassion and practical governance that was initially raised at the beginning of the chapter as an underlying factor of the Elizabethan Poor Law.

The role of senior childcare and education practitioners in any society in time or geography is inevitably to work within the systems they inhabit at the time, with a view to doing the best they can for the children under their care. This crucially involves a large amount of independent, analytical thought, reconciling what the practitioner knows from experience and theoretical knowledge to be good practice with the opportunities and pitfalls present in the policies and guidelines with which they are currently presented. In this way, ongoing changes can frequently be optimistically but cautiously viewed principally as opportunities, and planned for at an early stage. However, the informed, reflective practitioner also needs to heed the ongoing warnings of dissenting voices such as Alderson's (2008), which perform the essential task of alerting us to what may happen when policy documents are slavishly instigated by practitioners who think 'two dimensionally', taking little account of individual children's emotional, social and intellectual needs. With this word of caution in mind, the main areas of legislation and policy that currently (early 2012) guides the work of Early Years Professionals will be presented in summary below.

What are the key aspects of social policy legislation that underpin the work of contemporary Early Years Professionals, and how can they keep up with ongoing changes?

In January 2003, Lord Laming published his report into the death of child abuse victim Victoria Climbié, which found that health, police and social services missed 12 opportunities to save Victoria. It recommended that the Children Act 1989 should continue to function as the principal piece of child protection legislation, but made the following additional recommendations: a minister for children; a national agency for children and families; local committees and management boards to oversee children's services; a national child database and a 24-hour helpline for the public to report concerns about children. A government green paper, Every Child Matters, followed in September, signalling a cross-sector approach to policy for children and young people. It proposed an electronic recording system to track the developmental and educational progress of England's 11 million children; 150 children's trusts; a children's director to oversee local children's services; statutory local safeguarding children boards and an independent children's commissioner for England, to protect young people's welfare and rights. An amalgamation of social services, education and child health was to be accomplished by 2006, and a set of statutory guidelines for those caring for the youngest children also emerged: the original version of the Early Years Foundation Stage (2007).

Every Child Matters: the key outcomes

The Every Child Matters (ECM) green paper of 2003 identified five key outcomes for children and young people that are to be met through both changes in individual public and independent agencies working with children and through Improved Inter-Agency Working:

- *Being healthy:* enjoying good physical and mental health and enjoying a healthy lifestyle
- *Staying safe:* being protected from harm and neglect
- *Enjoying and achieving:* getting the most out of life and developing the skills for adulthood
- *Making a positive contribution:* being involved with the community and society and not engaging in anti-social or offending behaviour
- *Economic well-being:* not being prevented by economic disadvantage from achieving their full potential in life.

(DFES 2003)

Every Child Matters became the basis for a huge number of policy developments relating to education, health and social care and workforce development across the remaining period of New Labour Government, 2003–10. In 2004, the government passed a new Children Act to implement the main proposals of the green paper: electronic children's files, children's directors, local safeguarding boards, Ofsted inspections for the Early Years sector and the children's commissioner.

The Children Act 2004

Parts One and Two of the Act provide new structures and duties for England.

- To create a Children's Commissioner for England (already in existence in Wales and Northern Ireland)
- To establish more effective information sharing through electronic means between public authorities for children at risk of or who have been abused
- To establish a new structure for inter-agency cooperation in child protection - Local Safeguarding Children Boards (LSCBs)
- To Establish Local Authority Directors of Children's Services and a Lead Member for Children within Councils
- To Establish a New Inspection Framework for Children's Services
- To Establish Joint Area Reviews of Services for Children.

Parts Three and Four deals with the Welsh aspects of this legislation.

Part Five contains miscellaneous provisions that include some updating of elements of the Children Act 1989, the main points of which remain very much 'live', and work in partnership with all new legislation.

Part Six deals with some necessary administrative details.

(DFES 2004)

Reflection *Consider the principles of Every Child Matters and the contents of the Children Acts 1989 and 2004. Is there anything that you think should be added, removed, or more carefully defined? Make notes on this to discuss with your fellow students and tutors. Then consider the Coalition change of emphasis to 'Every Family Matters (see below) - what difference do you think this may make to your practice, and why?*

The Ten Year Plan for Childcare, which was unveiled in 2004, arguably instigated a new era in social policy. No post-Second World War government had previously legislated on care for pre-school children, or after school care for older children; as such the Childcare Act 2006 which followed the Ten Year Plan can be viewed as the first major legislative extension of the Welfare State, nearly 60 years after its instigation. It has been said that the politicians of the 1940s were very naive about the problems that would emerge with respect to funding the welfare state. As the situation unfolds, it appears that this may also be said about New Labour's optimism that, within a British taxation system, the modern welfare state would be able to support quality childcare for all.

The Ten Year Plan for Childcare 2004

Choice and flexibility: parents to have greater choice about balancing work and family life

- A goal of twelve months' paid maternity leave
- A goal of legislation to give mothers the right to transfer a proportion of this paid leave to the child's father
- Every family to have easy access to integrated services through children's centres. 2,500 children's centres to be in place by 2008 and 3,500 by 2010.
- For all families with children aged up to 14 who need it, an affordable, flexible, high-quality childcare place that meets their circumstances.

Supply and demand: Legislation for a new duty on local authorities in place by 2008 so that over time they will secure sufficient supply to meet the needs of families

- A goal of 20 hours a week of free high-quality care for 38 weeks for all 3 and 4 year olds
- An out of school childcare place for all children aged 3-14 between the hours of 8 a.m. to 6 p.m. each weekday by 2010.

Raising quality: high-quality provision with a highly skilled childcare and Early Years workforce

- All full daycare settings to be professionally led
- Transformation Fund of £125 million each year from April 2006 to invest in high-quality, sustainable, affordable provision
- Radical reform of the workforce, with consultation relating to a new qualification and career structure
- Reform of the regulation and inspection regime to improve standards and to give parents better information
- Affordability: families to be able to afford flexible, high-quality childcare
- In the long term, the aim was to reduce further the proportion of childcare costs paid by families, particularly those on the lowest incomes, making childcare increasingly affordable for all.

(DFES 2004)

The Childcare Act 2006

Enshrines in law parents' 'legitimate expectation of accessible high-quality childcare and services for children under 5 and their families'

- Local authorities to improve *outcomes* for all children under the age of 5
- Local authorities to *facilitate* the childcare market
- Emphasis on provision for working parents – particularly those on low income and those with disabled children
- Local authorities to ensure a full range of information to parents
- Introduction of the statutory guidance document, The Early Years Foundation Stage (2007)
- Reformed and standardised childcare and early years regulation across England.

(DFES 2006)

Reflection *Is a mass movement to publicly funded, collective pre-school/after school childcare a wholly positive development, or might there be potential underlying problems? A source that will help you reflect upon this are the UNICEF report 'The Child Care transition' (2008), which reflects 'the stakes are simply too high for the mass movement towards out-of-home child care to be seen as just another shake of the kaleidoscope in the rapidly changing lifestyles of advanced industrial economies' (p.13). Discuss issues arising with your fellow students and tutors.*

The Coalition years

A financial crisis created by worldwide failures in the international banking system cast a shadow over the last two years of New Labour governance, 2008–10. The small fall in the numbers of children officially 'living in poverty' that had been achieved over the first few years of the twenty-first century was reversed, unemployment figures began to rise, and public disillusionment fed into a narrow victory for the Conservatives in the May 2010 general election. As the Conservatives did not have a decisive majority, they made a pact with the Liberal party that allowed for a formation of a Conservative/Liberal Coalition Government. The Coalition have not formally repealed any of the New Labour legislation at time of writing (early 2012). They have also made it plain that they understand that the Early Years period is the most important stage of development, and therefore the period in which they are most willing to provide funding to provide financial and practical support for families (see Field 2010 and Allen 2011). However, their intentions are very much to support the child within the family, rather than the child as an independent entity in a collective setting. This was marked by one of the Coalition's first actions on arriving in governance: the cessation of the national child database

'Contact Point' and its subsequent dismantling, on the grounds that it was overly intrusive in the private business of individual families. Another example of a different political emphasis here has been the scaling back of government funding for universal daycare services. The Prime Minister, David Cameron has proposed that the intention is to 'take Sure Start back to its original purpose' (Coalition Government 2010, p.10); in the view of the Coalition Government this is defined as aiming the project at helping 'troubled' children and families solve the range of problems underlying their situation moving back to the 'Head Start' model that was more in evidence in the origins of Sure Start. Cameron proposed there were approximately 120,000 'troubled families' in the UK (see **http://www.communities .gov.uk/communities/troubledfamilies/**) living in 'areas of disadvantage', and that their problems need to be dealt with in order to break the cycle that will lead to the children themselves subsequently creating similarly 'troubled families' in the next generation; what Field (2010, pp.16–17) refers to as 'the intergenerational cycle of poverty'. The Coalition's overview of policy for children and families is summarised in *Supporting Families in the Foundation Years* (DFE 2011).

Supporting Families in the Foundation Years: A brief summary

The policy emphasises its focus on children's healthy development, so that by the time they are 5 years old, children are healthy and fully ready for the school years ahead. To this end, the Coalition Government propose to:

- Increase the health visitor workforce
- Introduce a reduced Early Years Foundation Stage from September 2012 with a greater focus on working with parents
- Retain a network of Sure Start Children's Centres located in areas of disadvantage, with a brief to work principally with troubled *families* rather than with individual children
- Offer free early education to the most disadvantaged 2-year-olds
- Revise the Code of Practice for early education to increase flexibility and reduce bureaucracy
- Promote quality and diversity across early education and childcare.

The government have proposed that they will further support parents by:

- Introducing new arrangements for more flexible parental leave
- Supporting the provision of flexible childcare so that parents can balance their working and family responsibilities
- Supporting the provision of online and helpline family-support services
- Working with charities and private providers to increase take-up of parenting and relationship programmes
- Supporting family learning and parental involvement in children's learning, for example by ensuring that Ofsted reports are clearly written and easy for parents to access and helping parents and communities to have a voice in the running of children's centres

➡

- Helping professionals to use all interactions with families as opportunities to identify any additional needs of both parents and other key family members and offer further help
- Requiring nurseries, pre-schools and childminders to give parents a short written summary of their child's progress around the age of 2
- Doubling the number of families benefiting from the Family Nurse Partnership
- Setting out a new 'core purpose' for children's centres, with 'early intervention at its heart'.

With regard to the children's workforce, the government intend to:

- Increase the quality of support that expectant mothers and fathers and families with young children receive
- Review how best to strengthen qualifications and career pathways for practitioners in the Early Years Foundation stage, and attempt to improve the gender balance of this workforce
- Continue to invest in graduate-level training in early education and childcare
- Make early years education professionals a central part of the remit of the new Teaching Agency, supporting the development of strong leadership
- Encourage partnerships between health and Early Years services, leading to stronger integrated working
- Clarify how information-sharing in the foundation years can work better
- Work with local authorities to address disadvantage and inequalities by securing sufficient early years provision
- Clarify how outcomes are measured in the early years
- Promote the development of an increasingly diverse sector with a strong role for private, voluntary, community and social enterprise organisations.

(DFE 2011)

The new Early Years Foundation Stage was published on 26 March 2012, and will become the new statutory guidelines within childcare/education settings in September 2012; The new Early Years Professional Status Standards were published in July 2012 and will 'go live' at the same time.

Reflection *Compare the contents of 'Supporting Families in the Foundation Years' with the New Labour legislation and policy outlined earlier in the chapter, and then consider the following questions:*

- *What do you think has changed and what remains more or less the same?*
- *The Coalition Government have proposed that they intend to work less with individual children and more with families, with a view towards helping them become self-supporting units, financially and socially. Where can you see this change of emphasis emerging from the new policy?*
- *Now look back across the whole of this chapter so far. Where can you see Labour 'collectivism' and Conservative 'individualism' emerging from the policies of the different administrations across the years?*

What are 'human rights' and 'children's rights'; how are these protected through legislation, and what is the relationship between 'rights' and inclusion?

Rights and responsibilities: a complex relationship

In 1942, as Beveridge was drawing up the plans for a post-war British welfare state, the US president Franklin D. Roosevelt wrote of his intention to lead the allies in the creation of a body of 'United Nations'. In 1945, the final year of the war, representatives of 50 countries met in San Francisco to draw up the United Nations Charter, which was signed on 26 June 1945 (UN 2012, online). The UN's first action was to produce the Universal Declaration of Human Rights (1948) (UN 2012, online) which set out what are now internationally agreed as the basic human rights that should be extended to all people by all nations, regardless of nationality, ethnicity, race or religion. This reflected international recognition of the additional suffering imposed upon minority ethnic groups by the highly xenophobic Nazi regime. Throughout its history, the United Nations has consistently demonstrated that it will only sanction international military action against a nation if it is obvious that the basic human rights of some or all of its citizens are being transgressed or ignored by the ruling regime. In 1998, following many years of discussion between the European Union governments, the New Labour Government passed a comprehensive Act of Parliament detailing the Human Rights of every person resident within and/or visiting England, including those who do not hold British nationality.

During the late 1940s and early 1950s, a great deal of psychological, sociological and health-oriented research was carried out to study the children and young people of Europe, many of whom had been killed or injured in the war, and many who, through the extensive displacement influences of the conflict, had lost contact with one or both parents either permanently or for a long period of time. John Bowlby, about whom you read in Chapter 2, developed his theory of maternal deprivation from his psychoanalytic work with children who had experienced separations in very early childhood, many of these due to displacement or evacuation. He gave evidence for the development of the Declaration of the Rights of the Child (UN 1959), where, for the first time, children were recognised on the world policy stage as 'special' human beings, in need of more care and protection from the state than adults.

The United Nations International Children's Emergency Fund, or 'UNICEF' grew out of the International Children's Fund, created in 1946 to collect money and resources to provide aid for children whose lives had been blighted in various ways by the Second World War. Since its adoption by the UN in 1947, UNICEF's mission has been to 'mount urgent relief programmes for children and adolescents in war-ravaged countries and for child health purposes generally, with such aid being distributed without discrimination due to race, creed, nationality, status or political belief' (UNICEF 2012, online). Its work over the years increasingly demonstrated that while the Declaration of the Rights of the Child had been a recognition of children's basic needs, a more comprehensive rights document for children and young people was needed. Many years were spent on its construction, and it was finally published 30 years after the Declaration of the Rights of the Child, being swiftly endorsed by all member nations of the UN apart from the USA and Somalia. For England, the discussions undertaken internationally also fed into national legislation, the Children Act 1989, which is outlined above. As you can see, both the United Nations Convention on the Rights of the Child (UNCRC) and the Children Act 1989 came into being in the same year.

The United Nations Convention on the Rights of the Child (UNCRC) 1989

The Convention lists 54 articles in all which outline a comprehensive set of international rights for children. Some of the most important ones that impact upon the work of Early Years practitioners are as follows:

Article 2: The Convention applies to everyone, whatever their race, religion, abilities; whatever they think or say, whatever type of family they come from.

Article 3: All organisations concerned with children should work towards what is best for each individual child.

Article 9: Children should not be separated from their parents unless it is for their own good. Even if they are separated for a good reason, e.g. if the child is being neglected or badly treated, in most circumstances, children have the right to stay in contact with both parents.

Article 10: Families who live in different countries should be allowed to move between those countries so that parents and children can stay in contact, or get back together as a family.

Article 12: Children have the right to say what they think should happen, when adults are making decisions that affect them, and to have their opinions taken into account.

Article 14: Children have the right to think and believe what they want, and to practise their religion, as long as they are not stopping other people from enjoying their rights.

Article 15: Children have a right to privacy. The law should protect them from attacks against their way of life, their good name, their families and their homes.

Article 19: Governments should ensure that children are properly cared for, and protect them from violence, abuse and neglect by their parents, and anyone else who looks after them.

Article 20: Children who cannot be looked after by their own family must be looked after properly, by people who respect their religion, culture and language.

Article 22: Children who come into a country as refugees should have the same rights as children born in that country.

Article 23: Children who have any kind of disability should have special care and support, so that they can lead full and independent lives.

Article 25: Children who are looked after by their local authority, rather than their parents, should have their situation reviewed regularly.

Article 27: Children have a right to a standard of living that is good enough to meet their physical and mental needs. The Government should help families who cannot afford to provide this.

Article 29 Education should develop each child's personality and talents to the full. It should encourage children to respect their parents, and their own and other cultures.

Article 30: Children have a right to learn and use the language and customs of their families, whether these are shared by the majority of people in the country or not.

Article 31: All children have a right to relax and play, and to join in a wide range of activities.

(UNICEF 2012b, online)

It was also recommended that every signatory nation should instigate the public post of a Children's Commissioner whose role it would be to oversee the instigation of national laws to comply with the UNCRC, and ongoing compliance with its articles within the relevant country. There was much debate about this in England, which was not finally settled until the Children Act of 2004 brought the post into being.

UNICEF further proposed: 'Many of the rights laid down in the Convention on the Rights of the Child have to be provided by adults or the state. However, the Convention also refers to the responsibilities of children, in particular to respect the rights of others . . . If children have a right to be protected from conflict, cruelty, exploitation and neglect, then they also have a responsibility not to bully or harm each other.

(UNICEF Children's Rights and Responsibilities leaflet, no date, online).

Reflection *Consider this concept of a balance between rights and responsibilities, and collaborate with your peers to make a table or chart that maps the principal rights and responsibilities of practitioners, parents and children within Early Years settings, discussing how these intermesh with each other. Introducing children to this balance of rights and responsibilities (for example, if you don't want him to call you names, then you should not call him names) is an extremely important part of children's early socialisation. Most children will be capable of this level of understanding early in the third year of life, quite a while before they begin to understand the more complex concept of showing contrition and asking for forgiveness.*

As you can see from the above, besides the balancing of rights and responsibilities, the UNCRC introduced the world to another relatively new concept: children's opportunities for developmentally appropriate participation in their wider society, and a developmentally appropriate 'say' in decisions affecting their own everyday lives, see in particular UNCRC Articles 12 and 14.

Reflection *How do you address children's participation rights within your setting, and how might you improve this aspect of your practice? Discuss this question with your peers and coworkers, considering where you might currently place yourselves on the 'ladder of participation', where you would like to be, and some ideas about how you might get there.*

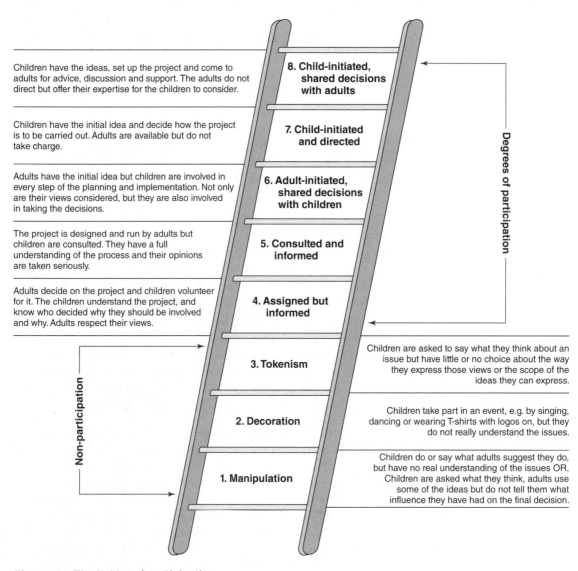

Children have the ideas, set up the project and come to adults for advice, discussion and support. The adults do not direct but offer their expertise for the children to consider.

8. Child-initiated, shared decisions with adults

Children have the initial idea and decide how the project is to be carried out. Adults are available but do not take charge.

7. Child-initiated and directed

Adults have the initial idea but children are involved in every step of the planning and implementation. Not only are their views considered, but they are also involved in taking the decisions.

6. Adult-initiated, shared decisions with children

The project is designed and run by adults but children are consulted. They have a full understanding of the process and their opinions are taken seriously.

5. Consulted and informed

Adults decide on the project and children volunteer for it. The children understand the project, and know who decided why they should be involved and why. Adults respect their views.

4. Assigned but informed

Degrees of participation

3. Tokenism

Children are asked to say what they think about an issue but have little or no choice about the way they express those views or the scope of the ideas they can express.

2. Decoration

Children take part in an event, e.g. by singing, dancing or wearing T-shirts with logos on, but they do not really understand the issues.

Non-participation

1. Manipulation

Children do or say what adults suggest they do, but have no real understanding of the issues OR, Children are asked what they think, adults use some of the ideas but do not tell them what influence they have had on the final decision.

Figure 4.1 The ladder of participation

Source: Adapted from Wong (2010).

In conclusion, leading practitioners need to gain a working knowledge of rights-based issues both nationally and internationally, and keep up with changes in this arena. Alderson (2008) gives a comprehensive overview of children's rights theory, practice and legislation as this impacts on Early Years, which will help you to build on the brief summary above, and the UNCRC area of the UNICEF website posts regularly on ongoing developments: http://www.unicef.org/crc/.

The emergence of the contemporary rights-based agenda also raises the issues of inclusion and equality of treatment; for example, consider UNCRC Articles 2 and 23. Such rights began to be represented in the legislation of most Western nations over the second half of the twentieth century, with most developing a comprehensive set of rights-based legislation in the years leading up to 2000. The following section considers the contemporary rights based agenda within the UK.

Rights, equality and inclusion: ethnicity, race, religion and culture

As an EYP and leading practitioner in a setting, creating an environment which reflects and values diversity in society is your responsibility. The most important aim in this endeavour is for the children in your care to be supported in their building of a positive self-image, and to respect the feelings of others, whatever their gender, culture, ethnicity or 'race', and whether or not they have a disability. If these concepts are successfully communicated, they will not enter adolescence perceiving the concept of 'normal' in the very limited fashion that had clearly been communicated throughout childhood to Micheline Mason, whose reflection on her mid-twentieth-century childhood is used as the opening paragraph in this chapter. The keys to this are the resources, activities and communication that you and your colleagues provide for the children and their families. Effective practitioners need to ensure that the environment they provide supports and values diversity through an awareness that is real and relevant, not tokenistic. In order to achieve this, practitioners may need to examine and reflect honestly upon any prejudices and biases they might hold. Practitioners may not always be aware of internalised stereotypes that can affect their expectations of children and families. The effective practitioner needs to question how and to what extent their setting works to value diversity in children and their backgrounds and avoid a 'colour/disability–blind' approach, where treating children 'equally' is translated into treating all children 'the same'. Iram Siraj-Blatchford suggests that Early Years practitioners should make children aware they all have an identity that is individually different and that difference should be celebrated:

> A positive self-concept is necessary for healthy development and learning and includes feelings about gender, race, ability, culture and language. Positive self-esteem depends on whether children feel others accept them and see them as competent and worthwhile.

(Siraj-Blatchford 2001, p.104)

A young child's self-esteem is easily damaged and research suggests that children as young as 2½ may show signs of discomfort with physical differences. By the age of 4, children from minority ethnic groups may feel unhappy with their appearance (Derman-Sparks and Ramsay 2006). Promoting and providing an inclusive environment that celebrates and values differences in identity, culture, religion, abilities and social practices is a difficult task, within a setting and without. No setting exists in a vacuum, but rather reflects the community it is a part of, with its share of discrimination, conflicts, issues over gender roles and ignorance with regard to disability (see Focus on practice boxes below). The effective practitioner, nevertheless, has to strive for and promote inclusive, anti-discriminatory practice by:

- Identifying and addressing any practices that are discriminatory within the setting
- Promoting self-esteem and positive group identity
- Valuing children and adults for their individuality and ensure a sense of belonging
- Respecting where children come from, what they achieve and what they bring to the setting.

In order to protect the equal opportunities of staff within the workplace, lead practitioners who have responsibility for employing and/or supervising and managing staff should be aware of the requirements of the Equality Act 2010, which updated and drew together the requirements of over 30 years of successive legislation mitigating against prejudice and discrimination on the basis of gender, disability, race, sexual orientation, religion or belief and age. A new category which has been added with the passing of this legislation is marriage or civil partnership.

The Equality Act outlines different ways in which it is unlawful to treat someone, such as direct and indirect discrimination, harassment, victimisation and failing to make a reasonable adjustment for a disabled person. It outlaws prejudice and discrimination in the workplace, when providing goods, facilities and services, when exercising public functions, in the disposal and management of premises, in education and by associations (for example a pre-school playgroup).

All Early Years settings must follow Equality of Opportunity legislation and guidance, and sometimes leading practitioners are instrumental in helping more junior employees understand their own and the setting's responsibilities in this respect. Consider the following practice examples:

Focus on practice

Lena has recently achieved EYPS. Two months ago she was appointed as Deputy Manager in a private day nursery. She felt that, based on the job description, the setting was looking for a lead practitioner, even if the title was 'Deputy Manager'. (A number of EYPs in her cohort had also echoed her thinking.) She is still finding her feet in this long-established setting, working with some long-serving, qualified and experienced staff.

A few days ago, she witnessed a conversation between a placement student and his supervisor, Bev, the toddler room leader. The student spoke to Bev in a polite and respectful manner when he informed her that as a student his college allowed him 'authorised absence' for Eid celebrations. He informed her of the most likely date for Eid, about three weeks away and promised to confirm the exact date as soon as possible. Bev refused the request and informed the student that if he took time off for Eid he would not be allowed to continue his placement.

Identifying good practice
Lena contemplates the following:

- What message does this give to the student?
- Is this a message from the setting or from one individual?
- Does the setting have a policy to cover the situation?
- What message does this send to the staff, children and families in the setting?

She accesses the guidance to the Equality Act 2010 on the internet at **http://www .homeoffice.gov.uk/publications/equalities/equality-act-publications/equality-act-guidance/** and notes the aspects of the situation that have violated legally required practices relating to equality and inclusion in employment. She goes to see the manager of the setting the following day and draws her attention to the situation. The manager expresses regret and says she will speak to the member of staff and to the student, and make sure he gets his Eid holiday. She thanks Lena, and asks if she will develop the staffing policies of the setting, which are very much in need of an overhaul.

Leading practice
Lena realises that the practice of experienced staff is often slow to change, so the following week she asks Bev to help her prepare a series of multi-faith activities for the children, initially focusing upon Eid. At the end of the month, after consulting again with the setting manager, Lena gives a presentation to all the staff to discuss and finalise some new policies relating to their employment. The following day she overhears Bev telling another member of staff that it is not fair that 'they' will get 'their' holidays and 'ours' as well. Lena then mentions at the next staff meeting that it has come to her attention that some members of staff may not have understood that, while practice will be planned around the expectation that both staff and children will take holidays on the feast days of their religion, the relevant number of days have to be taken from the adults' annual leave allocation if they are on the payroll. When the local authority circulates a flyer advertising inclusion training, Lena asks Bev if she will take the training programme with her.

Reflection *It is much easier if older members of staff can be persuaded to 'remain on board' as positive members of colleagues with many years of valuable professional experience. However, as national and international developments impact upon Early Years practice, misunderstandings may arise that lead to destructive 'us and them' attitudes developing among groups of staff. If such an issue degenerates into a serious dispute, all members of staff are likely to be* *affected, which is in turn likely to negatively impact upon the day-to-day practice and 'atmosphere' of the setting. As such, it is best to always try to deal with such issues in a conciliatory fashion, persevering if your initial efforts meet with failure or only partial success.*

Any setting that does not meet the equality and inclusion needs of its workforce is highly unlikely to be able to meet the diverse needs of individual children and their families. The importance of a team commitment to practice within the setting, and the leadership necessary to achieve this, is further discussed in Chapter 10 'Surviving validation', where the EYPS candidate's leadership of and other contributions to team coherence are presented as central concepts that must underpin both written and practical validation tasks.

Focus on practice

An Ofsted inspection report on a private daycare setting had revealed most areas of care, practice and provision to be 'good' with only one graded as 'satisfactory', this focused on 'inclusive practice' issues. The inspectors felt there was only 'limited' recognition of cultural diversity. The inspectors had taken into account the largely mono-cultural catchment area of the setting, but felt it was even more important in such circumstances to promote ideas of cultural diversity in preparing children for the wider world.

Andy, the setting manager, met with his lead practitioner, Jon, to discuss drawing up an initial action plan which would then be rolled out to staff for their opinions and ideas. Jon told Andy that a colleague, who worked in a local authority maintained setting, had recently been given some training on new initiatives around inclusive practice, and offered to find out more about this. Andy said that he would also contact the local Early Years service to ask for advice.

Identifying good practice

Andy had made initial contact with a local Early Years advisor, but had been too busy to follow this up, so Jon arranged a meeting with the Inclusive Development Programme Coordinator. After an interesting discussion, Jon came back with several ideas he felt could be included in their action plan. The adviser had mentioned the services of a teacher who supported traveller children, Angelica, who would be happy to come and talk with the children. Although the setting didn't currently have any traveller children, Jon remembered that it had some years ago. Angelica also suggested the centre carry out a survey to discover international and multicultural connections within the centre's existing families, as, she reflected, there was a lot more 'diversity' in the construction of present-day families than had been the case during previous decades, and the current craze for researching family trees was also turning up some very interesting international and multi-cultural histories of which families had previously been unaware. She also felt that the increasing numbers of children from eastern Europe now in primary schools would soon be reflected in Early Years settings, as some of these families settled permanently in the UK. Jon informed Andy of the outcome of his discussion with Angelica, and proposed that finding out about the 'diversity' of families of children attending the setting could be started with a topic on 'Myself'. He also felt, for the new children who would begin in September, that the information sheet each family filled in for their children's individual profiles should be more comprehensive, so that the full richness of the 'diversity' within children's family backgrounds could be identified and celebrated.

Leading practice

At the weekly meeting, all of the centre's staff were invited to comment upon the Ofsted Inspectors' findings. A number of them felt it was difficult to 'make diversity real' for young children if the culture used was completely outside the children's own experience. They evidenced the celebrations for Chinese New Year that a student had promoted during a block placement early in the year, which staff proposed had 'flown above the children's heads' and that they had seen it as 'just another party'. Jon felt that was a little harsh, that the student had been genuinely attempting to look at another culture, and that the artefacts, clothes and food she had brought into the setting had promoted conversation and interest among some of the older children. He told the staff about his meeting with the Early Years advisor, and showed them a brief 'family tree' he had drawn of his own family's diverse roots, asking them each to complete something similar for next week's meeting.

On the topic of 'traveller children', the staff had mixed feelings. Reactions locally to traveller families had not been very positive over recent times, after one of the local authority sites had been closed down, resulting in traveller families choosing their own areas in which to stay, which had not met with the approval of some of the local residents. Jon reminded them that exposing children to cultural diversity was a key aspect of preventing them engaging in stereotyping and discrimination in their later development, and also a way in which parents might begin to learn about the world outside their own cultural niche. He also reiterated a message from Angelica that she would be happy to come along and talk to staff and answer any concerns they might have.

The following week the staff's varied and interesting family trees promoted much discussion. It was realised by staff that they already had several sources of 'diverse culture' within the setting that they could use for the benefit of the children and support an action plan. The 'traveller children' topic was a success, with the teacher introducing a 'persona doll' that proved to be a favourite with the children. So much so, that a member of staff volunteered to go on 'persona doll' training and several other such dolls were bought as resources for the setting.

➡

The persona dolls
Courtesy of Persona Doll Training. www.persona-doll-training.org.

Reflections

● *Do you consider the manager's and lead practitioner's reactions to the Ofsted Inspectors' report were appropriate and adequate?*

● *Do you feel the lead practitioner led and supported the staff sufficiently in reflecting on their practice?*

● *Should there have been some involvement of parents/carers/the wider local community at any stage in drawing up the action plan?*

● *Have you experienced a 'mono-cultural' situation like the above? If so, how did that impact on your practice?*

As can be seen in the example above, Early Years practitioners have a series of tools available to them to assist in this task, but as is often the case the most effective tool is action based on sound working knowledge of theory combined with refection on practice. Local knowledge, gained through good working relationships with your local authority Early Years team, and effective local continuing professional development (CPD) are also invaluable to help settings and Early Years practitioners identify and respond to the needs of their communities. An EYP who aims to lead practice effectively will need this local information to help them to develop a suitable service for the local community including knowledge

Table 4.1 Deficit/difference models of disability

Deficit model	Difference model
Disability is a deficiency or abnormality	Disability is a difference
Being disabled is negative	Being disabled, in itself, is neutral
Disability resides in the individual	Disability derives from interaction between individual and society
The remedy for disability-related problems is cure or 'normalisation' of the individual	The remedy for disability-related problems is a change in the interaction between the individual and society
The agent of remedy is the professional who affects the treatment for the individual so they can 'fit into' society – probably in a reduced capacity	The agent of remedy can be the individual, an advocate, or anyone who affects the arrangements between the individual and society

of the local population – languages, cultures, religions, specific needs and knowledge of local services.

Equality and inclusion: disability

Nationally, guidance for practice in equality and inclusion is embedded within the Early Years Foundation Stage (2012) and The Equality Act (2010). As leading practitioners, you will have the responsibility to remove or overcome barriers children may face which could limit their ability to access opportunities to develop to their full potential. It is also every practitioner's responsibility to make sure that the child can access teaching and learning, not the child's or the parents'. The Equality Act (2010) outlines a clear set of responsibilities for practitioners which ensures that the defence that you did not know that a particular child had a disability/specific learning difficulty is unacceptable; the day-to-day curriculum/routines should be designed to be inclusive. The view of disability should be specifically that of difference rather than deficit. This can be expressed as in Table 4.1 above.

Focus on practice

I was once involved as a school governor in a school that pioneered inclusive practice during the early 1990s by taking a child into Reception who had severe cerebral palsy, who I will call 'Julie'. When Julie entered the school she was unable to walk, or to talk very much, but everyone who interacted with her realised that there was a keen intelligence working within, that had been nurtured up to this point by sensitive and patient parenting, and we worked very hard together to help her to realise her considerable potential. However, along the way, Julie's appearance met with some unfortunate comments from adults bringing other children to and from school, grandparents appearing to be particularly insensitive in this respect, perhaps because they were initially socialised in a society that viewed disability very much from the deficit point of view. Comments included references to 'the little crippled girl' and once a question as to whether she had come along with a parent to collect a brother or sister, and how kind the other children were being to include her in their play. When the person in question was told that Julie was a pupil at the school, the response was 'But the teacher must spend so much time with her – how is that fair to the other children in the class?' These fears were only slightly ameliorated by being told that Julie had a full-time special needs assistant! However, Julie (and the other children in her class) went on to thrive, and by the time she was 8, she was both walking and talking, and working within the normal literacy/numeracy range for a child of her calendar age.

Identifying good practice

One of the children in the older year groups of this school had a much older sister (whom we shall call Sandy) who had been born with severe spina bifida. When the admission of Julie raised the profile of special needs among the school community, Sandy, at that time in her mid-20s, came to a parent-governors meeting to tell us her education story. There had been no concept of inclusion during her primary years, but as she moved towards secondary school age, the Warnock Report on Special Educational Needs (1978) was published, putting inclusion firmly on the national education agenda. As such, Sandy and her physically disabled peer group in the 'special school' were all given a standard IQ test, the first test of intellectual ability that they had ever been given. Sandy scored around the 150 mark, indicating that not only was she not within the normal range . . . she was within the 'gifted' area of the IQ continuum. It was decided that on the basis of this discovery and the rapidly changing policy on the education of what were then called 'handicapped' children, Sandy should attend a mainstream secondary school. Warnock famously stated in 1986 'If I am to walk along a road, I need shoes; but there are those who need a wheelchair, or a pair of crutches, or a guide dog, or other things beside. These needs could be identified and met, and then off we could all go together' (Warnock 1986); however Sandy's experience indicated that this was very much an 'ideal' notion in the education world of the early 1980s. On arriving at her secondary school she found that some areas of the campus were not negotiable in a wheelchair, and, due to her very slow walking speed, she found it difficult to arrive at different rooms within the time allocated between lessons for 'changeover'. After some initial confusion (as Sandy was the only disabled pupil within the school, and the first that it had ever admitted), the Headteacher decided that the teachers should start their lessons at the stipulated time and if Sandy arrived late, she was not to be reprimanded, but that it would be her responsibility to 'catch up' from her point of arrival, without disrupting the rest of the class. This would not only now be designated extremely poor and *exclusive* practice – it would actually be illegal!

Leading practice

These two examples should help you to grasp the vast changes that have occurred within the whole education system over the past 30 years. As a Leading Practitioner within an Early Years setting, it will be your responsibility to ensure that the inclusion practice guidelines reflect the current laws relating to inclusion in education settings. It is hoped, however, that your aim would not simply be to comply with the law, but to move the inclusivity practice of the setting into the bounds of 'excellent'.

Reflections

- *How might you design training for staff in an Early Years setting on the 'deficit/difference' model?*
- *How would you develop the policies in your setting to aim for excellence in inclusion?*
- *What issues might arise within your setting relating to the design of the building if you had a member of staff or a child with the same types of disability as Julie and Sandy? How might you deal with this?*
- *How would you deal with a parent or grandparent expressing highly anti-inclusive views, and how would you expect your staff to respond to such comments?*

Focus on practice

'Cherry Trees', a large nursery for 3-5 year olds had to deal with a complex issue relating to special educational needs. A set of 4-year-old identical triplets, all of whom had been identified as being on the autistic spectrum had recently been admitted. Their mother, a single parent, had met with the Nursery's Lead Practitioner Elizabeth, and Pat, the setting's SENCO (special educational needs coordinator) and expressed the wish that the triplets should remain together and not separated into different areas.

Identifying good practice

Pat was supported by an Early Years Practitioner with special needs training and several teaching assistants, and the setting policy was to try and include children with SEN as much as possible in the daily routines, including free-flow play within the continuous provision, withdrawing the children into a small group only at the beginning and end of the day. Each child was usually allocated a class base and attempts were made to involve them at story or circle time, with support. Some staff felt concern at the prospect of the triplets being in one class base even with support. As the triplets displayed different levels on the autistic spectrum it was felt, in order to meet individual needs, it would be beneficial to separate them.

Leading practice

Elizabeth and Pat discussed this with their mother, Pauline, who was resistant to the proposal at first, but eventually agreed to a trial period. Over time, Tom, the triplet who showed the least overt autistic behaviours managed to gradually access circle and story time within his class base. Initially his support worker would sit beside

➡

him, but after a period, she was able to move away, as long as she remained in view. This had an effect on the rest of his play and involvement, as he gradually began to accept other children into his personal space. Peter, the triplet with most complex needs, was placed in a class base managed by a teacher whose initial degree was in art, where his obvious talents for drawing and painting were stimulated and praised. As time went by he began to quite happily access group times for short periods. Stephen, the triplet with the greatest need for cognitive and emotional support, preferred to play and explore in a one-to-one situation with a trusted adult, and would only actively seek out the company of his brothers. Elizabeth regularly coordinated with the boys' key workers and subsequently collated and communicated all these developments on a daily basis to Pauline via a home-school diary to reassure her that the triplets were happy, and enjoying their time in the setting.

Reflections

- *In this practice example, do you feel the mother's wishes were sufficiently respected?*
- *Do you feel the solutions reached supported each triplet's individual learning journey?*
- *Could this have been achieved by, as their mother had wished, keeping the triplets together?*
- *Was this a case of the triplets fitting in to existing routines and practice or a genuine attempt to meet individual needs?*
- *Have you experienced a similar difficulty in trying to meet individual needs within inclusive provision? If so, how did you deal with this?*
- *Discuss the above with colleagues, and define what you feel is good inclusive and anti-discriminatory practice.*

Conclusion

This chapter has addressed the following questions:

- How and why did legislation for children and families develop in England?
- What are the key aspects of social policy legislation that underpin the work of contemporary Early Years Professionals, and how can they keep up with ongoing changes?
- What are 'human rights' and 'children's rights'; how are these protected through legislation, and what is the relationship between rights, equality and inclusion'?

We have offered a brief journey through a national history of legislation and policy for children and families, considering how the political beliefs of governments impact upon the regimes that they offer to care for, protect and educate children, and to help their families to positively support and guide their children through the developmental period. We have explored the development of international rights-based policy, and traced its incorporation in British equality and inclusion policy and legislation.

How to keep up with such a relentless flow of legislation, policy and guidelines at both national and international levels is a challenge for all senior practitioners in childcare and education, across all ages and stages. In order to have some knowledge of the background to legislative and policy developments, it is necessary to keep up with current affairs, preferably by becoming a regular reader of a broadsheet newspaper, but at the very least by a daily browse on a good quality news website, such as those provided by the broadsheets, and/or the BBC. **It is the responsibility of the leading practitioner in every childcare/education setting to ensure that current guidelines are being followed on an ongoing basis.** The local authority is always available to provide advice, and the leading practitioner in a setting should always maintain good relationships with their designated advisor, who are most usually Early Years teachers, although there is currently (early 2012) a growing number of EYPs inhabiting local authority Early Years advisory roles. It is probably appropriate to close with the reminder that we offered in the first edition of this book: the advice on legislation and guidelines in this chapter, and, indeed, across the book as a whole can only be as up to date as the publication date stated on the flyleaf. You should not, therefore, use this chapter as your only source of information, but as a springboard into an ongoing quest to seek social policy and inclusion information to inform the development of your own practice, and that of other practitioners in the setting.

Reflection *How do you plan to keep up to date with current affairs and changes in the legislation and guidelines that apply to Early Years practice? Discuss plans and useful resources with your fellow students and tutors, making sure to note the location of useful websites and resources in your continuing professional development portfolio; then ensure that you keep this list up to date. You may also find it helpful to set up a website 'favourites' list on your internet browser program. You can start with the suggested reading list below.*

Further reading

Alderson, P. (2008) *Young Children's Rights* (2nd edn). London: Jessica Kingsley.

Allen, G. (2011) *Early Intervention: The next steps.* London: The Cabinet Office.

DFE (2011) *Supporting Families in the Foundation Years.* London: DFE.

Field, F. (2010) *The Foundation Years: Preventing poor children becoming poor adults.* London: The Cabinet Office.

UK Government publications

Office of Public Sector Information: www.opsi.gov.uk.

DoH	The Children Act 1989	HMSO
Treasury	Every Child Matters: Green Paper 2003	HMSO
Treasury	The 10 Year Plan for Childcare 2004	HMSO
DFES	The Children Act 2004	HMSO
DFES	The Childcare Act 2006	HMSO
DFES	The Education Act 2006	HMSO
DFES	The Childcare Act 2006	HMSO
Home Office	The Equality Act 2010	HMSO
DFE	The Early Years Foundation Stage 2012	HMSO

Journals

Children and Society

Children Now

Early Years – an International Journal of Research and Development

Early Years Educator

Educational Researcher

Nursery World

Psychological Review

Websites

Barnardo's: **www.barnardos.org.uk.**

Committee of Enquiry into the Education of Handicapped Children and Young People (1978) The Warnock Report: Special Educational Needs. Available at: **http://www.educationengland.org.uk/documents/warnock/.** Accessed on 16 June 2012.

Effective Provision of Pre-School Education (EPPE) project: **http://k1.ioe.ac.uk/schools/ecpe/eppe/.**

Guidance on the Equality Act 2010: **http://www.homeoffice.gov.uk/publications/equalities/equality-act-publications/equality-act-guidance/.**

NSPCC: **www.nspcc.org.uk.**

Sure Start: **http://www.education.gov.uk/childrenandyoungpeople/earlylearningand-childcare/delivery/surestart/a0076712/sure-start-children%27s-centres.**

UNICEF (2007) An Overview of Child Well Being in Rich Countries. Available at: **http://www.unicef-icdc.org/presscentre/presskit/reportcard7/rc7_eng.pdf.**

UNICEF (2008) The Child Care Transition: A league table of early childhood education and care in economically advanced countries. Available at: **http://www.unicef-irc.org/publications/pdf/rc8_eng.pdf.**

UNICEF Children's Rights and Responsibilities leaflet. Available at: **http://www.unicef .org/rightsite/files/rights_leaflet.pdf**.

UNICEF Convention on the Rights of the Child. Available at: **http://www.unicef.org/crc/**.

References

Alderson, P. (2008) *Young Children's Rights* (2nd edn). London: Jessica Kingsley.

Allen, G. (2011) *Early Intervention: The next steps*. London: The Cabinet Office.

Barnardo's (2008) History of Barnardo's. Available at: http://www.barnardos.org.uk/who_we_are/ history.htm. Accessed on 30 March 2008.

BBC (2001) Children as animals: origins of anti-cruelty laws. Available at: http://www.bbc.co.uk/dna/ h2g2/A640810. Accessed on 30 March 2008.

BBC (2008) Birth of the welfare state. Available at: http://www.open2.net/historyandthearts/ history/theservice_welfare.html. Accessed on 30 March 2008.

Beveridge, W. (1942) *Report to the Parliament on Social Insurance and Allied Services*. London: HMSO.

Campling, J. (ed.) (1981) *Images of Ourselves: Women with disabilities talking*. London: Routledge and Kegan Paul.

Children, Schools and Families Committee (2010) *Fifth Parliamentary Report – Sure Start Children's Centres*. Available at: http://www.publications.parliament.uk/pa/cm200910/cmselect/cmchilsch/130/13002.htm. Accessed 24 July 2010.

Coalition Government (2010) *The Coalition: Our programme for government*. London: The Cabinet Office.

Derman-Sparks, L. and Ramsay, P. (2006) *What if All the Kids are White?* New York: Teacher's College Press.

DFE (2011) *Supporting Families in the Foundation Years*. London: DFE.

DFES (2003) *Every Child Matters*, Green Paper. London: The Stationery Office.

Field, F. (2010) *The Foundation Years: Preventing poor children becoming poor adults*. London: The Cabinet Office.

Glennerster, H. (2006) *British Social Policy: 1945 to the present* (3rd edn). London: Blackwell.

Mansbridge, A. (1932) *Margaret McMillan: Prophet and pioneer*. London: J.M. Dent.

Marr, A. (2007) *A History of Modern Britain*. London: MacMillan.

National Head Start Association (US) (2008) About the National Head Start Association. Available at: http://www.nhsa.org/about/index.htm. Accessed on 24 March 2008.

Siraj-Blatchford, I. (2001) *Supporting Identity, Diversity and Language in the Early Years*. Milton Keynes: Open University Press.

Sure Start (UK) (2008) Sure Start: About us. Available at: http://www.surestart.gov.uk/ aboutsurestart/. Accessed on 24 March 2008.

The Effective Provision of Pre-School Education (EPPE) project 1998–ongoing. Available at: http:// k1.ioe.ac.uk/schools/ecpe/eppe/. Accessed 29 March 2008.

UNICEF (2008) The Child Care Transition: a league table of early childhood education and care in economically advanced countries. Available at: http://www.unicef-irc.org/publications/pdf/ rc8_eng.pdf. Accessed on 20 December 2008.

UNICEF (2012) *History of UNICEF*. Available at: http://www.unicef.org/about/history/index_ milestones_46_55.html. Accessed on 30 March 2012.

UNICEF (2012b) Children's Rights and Responsibilities leaflet. Available at: http://www.unicef.org/rightsite/files/rights_leaflet.pdf. Accessed on 30 March 2012.

United Nations (2012) History of the United Nation. Available at http://www.un.org/en/aboutun/history/. Accessed on 30 March 2012.

United Nations (1959) Declaration of the child. http://www.unicef.org/lac/spbarbados/Legal/global/General/declaration_child1959.pdf. Accessed 8 August 2012.

Warnock Committee (1978) Special Educational Needs: the Warnock Report. London: DES.

Warnock, M. (1986) 'Children with Special Needs in Ordinary Schools: Integration revisited', in A. and L. Cohen (eds) *Special Needs in the Ordinary Schools*. San Fransisco, CA: Harper Row.

Wong, N.T. (2010) A Typology of Youth Participation and Empowerment for Child and Adolescent Health Promotion, *American Journal of Community Psychology*, 46(1).

UK Government publications

DFES	The Education Act 1870	HMSO
DoH	The Public Health Act 1870	HMSO
DoH	The Children Act 1889	HMSO
DoH	The Children's Charter 1908	HMSO
DoH	The Children and Young Person's Act 1932/33	HMSO
DFES	The Education Act 1944	HMSO
DoH	The Children Act 1948	HMSO
DoE	The Housing Act 1980	HMSO
DFES	The Education Reform Act 1988	HMSO
DoH	The Children Act 1989	HMSO
Treasury	Every Child Matters: Green Paper 2003	HMSO
Treasury	The Ten Year Plan for Childcare 2004	HMSO
DFES	The Children Act 2004	HMSO
DFES	The Childcare Act 2006	HMSO
DFES	The Early Years Foundation Stage 2007	HMSO
DFES	The Early Years Foundation Stage 2012	HMSO

Part 3

Leading practice in the Early Years setting

5

Leading in children's learning and development

Wendy Holland

Chapter overview

The Standard addressed in this chapter is:

5. Make use of engagement, observation and assessment to meet the individual needs of every child.

Relating to the Standard we are focusing upon in this chapter, the following key questions will be addressed:

- What effective strategies can we develop for observing, assessing, planning, recording and reporting children's learning and development?

- How may we use such strategies to promote effective personalised provision based on a clear understanding of child development and possible next steps in children's learning?

- How can we achieve effective practice in supporting children's emergent language and communication skills, literacy and mathematics through sustained shared thinking and the provision of a language-rich environment?

Alice's progress

Alice, a twin aged 3 years, has been causing some concern. Her keyworker and Alice's mother have discussed how Paul, her twin brother, does all the talking for them. This practice seems to have increased since the arrival of their new baby brother. Alice's mother is particularly concerned about her language development and pronunciation. The twins are relatively new to the setting and Alice is still not separating well from her mother, despite her brother being there. Alice's keyworker has asked the Lead Professional, Jill, an EYP, to observe Alice for the afternoon.

At the beginning of the session, Alice settles after a tearful parting from her mother. She joins her brother at the water; filling containers seems to calm her and her sense of well-being appears to improve. Her levels of concentration and involvement appear to be high as she attempts to pour water from one container into another. Chelsea, a 4½-year-old, comes to join them. She talks to Alice rather than Paul. Over the few short weeks Alice has been in the setting, she has tended to seem more at ease with the older children.

Chelsea moves away to a painting easel and Paul decides it is time to play outside. Alice hesitates for a moment, then joins Chelsea who is humming to herself as she paints. The painting area is a favourite area for the twins, and Alice soon becomes absorbed in mixing colours on a palate, staying by herself at the easel when Chelsea has gone outside. She changes her brush from one hand to the other while mixing, then painting. Jill eventually draws up a small chair by the easel and looks at the painting Alice is involved in, asking Alice about her painting. Alice explains, with a reasonable amount of clarity, that it depicts a mother monster with a demanding baby monster. Jill records in her participant observation (see Chapter 3) and evaluation that:

- Alice's level of well-being has been sufficiently high for her to feel confident to engage in activities on her own without Paul.
- She showed ease in the company of an older child.
- Her concentration and involvement while painting were sustained for longer than was usual for her.
- Her communication with the practitioner evidenced language skills to a degree she had not shown previously on her own, although some sounds were not yet fully articulated.
- The topic of the picture suggests that she is coming to terms with her mother's involvement with her baby brother.

Jill made an extra note to ensure Alice's progress was shared with her keyworker so that, when Alice's mother came to collect the twins, they could discuss the **processes** that Alice had been engaged in to produce her painting, rather than just presenting her with the **product**.

Introduction

Two key elements of the EYPS are: (a) a practitioner's ability to demonstrate and model their own good practice, and (b) showing clear leadership of this effective practice with staff in order to support children's learning and development. This chapter will signpost research findings which underpin such effective practice for the reader, as well as providing examples from practice which exemplify the characteristics of effective leadership. The focus will be on those Standards that particularly identify the role of the practitioner in responding to the individual and holistic nature of children's learning, through the establishment of strategies for observation, planning, monitoring, assessment, recording and reporting, to enhance children's development. The use of such strategies in creating effective personalised provision will be examined. The importance of using such a framework to provide a language-rich environment, and the role of sustained, shared thinking between child and adult within that, will also be investigated.

What effective strategies can we develop for observing, assessing, planning, recording and reporting children's learning and development?

Before we consider which strategies to develop, we need to understand the rationale behind the need to observe, assess, plan, record and report children's learning and development. The Early Years Foundation Stage Statutory Framework (DFE 2012a) provides us with such a rationale for the implementation of the Observation, Assessment and Planning cycle for children from Birth to Five years.

Planning, to be effective for children this age, needs to be closely linked to their interests. It also needs to be flexible enough to absorb and use those spontaneous moments of learning that occur daily with young children. At the same time, it needs to ensure that all children receive exposure to experiences and activities that promote each individual's journey towards the Early Learning Goals (ELGs), reduced from 69 to 17 ELGs in the revised EYFS 2012 (see Chapter 2).

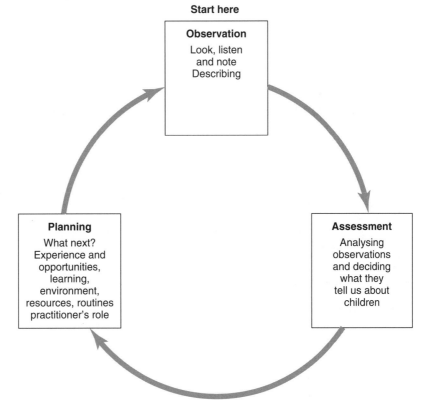

Figure 5.1

Observation is the means by which rich information can be gathered about each child (see Chapter 3). By doing close, regular observations, we can:

- determine children's particular interests, likes and dislikes through ongoing communication with children, parents and carers
- identify any special or particular needs
- establish levels of well-being and involvement
- gain knowledge of newly acquired skills
- assess individual progression
- plan next steps for personalised learning.

All of the above can be gained through regular participant observation while engaged in activities, talking with and listening to children. However, other forms of observation come into play; for example if there are concerns over a child's behaviour, event sampling may need to be employed and, by observing when a particular type of behaviour occurs, the triggers/causes for such behaviour identified. Concerns about areas of possible deficit or delay could involve the use of more detailed target child and/or focal child observations (see Chapter 3), in order to gather evidence to support further investigations by the Special Educational Needs Coordinator (SENCO). A key focus for such observations would be to consider the balance between the amounts of ludic (imaginative) and epistemic (investigative) play in which the child engages (Hutt *et al.* 1989), with a view to balancing this more carefully if the child is engaging in significantly more of one sort of play than the other.

On a broader level, observation can also highlight:

- gaps in resources that need to be addressed
- the imbalance between child-initiated and adult-led activities and experiences
- lack of sufficient access between indoor and outdoor environments for all children, including those with additional needs
- the need to provide more inclusive resources and activities to acknowledge and celebrate the diversity of children in the setting and the unique individuality of each child
- exemplary practice that can be cascaded to others or the need for further training in a particular area
- the need for more input from parents and carers to help support and develop the child's learning journey.

How we record observations is usually dependent upon the needs of individual settings. The EYFS CD-ROM includes examples of proformas and a template for a child's *Learning Journey* to use when observing. For new practitioners these can provide guidance and help. Effective knowledge of the three prime and four specific areas of learning and development outlined in the revised EYFS Guidance (2012) and their related aspects is also essential when ordering the information they gather under such headings as:

● Context for learning
● What did they do?
● Links to Early Years Foundation Stage
● How did the adult support the learning?
● Next steps.

The importance of committing the observation to paper, as soon as possible, lies in the need to provide more reliability and validity. The perspectives of several members of staff, as well as parents and carers, also provide triangulation of evidence for a child's profile. With the increase in the use of ICT, forms of recording, other than written narrative, are increasingly being developed. The use of digital photographs, video and audio recording which can be shared with the home all help to effectively build a child's profile or record of achievement.

Assessment, the next phase in the cycle, is the essential analysis and review of what has been observed. In order for this to be effective, sound knowledge of how children develop and learn is necessary (see Chapter 2). An understanding of schemas (Piaget 1951, Athey 1990) will help the practitioner and parent recognise, support and extend the child's developmental stage (Pen Green 2008). For example, how often has a **transporting schema** (where a child is fascinated by moving materials from place to place) not been recognised in a setting or at home and ignored or stopped because it is messy or inconvenient, instead of being supported and extended? The use of scales of involvement and well-being (Laevers 1997, 2005 and see Chapter 3) can help the observer assess the level of learning (on a continuum from deep to superficial) that is taking place. Effective knowledge of the six EYFS areas of Learning and Development and their related aspects is essential, in order for the child's progress towards the Early Learning Goals to be tracked (see Chapter 2). This *formative* type of assessment, assessment *for* learning, is an essential ingredient when attempting to plan for personalised provision and next steps learning for the child.

The EYFS (DFE 2012), as with the previous frameworks (EYFS, DCSF 2007a), provides clear guidance on assessment with a particular focus on assessment procedures around the new progress check for 2-year-olds. These are explained in the EYFS: 'A Know How to Guide' (DFE 2012b) and have been introduced to support the assessment of two year olds by a combination of views from parents, practitioners and health visitors on a child's development level, particularly in the areas of language and communication. The rationale underpinning this progress check is to provide earlier support/interventions for those children whose developmental levels are shown to be delayed between the ages of 24 and 36 months. Ongoing observation and assessment in all three prime and four specific areas of learning and development provide a summary of each child's progress that informs their EYFS Profile. The revised Profile (DFE 2012c) has 17 Early Learning Goals assessed on a three-point scale, where each individual child is seen as: *emerging, meeting or exceeding* the Early Learning Goals.

The new EYFS Profile is a **summative** form of assessment, assessment *of* learning, as it identifies the levels reached by a child at the end of the Foundation Stage, but can also be used in a **formative** way to inform the Year 1 teacher's planning.

Figure 5.2 The Common Assessment Framework process

Source: www.nelincs.gov.uk.

The Profile is one form of many available to record assessments (see Focus on practice box, ECERS and ITERS below). As with the previous profile documents (Foundation Stage Profile) (DFES 2003), EYFS Profile (DCSF 2007), some settings prefer to create their own specific document. However we document assessments, one important factor needs to be considered, that of ease of access for the child and parents/carers. Ongoing individual profiles or Records of Achievements have an important role in informing parents/carers of their child's continuing development. They also provide a vital opportunity for children to access their own learning and, in doing so, celebrate their achievements as well as being able to self-assess.

Practitioners need to familiarise themselves with other forms of assessment scales such as the Common Assessment Framework (CAF) (CWDC 2007). Holistic provision and assessment of children requires new skills, or at least new ways of thinking. The CAF is not solely for children practitioners have concerns about, or for children with additional needs.

This assessment requires practitioners to make connections between the child's home experience and how the child experiences the setting to a degree that has perhaps not happened before. Rather than being simply a referral mechanism, it needs to be seen as 'an assessment which is linked to a referral' (DFES RB740) on the EYFS CD-ROM (DCSF 2008). In this way the underpinning agenda of Every Child Matters for more effective multi-agency working (now a statutory requirement in the EYFS) can be progressed.

Assessing quality of provision

The use of Infant/Toddler Environmental Rating Scales (ITERS) for children from birth to 30 months and Early Childhood Environmental Rating Scales (ECERS) for use with children from 2½ to 5 years helps when a setting wants to assess its provision in a holistic way, by looking at such items as space and furnishings, personal care routines, listening and talking, activities, interaction and parents and staff; these have been used and developed by several high-profile Early Years research projects on both sides of the Atlantic over the past 20 years, including EPPE – Effective Provision of Pre-School education (1997–2003) and REPEY (Researching Effective Pedagogy in the Early Years) (2003) (Sylva, Siraj-Blatchford and Taggart 2003). Training in applying these scales to a setting can be offered by local authorities.

Focus on practice

The **ECERS (Early Childhood Environment Rating Scales)** are constructed as follows:

ECERS-R is based on seven subscales:

- Space and furnishings
- Personal care routines
- Language reasoning
- Activities
- Interaction
- Programme structure
- Parents and staff.

ECERS-E is based on four subscales:

- Literacy
- Mathematics
- Science and environment
- Diversity.

These aspects are scored along a continuum:

1	2	3	4	5	6	7
Inadequate		Minimal		Good		Excellent

The scales are used as follows:

1 = Inadequate

- Children's needs for health and safety are not met
- No warmth or support from adults is observed
- No learning is encouraged

3 = Minimal

- Children's basic health and safety needs are met
- A little warmth and support is provided by adults
- There are few learning experiences

5 = Good

- Health and safety needs are fully met
- Staff are caring and supportive of children
- Children are learning in many ways through interesting, fun activities

7 = Excellent

- Everything is good
- In addition, children are encouraged to become independent
- The teacher plans for children's individual learning needs
- Adults have close, personal relationships with each child

(Cryer 1999)

The **ITERS-R (Infant-Toddler Environment Rating Scale, Revised)** has seven subscales each of which yield a scale score, using the same scoring system as ECERS. The subscales are:

I. Space and furnishings

1. Indoor space
2. Furniture for routine care and play
3. Room arrangement
4. Display for children

II. Personal care routines

5. Greeting/departing
6. Meals/snacks
7. Nap
8. Nappy changing/toileting
9. Health practices
10. Safety practices

III. Listening and talking

11. Helping children understand language
12. Helping children use language
13. Using books

IV. Activities

14. Fine motor
15. Active physical play
16. Art
17. Music and movement
18. Blocks
19. Dramatic play
20. Sand and water play
21. Nature/science
22. Use of TV, video, and/or computer

V. Interaction
23. Supervision of play and learning
24. Peer interaction
25. Staff-child interaction
26. Discipline

VI. Programme structure
27. Schedule
28. Free play
29. Group play activities
30. Provisions for children with disabilities

VII. Parents and staff
31. Provisions for parents
32. Provisions for personal needs of staff
33. Provisions for professional needs of staff
34. Staff interaction and cooperation
35. Staff continuity
36. Supervision and evaluation of staff
37. Opportunities for professional growth

It is recommended that trained observers spend at least three hours observing and interview senior staff within a setting before applying measures from either scale. There are also manuals and grids that can be purchased or obtained from various local authority sources to ensure that the scoring measures are applied effectively.

(Harms *et al.* 2006)

Leading practice
As you can see, these are very detailed scales and staff wishing to use them to evaluate their own practice should seek training from their local authority in order to use the system properly. This would obviously be very useful for those who are already - or have an ambition to be - Leading Practitioners (LPs).

Task With the help of your colleagues and/or EYPS programme provider, seek out a training programme for ECERS and ITERS.

Planning, the other main ingredient of the learning cycle, is clearly dependent on effective **observation** and **assessment**. Planning can happen in a vacuum or be created by adults with more focus on meeting the dictates of a particular curriculum and learning outcomes. The danger is that an inflexible adult planning of environment and activities may lead to transmission teaching and a *passive* learning environment for children. Child development theory (see Chapter 2) and findings from contemporary research, such as the longitudinal study, Effective Provision of Pre-School Education (EPPE 1997–2003) and the REPEY report (Siraj-Blatchford *et al.* 2002), support the view that babies and young children are *active* learners.

The focus on play-based provision in the EYFS acknowledges such theory and research. Planning that is informed by daily observations and assessments showing children's interests, and that involves, extends and challenges those interests, has been shown to be more effective in helping progress children's development.

The EPPE research highlighted above found that settings where practice showed evidence of a mix of planning for child-initiated experience, child-led experience shared and extended by adults and adult-led experience were **centres of excellence.** Regardless of geography or socio-economic status, children in these settings appeared to make similar learning journeys. The importance of sustained shared thinking between child and adult, the use of open-ended questioning and, again, an equal balance between what the child initiates and the adult leads is underpinned by the REPEY findings. Good planning allows for these things to happen on a daily basis. For this to happen, practitioners need to have a clear understanding of the relationship between the different types of planning used by a setting.

- **Long-term** planning ensures that all areas of Learning and Development are addressed, and usually covers the whole year. It will also look at the provision of resources for special occasions, celebrations, festivals, and visits either out of the setting or visitors to the setting. The overall balance of the curriculum, for example effective access to both outdoor and indoor provision and the necessary resources, special projects that may be undertaken with creative partnerships, or any project that requires time to evolve. Any improvements recommended by Ofsted after a report will be included in the school's long-term improvement plan.

- **Medium-term** planning can act as a bridge between long-term and short-term planning, covering a period from three to six weeks. In the Foundation Stage, activities and themes tend to be of shorter duration, in line with children's changing interests and abilities. Medium-term planning could look at the access to and fair distribution of resources, the balance of topics and areas of focus within the six areas of Learning and Development and the ratio of child-initiated to adult-led activities and experiences.

- **Short-term** planning usually includes what will happen within one week. The key factor, as mentioned earlier, is to ensure that it is flexible to allow for children to follow their interests.

No plan written weeks in advance can include a group's interest in a spider's web on a frosty morning . . . yet it is these interests which may lead to some powerful learning.

(DCSF 2007b, p.12)

In order for planning to support holistic and personalised provision, it needs to reflect an inclusive approach – not by treating all children equally, but by building differentiated provision in order for children to *access* activities and experiences equally, to create enabling environments for all (see Chapter 7). It must also be informed by the formative observations and assessments of children's development that occur daily, so that children's interests and potential next steps are clearly in evidence, alongside any adult-led activities to promote particular outcomes in the seven areas of Learning and Development within the indoor/outdoor environment. (Examples of detailed short-term planning are still available on the EYFS CD-ROM 2008.)

A final element needs to be highlighted when looking at the planning cycle, that of **accountability**. As the EYFS has been given legal force under the Childcare Act 2006, settings need to ensure that all elements of the planning cycle are effectively in place. With regard to assessment and the EYFS Profile, the statutory arrangements allow for parents to receive a written summary of their child's progress against the early learning goals and the assessment scales and, where a parent requests it, a copy of the completed EYFS profile for their child. This may not differ too widely from earlier notions of good practice, where meetings were planned with parents to look at children's profiles/records of achievement before transferring to another setting.

Focus on practice

Reflection *Whether you are an experienced leading practitioner on one of the shorter pathways or a more recent entrant to the profession on the full pathway, you will no doubt have very quickly become involved in the planning within your current setting.*

Task Use your journal to reflect on your planning in the light of what you have learned so far in this chapter. Could you improve your planning? How would you go about this, with a 'real' rather than 'ideal' world orientation? See if you can arrange a session, either face to face or on a forum within your training provider's virtual learning environment (VLE) to discuss this with other EYPS candidates. You may also be able to continue this as an ongoing conversation, particularly if you can ask your tutors to set up a forum specifically for this purpose. In the college in which the editors of this book practise, such a forum has been set up in the 'Work-based learning' area of the Early Years VLE.

Having looked at the separate elements of the planning cycle and their rationales, we can revisit the initial question: *What effective strategies can we develop for observing, assessing, planning, recording and reporting children's learning and development?*

Effective observation: leading practice

Having to lead and show effective practice in this vital area at a time of change, when old practices may need to be revised to ensure they meet the new requirements of the revised EYFS, can aid the EYP in developing new planning strategies for children from Birth to Five years. How can the EYP create effective strategies that lead and support the first element in the planning cycle, *effective observation*?

- They need to assess practitioners' knowledge and understanding of child development in the 0–5 year age range to ensure that observations are effective and appropriate. Through the current cascading of practice in accordance with the EYFS framework, possible areas of confusion or lack of knowledge could be highlighted and staff then supported through the provision of additional training.

- The variety of observation techniques and their specific uses need to be understood and reinforced (see Chapter 3 and Focus on practice on ECERS and ITERS).

- Additional staffing needs to be factored into planning to allow for non-participant observations to take place when necessary.

- Differentiated proformas need to be created to meet the needs of differing age groups from babies to 4- and 5-year-olds. The EYP needs to involve staff working with the various age groups, to ensure practitioners understand the new formats and requirements, and through discussion to create and own observation procedures and proformas that meet their specific needs.

- Staff observations of children other than by their key person need to be seen as common practice and in some instances planned for, in order to increase validity and reliability.

- The importance and use of information/observations made by parents/carers of the child in their home environment needs to be acknowledged.

- There needs to be agreed practice on the recording of observations and how they inform children's profiles and future planning by staff involved in the different age groups.

The above, if implemented, with the EYP involving staff so that they feel real ownership of new practices, could help to promote and embed systematic and effective observation strategies within a setting.

Effective assessment: leading practice

How can the EYP lead and support effective practice within the next element of the planning cycle, **assessment**?

- Staff knowledge and understanding of the seven areas of Learning and Development in the revised EYFS 2012 need to be identified, in order for observed patterns of behaviour to be formatively assessed and recorded under the seven areas of learning, and against the revised early learning goals. The EYFS Practice Guidance (DFE 2012b) highlights the overlapping stages of development from 0–60 months under *Development Matters*, giving a brief résumé of children's learning and development at a particular age/stage.

- Discussion of or introduction to practitioners of other scales of assessment, for example scales of involvement where assessment is focused on *process* rather than *outcome*, and children are involved in 'deep level learning' (e.g. Laevers 1997 and see Chapter 3). Such research suggests that children need to feel a clear sense of well-being in order for learning to be truly assimilated and accommodated.

- Practitioners need to be well versed in the range of schemas that children may demonstrate. The recognition and assessment of schema that show how children are trying to make sense of the world around them, through testing out their ideas by carrying out the same action in a variety of contexts and with different objects, is an important stage in children's development, and needs to be assessed as such.

- The EYP needs to ensure that practitioners are reflective and can self-assess honestly. The EEL (Effective Early Learning) Project run at Birmingham University by Pascal and Bertram (1997) considered the quality of adult interaction with young children, and offered a broad set of guidelines for effective self-assessment.

- The EYP needs to ensure practitioners are familiar with the Common Assessment Framework, and understand it as an assessment framework, prior to referring a child. This kind of assessment is pivotal in helping to promote the provision of personalised and holistic provision for children, and requires practitioners to listen to and establish real dialogue with parents (Easen 1992).

- The EYP needs to be proactive in helping to create a profile of formative assessment for children that now spans from birth to five years. Not only will this help provide continuity of provision for individual parents and children to access, it will continuously inform personalised planning, and is now a statutory requirement under the EYFS framework.

- The EYP needs to help practitioners become familiar with the revised EYFS Profile (or its equivalent) as a summative assessment for each child at the end of the Foundation Stage. Staff must be assisted to understand that these statutory documents are moderated by the local authority as one assessment measure that is applied to the setting, and that they must always be easily accessible to parents. A summary of each child's achievements towards the Early Learning Goals must be provided before the child makes their transition to the next setting.

- The EYP also needs to model effective practice, by encouraging the use of learning journeys as a form of self-assessment with children to encourage self-evaluation.

- Infant/Toddler Environmental Rating Scales (ITERS) and Early Childhood Environmental Rating Scales (ECERS) may also form part of the EYP's strategies when holistically assessing the setting's provision (see Focus on practice box on ECERS and ITERS above). The assessment scales can be used with the help of staff, to improve provision by looking at specific areas of the physical environment, such as space and staffing ratios, furniture and resources as well as less tangible elements of the environment, such as interaction between child and adult, the quality of listening and talking, and available activities and planning.

Effective planning: leading practice

Leading and supporting effective practice in the final element of the cycle, **planning**, requires the following:

- The EYP needs to discuss with and support staff in implementing new planning structures, which incorporate the changes in planning and assessment required by the revised EYFS guidance 2012.

- By the creation of differentiated planning proformas that fit the individual needs of babies, toddlers and 3–5-year-olds, the EYP can help practitioners promote personalised and holistic learning. By talking to parents, the baby room staff could produce charts that reflect individual children's routines for feeding and sleeping, including transitional toys, or special, calming language that is family specific and will put the baby at ease.

- The EYP needs to ensure that planning at whatever age/stage reflects individual needs in, for example, patterns of attendance, routines that might be directly linked to the diversity of a child's culture, knowledge of a child's attendance at other settings, when and who will collect the child and the special requirements of a child with any kind of delay or deficit.

- The EYP should recognise the need for flexibility in planning that allows for children's interests to inform future short-term planning, while reflecting on links between the medium- and long-term plans of the setting in relation to topics and areas of Learning and Development, supporting staff who are unsure or lack the confidence to divert from planned provision.

- Planning needs to be accessible and visible to all staff, so that roles and requirements are clearly discussed and represented, and planning and preparation time needs to be built into the planning timetable to allow this and other tasks (e.g. the upkeep of individual profiles) to effectively happen.

- The EYP needs to ensure that time is given to evaluation of and reflection on daily planning, through discussion by staff teams involved, in order that next-day planning can be revised/extended to meet changing and individual needs.

- Planning needs to be accessible to parents, too. An overview of planned activities could be placed on the parents' information board, which might also include enlisting help with resources, encouraging participation in setting events (baby massage sessions, for example), or setting visits to look at print in the environment for older children.

- As with observation and assessment, the EYP needs to value the input of practitioners. Planning that has been created through whole staff involvement is more likely to be effective than planning that has been imposed.

Focus on practice

Sunflowers and caterpillars

Sue, a relatively new practitioner to the children's centre, whose previous employment had been in a school nursery class, had attended training on outdoor gardening activities. The head had been particularly keen for a member of staff from the

3 to 5's room to attend, as the setting had just finished re-designing, with the help of parents, some of the outdoor provision to include raised beds for the children to plant and grow things in. One project Sue developed involved the planting of sunflower seeds, initially in plastic cups filled with compost, which were duly planted out in one of the raised beds and nurtured by Sue and the children. It was a particularly hot summer, and the sunflowers grew to enormous heights. Eventually it was time to harvest them and Sue had planned to link the event to several areas of learning and development. She and Christine, the setting's Leading Practitioner, had discussed the timetable and planning for this older group of children who were due to leave that summer, and it had been agreed they would benefit from a slightly prolonged time of focused activity after lunch, before going out to play and the arrival of the afternoon children. The cut sunflowers were going to join a display of yellow objects in the room, which included a print of Van Gogh's painting of sunflowers. Sue had planned to look at one of the sunflowers in some detail, indicating in her planning the vocabulary she intended to introduce and the learning outcomes she hoped to achieve. The rest of the flowers were arranged in a vase and placed in the middle of an area that had been prepared with some 'thick' paints which some children had helped to create earlier using powder paint and glue (the thickness of the brush strokes in the painting had been commented upon by the children, and the idea of painting with thick paint using thick brushes appealed to them).

The largest sunflower had been selected for examination, and placed on sheets of large white sugar paper on the floor. The tallest child in the group lay down next to it and the children estimated the flower was three times as tall as him. 'As tall as a giant', was one reply. Sue reminded them how difficult it had been to cut them down. 'Like Jack and the Beanstalk', a child commented. Sue explained how the seeds in the seed head could be eaten, or planted, like they had a long time ago. She began to look at the flower, noting the 'hairs' on its long stem, its pale roots and the 'veins' in its leaves. 'We've got veins', said a boy, showing Sue his hands. 'Yes', she replied, then continued examining the sunflower. 'Yours are blue and knobbly', insisted the boy. This comment was ignored. Christine, who had been asked by Sue to observe the activity for the children's profiles, sensed some of the children had lost interest, and were no longer following the examination of the sunflower, but were concerned rather with something small and moving. A caterpillar had crawled from under a curled leaf and was slowly making its way to the edge of the paper. The children's interest in the sunflower immediately evaporated and all eyes focused on the caterpillar.

Sue tried several times to draw the children back to the focus of her careful planning, eventually looking to Christine for support. But Christine joined in with the children's interest, suggesting they made a 'home' of some kind for the caterpillar, and food for it to eat, gently persuading Sue that the sunflowers could be enjoyed another day, and the children could still experiment with thick brushes and thick paint. Sue was reluctant at first and concerned that her intended learning for the children and her planning would need to be fitted in to another period of focused activity or discarded. She was eventually won over by the children's enthusiasm for the new class 'pet', whom they named Vincent 'after the man who painted sunflowers'.

➡

Identifying good practice

Sue has shown elements of good practice in her initial training and the planting activity which had obviously been a continuing source of interest to the children. Her planning also shows she has tried to think about the learning outcomes for these older children who will be leaving the setting at the end of the summer. Her initial examination of the sunflower was interesting – getting the children to estimate its height and involving the children in an enjoyable way. Reminding them of the difficulties they had cutting the flowers down again taps into the children's imagination and interest, with the response about 'Jack and the Beanstalk'. Her introduction of new vocabulary starts well and again stimulates interest in the children, especially the boy who makes the connection between the veins on the leaf and the veins on our hands, which Sue should have explored in more detail. She does not, however, intend to be side-tracked.

Christine's refusal to support Sue in continuing with the sunflower activity also shows good practice. She is indicating to Sue that children's interests need to be listened to. The caterpillar had caught their imagination and interest. The planned activity could take place another time, when the children would be happy to re-engage with it. The resources Sue had prepared would not be wasted, as they could still form part of an activity in its own right.

Leading practice

Christine may empathise with Sue, who, having done the training, was keen to put it to use by planning projects for the newly developed garden area. The sunflowers had been a great success; not only Sue's group but the whole setting had enjoyed the sunflowers. Sue had obviously spent a lot of time and energy in planning the sunflower project, linking it in to the areas of learning and development with projected outcomes for the children, culminating in the activity she had asked Christine to observe in the belief that it would provide useful material with which to assess the children's understanding and learning. So Sue's reluctance to be side-tracked into a different focus was understandable; however, Christine needed to reinforce the need for flexibility, and the importance of letting children's interests influence planning.

After this incident, Christine asked for Sue's help in developing the 'Vincent the caterpillar' project. Sue soon became caught up in planning activities and resources around the life-cycle of the butterfly, as the children watched in fascination its building of a cocoon and its final transformation, not into the anticipated beautiful butterfly from the storybooks they'd listened to and the pictures looked at and searched out with Sue's help on the Internet, but a brown moth. The children were still fascinated as they released 'Spiky' the moth into the garden.

Reflection

- *Do you agree with Christine's decision?*
- *Could she have achieved her intentions in a different way?*
- *Did Christine's lack of support of Sue undermine her role as a Leading Practitioner?*

- *Was it more important for her to illustrate the need to be flexible?*
- *Was Sue at fault in planning and resourcing her project in advance?*
- *Was Sue right to try to challenge these older children, who were due to leave the setting, in the manner she did?*
- *Had her previous experience in a Nursery Class attached to a school predisposed her to view planning in a different way from Christine?*
- *Did the extension of the children's interest in the caterpillar justify Christine's actions?*

Task Try to reflect on the above, as well as other issues you feel this example raises, and where possible discuss these with peers. Consider too, have there been instances when circumstances out of your control have adversely influenced your own planning? How did you deal with them?

How can we use such strategies to promote effective personalised provision based on a clear understanding of child development and possible next steps in children's learning?

Personalised provision leads to effective personalised learning. The EYFS framework describes it thus:

> . . . providers to reflect the rich and personalised experience that many parents give their children at home. Like parents, providers should deliver individualised learning, development and care that enhances the development of the children in their care . . .

(DCSF 2007b, p.9)

In order for the EYP to lead and support practitioners in creating such an 'enabling environment' for every child, thorough understanding of child development needs to be modelled to and expected of practitioners. Only by understanding the norms within a range of behaviours can the practitioner identify the needs of individual children, and become alert to potential deficit and delay. Sheridan (1997) produced norms for children's development that have been widely used and adapted. Criticism of these norms consisted of the fact that they were too prescriptive in stressing age-appropriate levels of behaviour. The revised EYFS framework continues to provide a more generous overlap between expected behaviours for children from birth to 60 plus months (see Chapter 2), the first 'norm' or age stage beginning at birth to 11 months, followed by the next which starts at 8 to 20 months, and so on. This overlap allows for the range of abilities within any particular age stage. However, the EYP needs to ensure that the sequences that run through these norms are used with caution. Some babies will not crawl before they walk; not all children will process language in the same way, perhaps electing

141

to be mute until they are ready to speak. Nature and nurture will combine and interact to create the *unique child* (also see Bronfenbrenner's work in Chapter 2).

The EYP's responsibility in leading and supporting practice here depends upon their ability to ensure practitioners take all these factors into consideration. Home visits before a child is admitted to the setting, though sometimes expensive in having to provide supply cover, provide essential information about the child. In their home environments, parents often feel more relaxed, freely providing information about particular transitional toys, family language, friendships that have been formed with children already attending the setting. For babies and very young children, it could focus on their likes and dislikes when having nappies changed, their feeding and sleep habits, the way they prefer to be held or rocked. Such information can be gleaned during setting visits, but parents are sometimes ill at ease filling in an information sheet in a more formal situation, with the bustle of the setting around them. The home visit can also help the practitioner understand the child's position within the family, their relationship with other siblings, parenting styles, the family's position within the wider community, any possible fears the parent might already have about their child; in addition, expectations parents/carers might have regarding the setting and 'education' in general can be identified. It can also create a particular bond between the practitioner and child. Seeing this new adult in their home environment builds trust and helps the child during the transitional phase from home to setting.

This information, combined with initial careful observations and assessments during the child's settling-in period, can help the practitioner to provide and plan for effective personalised provision for that child. Looking at behaviour according to where it falls within a particular age norm against a particular area of learning and development is only part of the picture when trying to create personalised, holistic provision. What this will show is an individual child's particular learning style, so we can plan basic provision to allow for those children who are more visual or kinaesthetic in the approaches to investigating their environment. Such information will also help the practitioner to understand the schemas in which they are currently engaged, to help them make sense of the world. The amount of time children need to accommodate and assimilate ideas will vary, so the routines of the day should not be inflexible (see Chapter 7). Time should be built in to planning to allow for children to dwell for extended periods of time on a project or activity or to revisit projects/activities the next day. Children's creations need to be valued and their persistence in trying to build a model should be encouraged. They should not rush to finish and their creation should not be discarded at the end of the day during a hasty tidying-up routine (see the section on the Reggio Emilia approach in Chapter 6). If personal provision is carefully tuned, children's levels of well-being and involvement will rise and deep personal learning will occur.

Flexible planning around children's interests, too, should ensure diverse practice to encompass and celebrate the diversity of children's backgrounds and experiences within the setting. The use of sustained shared thinking with children as they create their products will show their understanding of process and give practitioners a clearer view of the next steps in provision needed for the child to progress, which may include revisiting an area of learning and development time and again until they have successfully assimilated and then accommodate the process. Keeping profiles up to date and regularly reviewing with children their own profile again helps to personalise provision through aiding the child to self-assess and see what their next challenge/step might be.

Personalised provision for children who may be giving cause for concern needs to be structured as soon as possible. Again this will have been arrived at by early conversations with parents/carers prior to the child's admission, or during the settling-in period. The child may have come from another setting or been assessed by another agency, and this needs to be taken into consideration when planning provision for the child. The EYP needs to ensure that practitioners are clear about the policies and procedures involved when a child is giving cause for concern, involving **early years action, then early years action plus and finally statementing: http://www .teachernet.gov.uk/management/atoz/s/senidentificationandassessment/.**

If the child already has a statement, the setting needs to ensure the additional financing can provide appropriate ratios of staff and resources to meet the needs of the child with SEN. If the child is giving cause for concern, and is not statemented, for example a child with behavioural issues or language difficulties, the EYP can discuss with the keyworker how to personalise provision to improve the situation for the child, using behaviour strategies that are already in place, in the first instance, or developing a new system of rewards that relate to the child's interests. The use of baby signs, Makaton or Picture Exchange Communication System (PECS) (Callcentre 2008, online) might be introduced for children with slight language delay. If further investigation is needed the EYP can liaise with the SENCO, keyworker and parents to arrive at an Individual Education Plan (IEP) for the child, to provide personalised provision that addresses the child's particular issues, as well as their overall development. IEPs must be reviewed at regular intervals; research suggests that many children will require temporary additional help at some time during their development. This requires staff to be alert and supportive of parents to ensure they understand the necessity for such temporary measures. It is the EYP's role in leading and supporting practice in this area to model good practice and ensure that staff feel comfortable, voicing and being proactive on behalf of a child they have concerns about, so that personalised provision can be adequately established for that child. The key person or worker is also a vital partner in the new EYFS progress check for 2-year-olds to enable earlier identification of developmental needs so effective support can be put in place (DFE 2012a).

Focus on practice

George had been a 'precious' baby in both the medical sense, being delivered prematurely at 28 weeks, and in the emotional sense, as the long-awaited child of older parents. He began in the Toddler Room at the setting, his parents having been loath to let him go, until financial necessity forced them to. George's behaviour had caused some concerns from the beginning. He was not intentionally aggressive to other children or adults as long as they did not attempt to persuade him to join in activities, meal times, or any other routines of the day. His reaction was initially to show frustration, then attempt to run away and hide. 'George ploughs his own furrow', Grace, his keyworker, had said to Janet, the setting Leading Practitioner, during one of their discussions about George, adding: 'Of course, it doesn't help when his parents don't have any routine with him at home.' Janet suggested she and Grace talk to his parents about George's lack of routine. His parents arrived late for the meeting, which meant George was present during their discussion, and it soon became apparent to Janet and Grace that they had little control over George's behaviour. Both parents looked exhausted, due partly to George's lack of sleep routine.

Janet and Grace both offered suggestions for helping ease George into some kind of routine. The parents were grateful and promised to try the methods suggested. Janet also asked if the setting SENCO might observe George, at the same time calming fears that anything more than immaturity and lack of routine were at the root of George's behaviour. George's parents did not manage to encourage him into a routine, and the SENCO, after observing George, agreed with Janet's initial diagnosis that George's behaviour was a product of his immaturity due to his premature birth and lack of routine at home, suggesting they should try to get the parents to cooperate. When George was due to transfer into the 3-5 years room the suggestion was made to his parents that he would benefit from a longer stay in the Toddler Room, but his parents were adamant they wanted George to 'go up with his friends'. In the 3-5 room, where the planning and focus were on more adult-led activities that challenged children's learning and development, more demands were placed upon George to join in activities and be sociable. This in turn led to more behaviour difficulties. 'He just ignores you', his new keyworker had said to Janet, asking if Janet would observe George to see if his behaviour was simply due to the transition into a new room with new expectations or if any other triggers for George's behaviour could be identified.

Identifying good practice

Janet observed George over a period of days. He had a cold and a cough, which his keyworker described as 'semi-permanent'. Janet noticed that George tended to engage in solitary play, but would on occasion choose to play alongside particular children who were, in the words of one staff member, 'noisy and boisterous', and 'not a particularly good role model for George'. Janet noticed George would sometimes stand very close to a child and peer into their face if he wanted to communicate with them. His language skills were immature for his age, some sounds being entirely absent from his speech, and some children would turn away, but George would gently turn their faces back to him. During one observation, a child playing with musical instruments dropped a cymbal, which stopped most of the children nearby in their tracks. George, however, had his back to the incident and carried on building a tower with plastic blocks. Janet felt George's hearing needed to be investigated and, after speaking with the SENCO, contacted his parents.

Leading practice

After his hearing assessment, George was found to have a severe conductive hearing loss in both his ears, and an operation for grommets to be inserted was arranged. Janet researched information on grommets and knew they were sometimes only partially successful (not like fitting a pair of spectacles). She informed staff and, on George's return, asked his keyworker and other staff in the 3-5 room to note down any differences in his behaviour. 'He keeps putting his hands to his ears', one member of staff noted. But his keyworker recorded, 'he now stops, turns and looks at you when you call his name'. Janet decided to arrange a meeting between herself, George's keyworker, the SENCO and George's parents. He was still operating at a less mature level than his peers. So an Individual Education Plan was agreed for George, with reviews every two months. Initially, there seemed to be no difference in George's behaviour. After four months one of the grommets had worked its way out, and at an IEP meeting with parents they confirmed that they were managing to establish a routine for George, and really felt the staff support was making a difference.

Reflection

- *Did Janet, along with other members of staff, too easily accept that George's behaviour was the result of (a) being premature and (b) being the only child of overprotective parents with a 'permissive' approach to parenting?*

- *Could one of the reasons for George's behaviour, i.e. his conductive hearing loss, have been detected earlier?*

- *Did Janet, his keyworker and the SENCO handle the situation with the parents appropriately?*

Task Discuss the above and any other queries you might have about this situation with your peers/colleagues if possible. Have you been in a similar situation where behaviour issues have been wrongly or inadequately dealt with? As the EYP in this situation, what steps would you have taken?

How can we achieve effective practice in supporting children's emergent language and communication, literacy and mathematics skills through sustained shared thinking and the provision of a language-rich environment?

The EYP, in order to lead and support practice in this area, needs to have a sound knowledge of the possible developmental stages children go through in acquiring language and communication skills (see Chapter 2 and associated reading). Again, as with the use of developmentally appropriate stages, caution must be used. For many children, however, a sequence of development can be evidenced, and the EYP needs to familiarise themselves with these general stages. Research into the kinds of language we use as practitioners with children can also have an important effect (Bernstein 1976, Tough 1974). From the baby's attempts at early vocalisation to the rapid fire 'why?' question of the older child, children naturally engage in trying to communicate with significant others in their lives. The EYFS practice guidance suggests that effective practice in encouraging children's developments in this area of learning requires **positive relationships** to be built with **people who have meaning for them** (DCSF 2007b, p.39). Without the sense of security and trust such relationships engender, it is suggested that communication and language skills may not fully develop in the young child (see reference to 'Genie' in Chapter 2). It is the EYP's task to lead and support practitioners in creating such warm, trusting, **enabling environments**, through, for example, establishing open and trusting relationships with parents/carers, accepting and using their specialised knowledge of the child's daily routines, the forms of language used by the family that the baby or child responds to best. Where a child comes from a home where the principal language spoken is not English, it can help to request tapes/CDs in the baby's home language. Ensuring the keyworker for a child fully understands the importance and remit of their role is also essential in ensuring that babies and young children entering the setting can experience a warm, supportive, trusting environment.

Within such key relationships, a baby will learn to link sounds and voices to the new routines of their day, for example music being played during nappy changing, as well as the practitioner's calm voice, or a favourite story being read before they fall asleep. In a trusting, caring relationship, children will more readily express feelings, thoughts and ideas. The EYP needs to ensure that planning and organisation incorporate daily opportunities to explore language through rhymes, songs, poetry and stories, and for older children to access fiction and non-fiction materials, and that the language accessed is also reflective of the diverse nature of children's individual personalities and cultures. Books and signs around the setting written in their home language will enable children from diverse backgrounds to feel welcomed as part of the community, creating an environment rich in language for every child. The *Hundred Languages of Children* suggested by the Reggio Emilia (Edwards, Gandini and Forman 1998) schools implies that children's communication is not limited to the use of speech, but can be seen through dance, music, mark-making, drawing, modelling, painting, expression and body language, to name but a few. Young children learn best when all their senses are engaged.

The EYP needs to lead and support practitioners in promoting this rich language environment, through the use of 'conversations' and early 'proto-conversation' turn-taking with babies and toddlers (see Chapter 2), daily sessions with rhymes, songs sung in diverse languages and repetitive and familiar stories, linking sound to movement as children become more mobile. Song books can be created for parents to use at home to encourage familiarity with rhymes and language, accompanied by pleas for help in compiling story sacks, songs and rhyme bags. As children progress they can be encouraged to 'read' a story to peers, or recreate a familiar story with such visual aids as home-made puppets and props and magnet boards; to listen to and act out story and rhyme tapes, as well as having access to books both fiction and non-fiction, big books, pop-up books, board books and interactive multimedia sources. Musical instruments can be used to emphasise the beat and rhythm of language, tapping out the beats, for example, in a child's name, trying to repeat a pattern played by an adult or peer. Later still comes the introduction of different uses of language for different audiences; the chance, time and encouragement to discuss, argue, share experiences, re-tell narratives in the correct sequence, showing an understanding of language patterns in stories. Children in a rich linguistic environment with access to a range of printed materials will begin to link sounds to letters, using their growing phonic knowledge to write simple words. Any language-rich environment needs print in all its forms, with outings, perhaps, into the local community to look at print in the wider world – the huge neon sign naming a supermarket or the street name of where they live. The revised EYFS practice guidance: *Development Matters* (DFE 2012b) has created a new area of learning by making changes to the previous Communication, Language and Literacy (CLL) area of learning. A new prime area of learning has been created called: Communication and Language, its aspects being: Language and attention; Understanding; Speaking. This reinforces the importance of a child's early ability to communicate, listen and understand. Combined with the two other newly created prime areas: Personal, Social and Emotional Development, and Physical Development, it supports child development theories around children's maturational stages of development. Confirmation if needed of the necessity for young children to gain some mastery over these basic, essential skills before moving on to achieve more advanced skills. These are outlined in the newly created Specific Areas of Learning: Literacy, Mathematics, Understanding of the World and Expressive Arts and Design.

Alongside this exposure to and experience of language, the EYP has to look at how practitioners use language with children in their daily practice. Both the EPPE and REPEY research studies emphasise the importance of using language in sustained shared thinking with children. As Siraj-Blatchford *et al.* (2002) suggests, this is not always an easy thing to achieve: 'The challenge in enquiry is to interact with the child so as to capture their interest and attention without telling them to stop what they are doing.' The use of certain forms of language by the practitioner is also highlighted, particularly the form and phrasing of questions, e.g. the use of open-ended questioning: *I don't know, what do you think? or what would happen if we did . . . or what rhymes with . . .* The EYP needs to model and support practitioners in the *art* of open-ended questioning. The EPPE findings showed that, even in those 'centres of excellence' where very good practice was reported, only approximately 5 per cent of questions used by practitioners were of the open variety. Practitioners need to plan for such shared thinking to happen, but also to seize the spontaneous moment from some child-initiated experience. For the practitioner to be genuinely involved in shared thinking with a child, they need to understand the world from the child's perspective. The EYP also needs to model how a language-rich environment underpins not only the acquisition of language itself, but all the areas of learning, including helping children to problem solve, guess and estimate numbers, quantities, the properties of shapes, the patterns in the world around them, abilities essential to the understanding of early mathematics.

Focus on practice

Zahir's world

Susan, the setting Leading Practitioner, had been monitoring the profiles of the 4-5-year-olds who would be leaving the setting to go to school after the summer. She had already had a discussion with the keyworker responsible for Zahir, a 4-year-old who, against the setting's advice, would be leaving that summer. His keyworker, Josie, explained why his profile which had started so promisingly, with his observations showing a lively and active boy, interested and engaged in a number of areas of development and learning, suddenly seemed to decrease and were almost non-existent for the last few months. Around that time Zahir's mother had become seriously ill, and had been undergoing tests involving short stays in hospital. Zahir's aunt, who usually collected him, spoke very little English, and the dialect she spoke was not well understood by the member of staff who acted as interpreter in these situations. Zahir's father did speak good English, but on the rare occasions he collected Zahir he was in a hurry, reluctant to discuss the situation. Zahir had become reclusive, preferring to be at the design and technology table, building quite intricate, solitary models that he did not want to discuss. In the outdoor area he spent his time making larger models, re-arranging milk crates, tyres, hollow blocks and any other building material to hand. When other children offered to help or showed interest in his building, he would shout at them, often becoming excitable, using his home language. At times when the member of staff was asked to interpret, she would say he did not want anyone near, adding that he was too old to be using his 'mother tongue' in the setting environment, and the family should be helping to teach him English. While not openly defying the adults in the setting, he would only take part in focused activities reluctantly, refusing to communicate, except for the briefest of exchanges with other adults or children. Story time was the only time he seemed to give his full attention, listening intently to the stories, but again refusing to role-play or take part.

Identifying good practice

Susan decided to read the story in Zahir's room one afternoon. She took in a large empty cardboard box, telling the children they needed to listen carefully to the story so they would know what to do with the box afterwards. She read the story *This is Our House* by Michel Rosen, where a group of children from a block of high-rise flats find a large empty cardboard box. They argue over what it should be – a boat, a plane, a house. In the process of arguing they wreck the box, then decide to work together to rebuild it into 'our house'. Zahir had sat listening intently to the story. As soon as it had finished, he leapt up and said, 'mine', attempting to put his arms around the cardboard box. Several other children began to argue and pull at the box. Susan got their attention by telling them they were behaving just like the children in the story. This cardboard box was now also in need of repair. The children carried it over to the design and technology area and began to repair it, under Zahir's minimal instructions. The children trusted Zahir as he always built interesting models which others tried to copy. Susan began to take some pictures of the process with a digital camera, then remembered the setting had recently acquired a video camera. By this time, the group had decided not only to repair the box but to make it into something under Zahir's direction. When Josie returned, Susan suggested that she video the proceedings, but Josie was unsure how to use the camera; she had been absent for the training due to illness and had not caught up. Susan continued taking digital images, but when she tried to show Zahir what she had taken and engage him in conversation, he looked away and continued with his task. The video camera, however, did catch his attention, along with the rest of the group. After they had been filmed for a while, Susan would stop filming and ask some children to talk to the camera. 'Like on the news', a child suggested. Susan agreed. Afterwards she showed the 'interview' back to them. Zahir had refused to take part until he saw the re-run, then he became animated, trying to explain his vision for the 'skyscraper house' his 'team' were building. In his excitement he slipped into his home language, then corrected himself, answering Susan's questions about windows, doors, lifts and stairs, as she probed how and why they were making a 'skyscraper house'.

Leading practice

Reflecting on the situation Susan notes the following:

- The issues around Zahir's behaviour should have been picked up sooner, not left until he was due to leave the setting.

- This had resulted in a sad little boy developing defensive behaviour. His sense of well-being had been allowed to reach very low levels. He had shown involvement (in model making), but this had almost been a displacement activity to hide from what was really troubling him.

- No real attempt had been made to discuss or talk with members of Zahir's family.

- There were issues that needed addressing around staff in the setting and the use and encouragement of home language.

- There needed to be some system whereby, if staff missed important training through no fault of their own, a way of inducting them should be found.

After discussion with the deputy manager the following course of action was decided:

- As well as the usual observations based on areas of development and learning, scales of well-being would be introduced (see the Leuven Scale in Chapter 3). Susan, who had used these in her last employment, would organise training for the staff.

- Better procedures for talking with and involving parents needed to be established. With only one part-time member of staff able to speak Urdu and Punjabi, the setting was limiting its ability to reach out to the increasingly diverse community it now served. The deputy manager said she would discuss with the manager the possibility of employing another bilingual member of staff who would work both in the setting and as a family support worker.

- Clear guidelines would be drawn up with regard to the use and encouragement of home language, and this would need to be reflected in the wider setting environment.

> **Task** With your colleagues/fellow students consider the following points:
>
> ● What actions by Susan can be seen as 'good practice' in the above scenario?
>
> ● What other choices were available to her?
>
> ● If the manager does not agree to the employment of another bilingual member of staff, how will the setting deal effectively with communicating meaningfully with families from culturally diverse communities?
>
> ● Some settings have an increasingly diverse population; for example, a setting we visited last year housed children speaking more than 20 different home languages from Africa, Asia and eastern Europe. How might a Leading Practitioner develop an inclusive approach towards these children and their families?

Conclusion

What effective strategies can we develop for observing, assessing, planning, recording and reporting children's learning and development?

This chapter has emphasised the vital importance for the EYP to ensure the establishment of sound knowledge and understanding by staff of the **planning cycle**; the importance of good practice in the ongoing **formative observation** of children, and the linking of information collected through various kinds of observation to the assessment of each individual child's needs, in order to create personalised learning for the child. **Planning** should therefore allow for, in the **short term**, careful observation by staff of groups of children and the individual child, in order to provide activities and experiences that promote learning for every child on their journey towards achieving the revised Early Learning Goals (ELGs). Clear, whole school planning needs to be created to inform staff, provide proformas and promote discussion of, for example, resources, school trips, festivals, and the use of both indoor and outdoor spaces. Above all, in line with the play-based emphasis of the new EYFS framework, planning needs to be **flexible** enough to take into account children's individual interests. **Triangulation** of observations obtained by several members of staff, not only the child's keyworker, will provide the necessary **reliability** and **validity**. **Formative assessment** of young children from 0 to 5 years is an essential and statutory requirement of the EYFS framework (2012). Assessment scales that recognise involvement and well-being as well as assessments against the seven areas of learning will help to provide a holistic view of the individual child's development. The EYFS Profile can be seen as a **summative** document, detailing the stage the child has reached in relation to the ELGs by the end of the Foundation Stage, which will help with the child's transition to Key Stage One. Knowledge of the ITERS and ECERS scales can also help the practitioner assess and improve the environment and support good practice (see Focus on practice box above). An understanding of the Common Assessment Framework is necessary for practitioners to be able to respond to children about whom they may have concerns. **Recording** of observations and assessments can take many forms; often a setting will design its own proformas to meet its particular circumstances. Again, in the new EYFS, this is a statutory requirement. Examples of proformas for observing, planning and assessment can be accessed on the CD-ROM accompanying the EYFS guidance. **Reporting** children's achievements and development to parents has been and continues to be a statutory requirement (at least once a year). Other agencies, for example local authorities, Ofsted, and certain government departments, also require information such as the data from EYFS profiles for individual settings. Reporting also happens on a daily basis, between members of staff, between staff and parents and, most importantly, between practitioners and children, in order to help each child become self-reflective.

How may we use such strategies to promote effective personalised provision based on a clear understanding of child development and possible next steps in children's learning?

Knowledge of child development theories, research and initiatives is essential for **personalised** care and learning to take place. This has to be applied in conjunction with a sound understanding of the personal circumstances of each child. Bronfenbrenner's (1979) theory of the relationships within a family, between a family and settings and the larger world, Baumrind's view of parenting styles (in Oates, Lewis and Lamb 2005), Dunn and Kendrick's (1982) work on sibling relationships, all show the necessity for the practitioner to be knowledgeable about each child's individual circumstances if effective personalised provision is to be established. **Working with parents** and carers to establish effective personalised learning for the child is essential, together with ongoing formative observation and assessment. **Shared thinking** between the practitioner and child helps extend the child's development and learning potential, through the use of open-ended questioning. Allowing time for a child to revisit projects and self-reflect must be built into the routines of the day, if real and effective personalised provision is to be achieved.

How can we achieve effective practice in supporting children's emergent language and communication skills through sustained shared thinking and the provision of a language-rich environment?

As this chapter demonstrates, the practitioner needs a sound knowledge of the stages of **language acquisition** (see the Practice Guidance EYFS, DCSF 2008) for children from 0 to 5 years. The need for **positive relationships** to be established during the child's initial **transition** from home to setting is essential, with links to home provided by transitional toys, music or objects to reassure the child. Only in such a supportive and **enabling** environment, will children feel able to express themselves. The practitioner needs to recognise that children from 0 to 5 have *the hundred languages of children* through which to communicate with others, the diversity and variety of which needs to be recognised and celebrated by the practitioner. The provision of a **language-rich** environment, through book corners, story sacks, role play, puppets and regular sessions playing with language through rhymes and songs, are again essential for the development of a child's language.

The real acknowledgement of the diversity of languages within a setting, as well as the celebration of that diversity and difference, is important for establishing positive relationships and a confident sense of self in young children. The means to create music, dance and rhythm as ways of expression, both indoors and out, need to be resourced. **Listening** to children and taking their questions seriously, sharing their thinking as they engage in activities and experiences, both self- generated and adult-led, are important in encouraging the development of a language-rich environment.

Further reading

Bee, H. (1997) *The Developing Child*. Harlow: Longman.

Bruner, J. (1983) *Child's Talk: Learning to use language*. New York: Norton.

Cohen, D. (2002) *How the child's mind develops*. London: Routledge.

David, T., Gooch, K., Powell, S. and Abbott, L. (2003) Birth to three matters, a review of the literature. Available at: **http://www.standards.dfes.gov.uk/eyfs/resources/downloads/rr4444.pdf**.

Donaldson, M. (1978) *Children's Minds*. London: Fontana.

Lindon, J. (2008) *Understanding Child Development: Linking theory and practice* (2nd edn). London: Hodder Arnold.

Nutbrown, C. (2006) *Threads of Thinking: Young children learning and the role of early education*. London: Sage.

Piaget, J. and Inhelder, B. (1969) *The Psychology of the Child*. New York: Basic Books.

Smith, P., Cowie, H. and Blades, M. (2003) *Understanding Children's Development*. Oxford: Blackwell.

Vygotsky, L. (1978) *Mind in Society*. Cambridge, MA: Harvard University Press.

Websites

EPPE: **http://www.ioe.ac.uk/schools/ecpe/eppe/**.

EYFS (2012) **www.foundationyears.org.uk**; **www.education.gov.uk/publications**.

REPEY report: **http://www.dcsf.gov.uk/research/data/uploadfiles/RR356.pdf**.

References

Athey, C. (1990) *Extending Thought in Young Children: A parent-teacher partnership*. London: Paul Chapman.

Bernstein, B. (1976) *Class Codes and Control*. New York: International University Press.

Bronfenbrenner, U. (1979) *The Ecology of Human Development: Experiments by nature and design*. Cambridge, MA: Harvard University Press.

Callcentre (2008) Picture Exchange Communication System. Available at: http://callcentre.education.ed.ac.uk/SCN/Level_A_SCA/Using_Symbols_SCB/Hot_PECS_News_HTA/hot_pecs_news_hta.html. Accessed on 18 February 2009.

Cryer, D. (1999) 'Defining and assessing early childhood program quality'. *Annuals of the American Academy of Political and Social Science*, 563.

CWDC (2007)'The Common Assessment Framework for Children and Young People – A Guide for Practitioners'. Leeds: Children's Workforce Development Council.

DCSF (2008) *Early Years Foundation Stage Practice Guidance*. Nottingham: DFES Publications.

DCSF (2007a) *Early Years Foundation Stage Profile*. Nottingham: DFES Publications.

DCSF (2007b) *Statutory Guidance in the Early Years Foundation Stage*. Nottingham: DFES Publications.

DFE (2012a) *Early Years Foundation Stage Statutory Framework*. Cheshire: DFE Publications.

DFE (2012b) *Early Years Foundation Stage Practice Guidance*. Cheshire: DFE Publications.

DFE (2012c) *Early Years Foundation Stage Profile*. Cheshire: DFE Publications.

DFES (2000) *Curriculum Guidance for the Foundation Stage*. Nottingham: DFES Publications.

DFES (2003) *Foundation Stage Profile*. Nottingham: DFES Publications.

DFES (2006) *Common Assessment Framework*. Nottingham: DFES Publications.

Dunn, J. and Kendrick, C. (1982) *Siblings: Love, envy and understanding*. Cambridge, MA: Harvard University Press.

Easen, P. (1992) 'Parents and educators: Dialogue and development through partnership', *Children and Society*, 21(5), pp.376–89.

Edwards, C.P., Gandini, L. and Forman, G. (1998) *The Hundred Languages of Children: the Reggio Emilia approach – advanced reflections*. New York: Alex Publishing.

Harms, T., Cryer, D. and Clifford, R.M. (2006) *Infant/Toddler Environment Rating Scale*, (rev. edn manual). New York, NY: Teachers College Press.

Hutt, S.J., Tyler, S., Hutt, C. and Christopherson, H. (1989) *Play, Exploration and Learning: A natural history of the pre-school*. London: Routledge.

Laevers, F. (1994) *The Leuven Involvement Scale for Young children*. Leuven, Belgium: Centre for Experiential Education.

Laevers, F. (1997) 'Forward to basics! Deep-level-learning and the experiential approach', *Early Childhood Research Quarterly*, 12(2), pp.117–43.

Laevers, F. (2005) 'The curriculum as means to raise the quality of ECE: Implications for policy', *European Early Childhood Education Research Journal*, 13(1), pp.17–30.

Oates, J., Lewis, C. and Lamb, M. (2005) 'Parenting and attachment', in S. Ding and K. Littleton (eds) *Children's Personal and Social Development*. Oxford: Blackwell.

Pascal, C. and Bertram, A.D. (1997) *Effective Early Learning: Case studies of improvement*. London: Hodder and Stoughton.

Pen Green (2008) *The Pen Green Framework for Engaging Parents*. Corby: Pen Green.

Piaget, J. (1951) *Psychology of Intelligence*. London: Routledge and Kegan Paul.

Rosen, M. (1996) *This is Our House*. London: Walker Books.

Sheridan, M.D. (1997) *From Birth to Five Years*. London: Routledge.

Siraj-Blatchford, I., Sylva, K., Muttock, S., Gilden, R. and Bell, D. (2002) *Researching Effective Pedagogy in the Early Years*. RB 356. London: DFES Publications.

Sylva, K., Melhuish, E., Sammons, P., Siraj-Blatchford, I., Taggart, B. and Elliot, K. (2003) *The Effective Provision of Pre-School Education (EPPE) Project: Findings from the pre-school period*. London: Institute of Education.

Sylva, K., Siraj-Blatchford, I. and Taggart, B. (2003) *Assessing Quality in the Early Years Early Childhood Environment Rating Scale*. Stoke-on-Trent: Trantham Books.

Tough, J. (1974) 'Children's use of language', *Education Review*, 26(3), pp.166–79.

6

Promoting emotional security and positive behaviour

Wendy Holland

Chapter overview

The Standards addressed in this chapter are:

2. Work directly with children and in partnership with their families to facilitate learning and development.

4. Set high expectations which inspire, motivate and challenge every child.

Relating to the above standards, the following key questions will be addressed:

- What effective strategies can we develop that reflect our knowledge and understanding of how children learn and develop and our commitment to ensuring each child achieves their full potential? How do we create fair, respectful and supportive relationships while achieving such effective practice?

- What effective behaviour management strategies can we create to support the development of positive, emotional, behavioural attitudes and independence in children?

- What constitutes effective practice in the identification and support of children whose development, progress or well-being is affected by changes or difficulties in their personal circumstances? What strategies do we need to establish and implement to ensure that, where necessary, appropriate specialist support is provided?

- How can we develop practice to ensure effective and sensitive communication with children through listening to and respecting the views of children from birth to the end of the foundation stage is achieved?

Providing for John's individual needs

John had attended the children's centre since he was 2. Now at 3 years of age he was about to move into the attached nursery for 3 to 5 year olds. It was essentially the same building his elder brother and sister had attended several years before when it had been an LEA nursery school. John's brother and sister had been seen by both parents and nursery staff as exceptionally able children, the label 'gifted' having sometimes been applied to them, especially in relation to their early reading and number skills. As his parents had been vocal about their two older children's achievements and 'gifts', they were equally open and forthright about their disappointment in John's apparent lack of literacy and numeracy skills. The Centre had found John to be a quiet child, 'almost reclusive', one member of staff had said, given to sudden short outbursts of 'difficult' behaviour. On looking through the new entrants' profiles, Angela, the centre's EYP, felt that John was making age/stage appropriate progress in most of the six areas of learning. What did concern her, however, were his keyworker's comments regarding his reclusive nature, punctuated by sudden acts of aggression towards either staff or children. Often he would soil himself after such an episode, which nearly always seemed to occur at the end of the day. The soiling was seen by his parents as a particularly 'backward' step, even after Angela tried to explain that transitions sometimes had this effect on a child and they should be patient. John's parents got into the habit of expecting to talk at some length on a daily basis to his keyworker or, failing that, another member of staff about their son's progress, often making comparisons, within John's hearing, between him and his elder siblings. When his keyworker discussed this with Angela, she suggested the keyworker made more regular close observations of John. These highlighted his interest in dinosaurs and model making, as well as his skills on the computer and on the outdoor apparatus. He particularly liked to find original ways to negotiate the obstacle courses and spent time setting up complicated 'dens' from twigs and other materials at hand. However, John's parents were not responsive to his keyworker's reports of such positive activities; what they wanted to see was some clear evidence of writing or mathematical skills.

In discussion with John's keyworker, Angela subsequently suggested an approach similar to one she had seen developed at Pen Green Children's Centre, where children were filmed engaging in play-based activities, and this material was then used in discussions with parents/carers to provide insight into children's learning through play. She suggested they should include film of John building one of his special dens, which could then be used to inform parents during the twilight sessions that had been arranged for looking at the new EYFS framework. John's parents were regular visitors at the twilight sessions, and after watching the evidence (especially their own son being quite articulate about something that really interested him) their views began to change. This resulted in more praise and celebration of the activities their young son engaged in and, while still remaining proud of their older offspring, they began to accept and enjoy John's uniqueness. Slowly, this had a positive impact on John's behaviour and his aggressive outbursts gradually began to lessen.

Introduction

As can be seen from the above scenario, the standards to be focused upon in this chapter are those that particularly identify the role of the practitioner in having high expectations of all children, both in their behaviour and in each child's ability to achieve their full potential. The practitioner's role in developing children's social and emotional competency will be examined, through their use of effective strategies which promote positive behaviour, self-control and independence. In helping children to develop to their fullest potential, focus will also be placed on the practitioner's role in identifying and supporting children whose progress, development and well-being are affected by changes or difficulties in their personal circumstances. The remit of the practitioner's role in the referral process for children who may need specialist support will also be discussed.

The positive values, attitudes and behaviour this particular group of standards reinforce will only be achieved effectively through the establishment of trusting, positive relationships with children. How such fair, respectful and constructively supportive relationships can be developed will be examined. In particular, the practitioner's role in communicating sensitively and effectively, through careful listening to children and valuing their ideas and contributions, will be investigated. This chapter will, as in previous ones, signpost relevant research findings which underpin effective practice for the particular standards being addressed, as well as providing examples from practice which exemplify the characteristics of effective leadership. The Further reading list suggests texts that will provide a more detailed approach to some of the key issues discussed here.

> **What effective strategies can we develop that reflect our knowledge and understanding of how children learn and develop and our commitment to ensuring each child achieves their full potential?**
> **How do we create fair, respectful and supportive relationships while achieving such effective practice?**

For the practitioner to address these questions we need to look at the following:

- Sound knowledge of the emergent principles, theories and research underpinning child development (also see Chapter 2)
- Secure knowledge of the individual child through home visits, meetings with parents and carers
- Observations, assessments and the planning of personalised provision (also see Chapter 5)
- Good inclusive provision which challenges stereotypes that may inhibit development, whether from parents, practitioners, other agencies or children themselves (also see Chapter 3)
- Establishment of positive relationships which take into account children's levels of well-being and involvement, as well as practitioners' levels of engagement and support
- How we in the UK can learn from the best practice embedded in international approaches to early childhood care and education that support and challenge the child's development and learning (also see Chapter 4).

In order to develop effective strategies that reflect our high expectations of children, it is essential we understand each individual child. As stated in previous chapters, the practitioner needs a sound knowledge and understanding of child development in all areas – cognitively, linguistically, emotionally, socially and physically. With such knowledge, the practitioner needs to be able, through observation, to identify individual stages of development, in order to provide appropriate challenges for the child. Sound knowledge of the child's **prior learning and experiences** has to be in place, before reasonable, achievable and challenging expectations can be created. The gaining of such knowledge takes energy and commitment. The detail needed is not found in a single proforma that a parent or carer might have hastily or anxiously filled in when the child first attends a setting, or a brief observation of the child during the initial settling-in period. In order for the information to be detailed and meaningful, a holistic review of the child's experiences needs to be undertaken.

Ideally, this would begin with a home visit prior to the child's attending the setting. A wealth of information can be gained from such a visit:

- How the child relates to the significant others in their home environment
- How they communicate with parents/carers, younger or older siblings
- The quality of such relationships: are they warm, affectionate, supportive?
- What kind of behaviour strategies does the parent/carer use?
- What kinds of parenting style(s) does this suggest and how can we provide support and balance of experience for the child?

Parents may feel more at ease in their home environment, better able to tell you about the child's particular likes and dislikes, or the important routines of their day. They may discuss, too, any possible concerns they might have, which they have not really voiced yet to anyone 'official'. The practitioner is not there to judge, but to gain a picture. As the EPPE study (2003) has shown, it is what parents **do** to support their children's development and learning and how they do it that is important, more important than other influences such as the parent's occupation, education or income. Within the security of the home, rather than the strangeness of a new setting, the practitioner, hopefully, will be able to create the beginnings of a positive relationship with the child that will transfer when that child eventually arrives at the setting. Leaving a toy, game or book for the child to enjoy and bring with them, during their settling-in period, is one way of creating what needs to be a trusting, warm and respectful relationship.

It is not only the child who needs to feel comfortable enough to engage, but the parent too. As Every Child Matters states:

> The bond between the child and their parents is the most critical influence on a child's life. Parenting has a strong impact on a child's educational development, behaviour and health.

(DFES 2003, p.39)

There may be barriers, spoken or unsaid, that make the particular relationship between practitioner and parent/carer more problematic. The parent/carer might, as a child, have undergone difficult experiences within their family and/or the education system. In the case of very young children, the parent might be afraid, consciously or subconsciously, of their role being usurped, for example because the practitioner witnesses the child's 'milestones' first. Good, open and honest rapport needs to be established from the very beginning so that such sensitive issues can be explored. Essential is a real recognition too, by the practitioner, that the parent/carer is the child's first and enduring educator, whose intimate knowledge of the child will, if shared, provide the practitioner with the kind of detailed knowledge and understanding to be able to create an exciting, engaging environment that reflects the child's interests, while stimulating and challenging them within the areas of learning and development.

The cultural diversity of families needs to be acknowledged and celebrated. Questions about the use of home language and English, for example, might need to be raised. A review of research on bilingualism (Siraj-Blatchford and Clarke 2000, p.30) suggests numerous advantages to being exposed to more than one language from birth. Whitehead (1996) is quite clear the research findings suggest that language mixing in the early years is not an indicator of 'muddle and inadequacy', but rather that children are making choices in how to express their feelings. She further suggests that,

> It is absolutely essential that early years carers and educators respect the languages of the young children for whom they are responsible. This must go deeper than vague goodwill or tolerance.

(Whitehead 1996, p.21)

If a home visit is not possible, for example because of insufficient staff to provide cover, or the visit is not wanted by the parent/carer for any number of reasons, the practitioner needs to ensure that they take time to talk with those parents/carers when the opportunity arises to gain a fuller picture of the child's prior knowledge, experience and interests than the usual admissions documentation generally provides.

A strength of good inclusive practice is that it challenges stereotypes and misconceptions of all kinds. This includes the possibly lower expectations that parents/carers, practitioners and children themselves may have about what is possible or achievable. A new parent might perhaps be finding it hard to adjust to their child's attending the setting and is being overprotective. This may well be preventing the child from settling in and taking full advantage of all the setting offers. It is the practitioner's task to explain this sensitively to the parent. It may be that an inexperienced practitioner is 'taking over' children's activities, thinking they are helping children who are 'struggling', when what they are really engaged in is the celebration of their own artistic talents! Again it is the Lead Practitioner's duty to model and explain good practice, while not dampening enthusiasm. In the case of children about whom there are concerns, or who have already been statemented, the Lead Practitioner needs to ensure that all parties involved communicate. The setting's **Special Educational Needs Coordinator (SENCO)**, the child's parents/carers and any other relevant agencies, when discussing and creating the child's **Individual**

Education Plan (IEP), need to ensure that expectations of the child are realistic and achievable. Such a plan will need to be revisited on a regular basis to assess the child's learning and development and ensure progress is built into expectations.

In attempting to raise expectations for each and every child, the practitioner should not accept stereotypical thinking, regardless of where it originates, but look at each child with knowledge and understanding of their capabilities, interests and particular learning styles and plan to promote and encourage whatever next steps are relevant and appropriate. The EYP needs to lead and support practice in this area by demonstrating through their own planning and assessment how differentiated progression is possible and, indeed, necessary for each child.

We need to keep in mind the **personalised learning needs** of the child when considering how to develop and challenge their learning (see revised EYFS 2012: *Development Matters* for age-staged progression across the seven areas of learning towards the **Early Learning Goals**)(DFE 2012).

- The observation, assessment and planning cycle (see Chapter 5) is essential to maintain in order for the practitioner to be informed of children's individual interests and needs as they change and develop.

- Triangulation of team observations, through discussion at daily planning meetings, guides the planning of appropriate and challenging adult-led, child-led and adult-extended activities, within rich, supportive and well-resourced continuous provision (see summaries of EPPE and REPEY findings, Chapter 5).

- Careful observation also identifies not only developmental stages but the levels of an individual child's self-esteem and involvement (see Chapter 3, the Leuven scales of well-being and involvement).

- Observation of staff levels of sensitivity and engagement (see EELS research scales of staff engagement in Chapter 3) also provides material for reflection on practice. It is the Lead Practitioner's duty to ensure all members of staff are aware of the need to promote a consistent and committed whole setting approach to principles, policies and practice.

The EYP also needs to be knowledgeable about best practice within international approaches to early years care and education, in order to enrich practice within the UK by reflection on their own principles and practice. The Reggio Emilia pre-schools in northern Italy promote the picture of the child as 'rich' in imagination and abilities, a curious and determined investigator and researcher of the world around them, whose questions are taken seriously.

Focus on policy and practice

The Reggio Emilia approach

The Reggio Emilia approach was initially created in the mid-twentieth century in a political context in which it was conceived as a reaction against fascism. Louis

Malaguzzi, its creator, left the state school system to become involved in community initiatives in Reggio Emilia, a region of Northern Italy. The approach was pluralistic, involving children, parents, teachers, administrators and politicians. It took its influences from social constructivism (e.g. Vygotsky 1978), and aimed to develop children's knowledge through a collaborative partnership. Its opposition to standardisation, outcomes, targets and focus upon economic productivity means that the approach is often difficult to integrate into current Western curricula – a point that should make us consider where our own pedagogic practices have been heading over the late twentieth century and first decade of the twenty-first century.

The child is viewed as rich in potential, strong, powerful and competent and able to develop their own theories about the world and how it works – a self-confident explorer/investigator with a sense of curiosity and the freedom of spirit to venture beyond the known/given. They are believed to have the capacity to explore such ideas in collaboration with other children and adults, using a 'hundred' languages with which to express themselves, including sign, art, dance etc., all of which are equally valued. Great emphasis is placed on adults and children learning together, valuing each others' opinions, viewpoints and interpretations. The welfare of young children is seen as the collective responsibility of the community, creating feelings of 'ownership' among all involved.

Children are encouraged to be aware of the present, build on the past and look to the future, and priority is given to setting aside the necessary time for children and adults to discuss and debate and reflect. Revision and reflection are considered central to children's learning, therefore projects unfold at the child's own pace. Children are encouraged and expected to concentrate for long periods of time from a very young age, while caring adults spend much time documenting, interpreting and sharing information with colleagues and parents. There is no set curriculum; both children and adults are viewed as researchers, and adults give great respect to children's theories and hypotheses, allowing children to make mistakes. It is common to find an artist in residence in Reggio Emilia settings, working with the children to express their ideas in art and craft forms.

Practitioners are expected to try to understand children's learning processes rather than acquire skills and knowledge that they will then expect to 'transmit' to children in turn; the practice of teaching is not seen as being about how to transmit information, but about developing understanding of how children learn. They are encouraged to meet and talk with people working outside the boundaries of education – for example, scientists, musicians, writers, architects – and both to take ideas from such professionals back into the setting and to invite those who are willing to visit and share their knowledge with the children. Reggio Emilia practice is distinguished by its rejection of hierarchical staff structure, externally imposed policies, manuals and curriculum guidelines.

The Reggio Emilia learning environment is designed to give space and light, with white walls, mirrors, three-dimensional pyramids and light tables. Above all, within the social constructivist model of learning, the environment must be flexible. The dining room is at the heart of the school, with the kitchen area visible at all times, underlining the importance given to preparing and sharing food. The furniture is multi-functional and open to modification, so that the children shape the room, and in turn the room shapes them (Rinaldi in Cadwell 2003). There is always an *atelier* (art studio or area) and a creative and discovery area available, containing a range of materials that are not for 'set' or restricted activities but intended to lead to investigation.

Identifying good practice

In the Reggio paradigm, practitioners are seen as *facilitators* and *researchers* who help children make sense of the world. A question like: *'Where does the water come from'* (perhaps asked by a young child seeing water pouring from a tap) might lead to the child's being challenged to find out. Donning hard hats, young children between 3 and 6 years, accompanied by practitioners/facilitators, might begin a field trip to investigate the setting's plumbing system and develop a project around the properties of water. The Reggio Emilia pre-school approach sees the environment as a *third teacher*, where the environment is carefully planned and resourced to encourage light and space and challenges the children to use it imaginatively and autonomously, with free-flow movement both indoors and out. If we are to have high expectations of children and their achievements, we need to provide similar environments rich in resources and potential.

Leading practice

- What value is placed on children's theories/ideas in your setting?
- How are different learning styles accommodated?
- How do children use their many 'languages of expression'?

Task Consider these questions with your colleagues and peers, and, on the basis of your answers, consider how you could improve practice in your setting, particularly so that children are given more uninterrupted time, allowing them to leave unfinished investigations, knowing that they can return to them later, and that not all will be tidied away at 'tidy-up time', and then deemed 'finished'.

Reflection *What problems might a Reggio approach create within a regime that runs on the statutory guidelines of the EYFS?*

Task Consider this point with your colleagues and peers, and how you might come to a satisfactory conclusion in terms of developing good practice, while maintaining the statutory requirements. (Note: This may not be an easy prospect!)

Focus on practice

Peter's progress

Peter was a summer-born child. When he was just 3 years old, he attended a local nursery as his mother, a single parent, was new to the area and had found part-time work. She was anxious for Peter to take advantage of his full afternoon entitlement as soon as possible, and appeared reluctant to adhere to the setting's settling-in policy of a gradual introduction for new children. Parents were encouraged to stay until their child was settled for the first couple of weeks, and return to collect their child a little earlier each afternoon, until it was felt by practitioner and parent that the child was ready to separate for the whole afternoon session. So it was with reluctance that the setting agreed to shorten Peter's settling-in period.

To the practitioners, Peter presented as a particularly immature child, who appeared to need to investigate new experiences orally (Freud 1965). When engaged in using PVA glue for the first time, he discarded the spatula, dipping his fingers into the glue pot and proceeding to eat the glue and anoint his face with it. The same process happened with play dough, sand, cornflour 'gloop', virtually every new substance Peter experienced. He spoke very little at first, pointing or nodding his requirements, showing his displeasure by sitting down and refusing to move, hitting out and occasionally trying to bite other children and adults. This latter behaviour would occur if he did not manage to have first choice of the 'trikes' outside. If left to his own devices, he would happily ride silently round and round all afternoon. He was particularly restless at the end-of-session story time, so much so that practitioners had to ask his mother to revert to collecting him earlier, until he was happy to concentrate for slightly longer periods. She was distressed by this, informing staff that she was putting Peter into nearby daycare after his nursery session had finished, because of the demands of her job, and was not sure if this new setting could accommodate the earlier finishing time. So nursery staff persevered with Peter's distracting behaviour at the end of the day.

Over time, the slow level of progress in Peter's behaviour and communication skills began to concern some staff, but it was difficult to arrange time with his mother, who now had a full-time job, and had arranged for Peter to attend daycare before and after his time at nursery. Notes sent with the daycare staff at the end of a session were rarely replied to, and when meetings were arranged his mother often did not turn up. At staff meetings, when Peter's development was discussed, the view was often expressed that his immaturity was due to his young age and the number of changes he had had to surmount in a relatively short time. The fact that he preferred to spend his time outdoors engaged in physical activities was regarded as normal 'boyish' behaviour.

Identifying good practice

Helen, a newly appointed EYP, took particular interest in the young boys who were in their final term at the nursery. There appeared to be a staff culture that supported leaving the boys to their 'boisterous' outdoor play – a view underpinned by the belief that this was necessary, given the formal provision that awaited them in the Reception class of the neighbouring primary school. Helen, who was familiar with the contemporary debates around boys' underachievement, having recently read the Primary National Strategy guidance for Early Years practitioners on supporting boy's achievements (DFES 2007), decided to look in detail at the profiles of all the boys who would be going through the transition to the mainstream school's Reception class at the end of the semester. Peter's profile was of particular interest to her. Towards the end of Peter's final semester at the nursery, Helen managed, where staff had been previously unsuccessful, to arrange a meeting with Peter's mother, by being flexible and staying behind one afternoon. At the meeting, she tried to suggest that Peter should delay attending the neighbouring primary school in September, when he would be almost a year younger than most of the children in his Reception class, explaining that his young age and personality were better suited to another term at nursery. His mother replied that this was the first she had heard of it, as none of the other staff had mentioned the possibility of Peter staying 'back', and, anyhow, she felt Peter was 'ready' for the 'proper work' experience the mainstream Reception class would provide.

Leading practice

Having looked at all the boys' profiles, Helen noted they related to the six areas of learning mainly through lots of photographs of the children engaged at the sand and water trays, creating models with recycled materials, enjoying outdoor activities, or using construction both large and small within the setting. Some profiles contained examples of emergent writing and painting, or artwork done on the computer accompanied by scribing from setting staff to explain the process the children had been engaged in. A few examples of the boys' attempts at number recognition had also been recorded. The contents of Peter's profile were particularly sparse. What Helen noted was the circular schema that seemed evident when looking at the few examples of his paintings and emergent writing and his physical play. Helen decided that, in order to encourage the leavers to engage effectively in the development of their emergent writing skills, the outdoor provision needed to reflect more what was available to children inside the setting. Initially, she would put out large sheets of paper, either anchored on the ground or fixed to a wall, informing staff that these 'graffiti zones' would hopefully encourage the boys to mark-make outside. She also encouraged staff to set up and engage in role-play situations outside where emergent writing was needed (a ticket office for the train, receipts for petrol at the petrol station and menus for the alfresco coffee shop/café). Although Peter did access these new resources and activities, his input was limited, until the week Helen planned *looking for mini-beasts* as an ongoing outdoor activity. With the use of magnifying glasses and collection boxes, the children went on mini-beast hunts and Peter found a ladybird, or rather a ladybird found Peter. Helen watched as this boisterous boy stood perfectly still, arm extended, as the tiny creature slowly crawled up his arm, on to one hand, then the other and finally into the collection box another child held at the ready. Peter took his find into the classroom, lying full length in the carpet area, watching the creature inside the Perspex box. Staff commented it was the quietest and the most calm they had ever seen him. Later that day, he began painting the circular shapes staff had got used to seeing him produce. This time, however, there were circles within circles and curly lines spiralling around the circles. Helen was called in by a member of staff who proudly showed her Peter's creation and the adult scribing alongside it describing the 'ladybird' Peter had painted. He began a small production line in the days that followed, producing painting after painting, until his mother, on one of her rare visits to collect him, suggested he painted something else, looking for support from Claire, the new young member of staff handing her yet another of Peter's ladybird paintings. Claire, trying to be supportive to a parent she had been told was rather 'difficult', agreed it was perhaps time Peter tried to draw something else. Helen, on hearing of the incident, decided to approach the manager of the nursery about delivering some staff training. A number of areas of development concerned her:

● The limited use made of the children's profiles to guide planning for both individual and whole group development.

● The laissez-faire approach to boys' development and learning, particularly their inability to persist with difficulty, their fine motor skills and emergent writing. Taking good practice from the EYFS guidance, she hoped to introduce to staff the idea of 'learning diaries'.

● The need to revisit work on understanding and supporting children's individual schemas.

● The need to have a more equal and sustained approach to partnership with parents, to ensure that those parents who were hard to reach due to work or other commitments were not discriminated against when it came to discussing their child's interests and developmental needs.

Reflection

● *Is Helen right to challenge the staff perspective on boys' 'boisterous' outdoor play being necessary in this situation? How might the staff react to yet more 'paper work'? Is she going too far too fast?*

● *Was she being unreasonable in her expectation of staff to accommodate 'hard to reach' parents with more flexibility? How might this have affected the relationship between Peter's mother and the setting?*

● *Discuss with other members of your cohort what changes Helen might make to staff use of children's profiles in planning.*

Task Discuss the above and any other queries/questions you feel this scenario raises with peers/colleagues where possible.

What effective behaviour management strategies can we create to support the development of positive, emotional, behavioural attitudes and independence in children?

Standards 2 and 4 focus on the behaviours of both adult and child and also the behaviour management strategies used by both adult and child to develop and promote positive behaviour. The potential EYP must demonstrate the ability to:

● Consistently apply a behaviour policy that has clear boundaries and concise rules, on a daily basis, and one that sets reasonable, age-appropriate expectations of children's behaviour.

● Promote children's self-control and independence and demonstrate they can plan for opportunities to develop children's social and emotional skills.

- Give children opportunities to be responsible, make decisions, errors and choices, while continuing to feel secure.
- Help children to develop skills of negotiation in solving problems with other children and model such skills appropriately.
- Set a tone of high expectation of individual behaviour by being assertive and challenging unacceptable behaviour, making it clear to the child that it is the behaviour that is being focused upon and not the child themselves.
- Support children who attempt to talk through conflicts and seek resolutions that are fair and equitable.

In showing leadership and support of others, the EYP needs to:

- Demonstrate the importance of positive values and attitudes, by actively promoting and modelling strategies to encourage appropriate behaviour in both staff and children.
- Reinforce the need for consistency in creating boundaries, and applying rules with both colleagues and parents/carers.
- Show the ability to be able to preempt potential behaviour problems through effective management of the physical environment, experiences, activities and resources, including sensitive scheduling of daily routines.
- Demonstrate through their own professional behaviour the importance of punctuality, time-management and reliability, as well as skills in listening, empathy and respecting differing views.
- Recognise the importance of working in partnership with parents/carers, and with appropriate professionals from other agencies, in order to help children with particular behavioural difficulties to fully access the provision.

Before we look in detail at the above desired requirements, we need to consider the wider picture of child development (see Chapter 2). As has been reiterated previously, it is only through a sound understanding of child development that successful practice can be achieved. This is certainly the case when looking at behaviour management strategies.

For babies and infants the practitioner needs to have a clear understanding of what is appropriate and age/stage related behaviour, in order to create effective behaviour strategies. The practitioner needs to pay attention not only to the child's cognitive, linguistic and physical development but also to their *emotional competency* (Denham 1998). It is through the development of the child's emotional competency that empathy for others, self-control, perseverance, social awareness and sensitivity can be encouraged (Goleman 1995). Research suggests (Dunn 1993, Barnes 2001, Smith, Cowie and Blades 2003) that children by the age of 2 years have developed 'person permanence' as well as the basic emotions. Between 4 and 5 years personal emotional styles become established and from 3 years the development of social emotions, for example the ability to empathise, has begun (Harris 1989). Research also suggests (Barnes 2001, Dunn 1993) that where parents/carers talked to their infants and young children about their feelings, children were more likely to talk about their own and others' feelings from 2 years of age.

Another important aspect related to emotional competency is the theory of mind, the beginnings of a child's ability to understand that other people have 'minds', feelings and an internal self (see Chapter 2). For the child this means tuning in to the fact that others will have desires, needs or feelings that may be different from their own. Along with this growing appreciation of themselves and 'others' as distinct and different, children placed in regular social situations outside the family environment need to develop the skills to organise and/or control their own emotions and behaviour to facilitate their interactions with peers.

Maccoby (1980) describes the basically impulsive nature of young children's behaviour and their limited ability to sustain attention. The average attention spans in physical play she identified as:

- 30 seconds at 2 years
- 42 seconds at 2½ years
- 55 seconds at 3 years.

Control and organisation of young children's impulsive behaviour needs careful handling and the understanding, for example, that a 2-year-old, experiencing the emotional 'storms' that are frequent at this age, needs to be soothed and calmed before they can re-engage with others in the world around them. The 'coping strategies' that children themselves develop in order to control and organise their behaviour are not simply maturational, but influenced by their social environments in both negative and positive ways. Practitioners, for example, need to be aware and wary of any cultural or social stereotyping that may happen in a setting, either between children, staff or parents/carers. Research has shown that children as young as 2 and 3 years develop an understanding of and reactions to skin tone and gender which can result in cultural/racial stereotyping or, for example, gender stereotyping of types of play or toys or behaviour. Any and all of the above can have a definite and sometimes lasting effect on children's self-identity and consequently their behaviour and emotional competence, as well as their cognitive growth and development, as discussed in the previous chapters (Laevers 1994).

The practitioner's ability to respond positively to children's behaviour requires the ability to openly and honestly self-reflect. Webster-Stratton (2000) argues that practitioners need to be able to distinguish between their own feelings and thoughts, as well as be aware of their negative and positive thoughts in any conflict situation. The ability, after such reflection, to find ways to manage their own emotions and responses will make them more effective practitioners in meeting the children's needs.

What does knowledge and understanding of the above mean for the practitioner? Perhaps we should now return to the beginning of the section on behaviour and apply what the above theory and research together with further initiatives suggests to the creation of effective practice.

The EPPE report, in looking at 'excellent' settings, found they had adopted discipline/behaviour policies where staff supported children in rationalising and talking through their conflicts, using a 'problem solving' approach, supported by a strong behaviour management policy which all staff understood and to which they all adhered. In the less effective settings it was found that there was often no clear response to children's misbehaviour and/or conflicts and, on many occasions, children were told to stop or distracted.

One of the recommendations of Ofsted (2005) in a report on managing challenging behaviour was to underline the need for consistency among staff in the way expectations of behaviour are set and maintained.

An extract printed in the EYFS Primary National Strategy document on developing positive relationships by Julian Grenier, the head of Kate Greenaway Nursery School (http://www.kategreenaway.ik.org/), proposes the need for 'consistency and a whole-staff approach . . . as a team we need to ensure that we are being fair and consistent' (Grenier *et al.* 2008, online).

In terms of leading and supporting practice, then, the potential EYP needs to ensure there is a whole-team consistency in implementing behaviour policies/ strategies for effective practice to occur. This, of course, requires discussion, a feeling of ownership on the part of staff, and agreement with the philosophies on children's behaviour that underpin the policies created. It requires, too, support for an individual practitioner by other members of the team. Again, as Grenier (2008, online) suggests, 'nothing undermines a staff member more than when their careful work with a child is dismissed as "fussing" or "spoiling"'.

The relevance and age-appropriateness of behaviour policies/strategies is also key when considering good effective practice. Thinking back to the research on emotional competency, to ask a 2-year-old to 'say sorry' will not mean much to the child, who may not even be able to understand the words, when a hug might be much more effective. 'Why did you do that?', when aimed at a child too young to be able to articulate reasons for their actions, is inappropriate, especially as on occasion their inability to reply is seen as stubbornness and seen as further evidence of misbehaviour! Age appropriateness needs to be built into every successful behaviour policy, especially as within many Early Years settings practitioners are dealing with the full age range from birth to five years. The EYFS in its Learning and Development section gives guidance on what to look for in terms of age/stage appropriate behaviours and the good practice that supports children's behaviour and self-control.

Assessing children's emotional competency and therefore their ability to understand and comply with the setting's behaviour policies can be achieved through observations in the same way information on cognitive development is gathered (see Chapter 3). Again the EYFS guidance gives suggestions of what to look for and notes that are age/stage related. In this way, individual behaviours can be more accurately understood and steps to help the child progress developed. The practitioner needs to provide experiences that help young children understand how adults and other children are feeling, and also experiences/activities that challenge the child's own interpretation of events and explanations of other perspectives. The Primary National Strategy's programme, *Excellence and Enjoyment: Social and emotional aspects of learning* (see http://www.standards.dfes.gov.uk/primary/publications/banda/seal/), is comprehensive and linked to early years practice, providing the practitioner with numerous examples of good practice in encouraging young children to build positive relationships, feel good about themselves and others, and talk about their thoughts and feelings.

Helping children to resolve conflict by rationalising and talking through their feelings, as the EPPE research (2003) suggests, fosters children's ability to identify what they and others are feeling, and so realise the impact of their actions on others, helps them find solutions to problems, and builds self-esteem. The High/ Scope approach (Schweinhart 2003), which some Early Years settings in the UK have adopted, similarly emphasises this need for children to reflect on their own behaviour, not through isolating the child, but by encouraging the child to discuss the problem with the adult or others involved.

Sometimes, for example in the case of bullying, other strategies are needed. The use of empathy or persona dolls (see Chapter 3) is an effective resource here, where issues relating to behaviour management can be addressed. If a child is being bullied, or is the one being aggressive to others, this can be explored through the use of the 'doll', without specifically identifying the child/children involved. This allows for the unacceptable behaviour to be effectively discussed without 'naming and shaming' or embarrassing either the child being bullied or the child doing the bullying, building an awareness that, while the behaviour is disapproved of, the child as an individual is still valued. To act otherwise would damage the child's sense of self-esteem and self-worth, and could well lead to progressively more 'difficult' behaviours as a result. Often, while the doll is being passed round for 'comfort', the child responsible for the unacceptable behaviour will console the doll and offer advice.

As mentioned earlier in this chapter, the environment is an essential factor in children's development. The EYFS, in its promotion of 'Enabling Environments', clearly states the importance of what is sometimes called 'the third teacher' (see earlier reference to pre-schools in Reggio Emilia). Ensuring that the environment has enough space, light and resources both indoor and out for children to explore and be challenged by can be a stabilising factor in behaviour management. Overcrowding around an area of continuous provision, for example, can be easily remedied by establishing 'fair' rules with the children on the numbers allowed access at any one time. As with adult participation in policy making, children's input in helping to create 'class rules' also shows positive results. Scarce or poorly planned resources can again cause unnecessary conflict. If the scarcity cannot be remedied very quickly, for example the provision of extra tricycles in the outdoor area, then, again, rules for fair use of the equipment need to be clearly established. The use of a visual reminder, for example a large egg-timer, again with the children's cooperation, helps reinforce fairness and responsibility in turn-taking. Planning activities/experiences can also affect children's behaviour. If the day is over-planned, being divided into too many routines, this can create conflict, with children having insufficient time to establish themselves or settle into areas of provision, time to finish or reflect on the processes they are engaged in. Alternatively, if too much time is allocated to very young children being expected to sit still, for example during overlong 'circle' or 'carpet' times, this too can lead to conflict and behaviour management issues. Planning, like the behaviour strategies themselves, needs to be age/stage appropriate. Again, involving children in the planning can have a positive effect, with ownership creating respect for and interest in the planned activities.

Involving children in the behaviour management strategies, where they have to take some responsibility for their implementation, is also successful. A 'kindness' tree, where young children discuss and elect who they feel has done a kind act that day, a 'happy smile' chart, where children decide, depending on their feelings about a particular incident, to display a happy or sad face, the shared responsibility for a class 'pet', all provide children with the chance to reflect, take responsibility for their behaviour and act autonomously.

Focus on practice

Nathan, a 4½-year-old boy of mixed race (a white English mother and black West Indian father), was not his usual cheerful self. Catherine, the EYP at his setting, mentioned this to his keyworker at a staff meeting, when the children who were due to transfer to mainstream schools that September were being discussed. Most of the other 'leavers' were showing signs of real confidence at being the 'big children' at the setting. Nathan, however, had become uncharacteristically withdrawn. His keyworker told Catherine that she had discussed this with his mother, who was herself baffled at the change in Nathan. She had put it down to his realising he would soon be leaving the nursery and unfortunately having to say goodbye to some of his friends who were going to different mainstream schools. Later that week, Nathan's father came to collect him. He no longer lived with Nathan and his mother, but was still, it seemed, amicably involved in the childcare arrangements.

Identifying good practice
The keyworker mentioned her concerns about Nathan's withdrawn behaviour to him, but he dismissed it as 'a phase', saying he had started taking Nathan to a local judo club 'to toughen him up a bit'. Apparently Nathan really liked learning judo. Catherine, who continued to observe Nathan, suggested that his keyworker built in some one-to-one time with him. It was during such a quiet one-to-one session in the book corner that Nathan confided that he didn't really like going to the club. He loved doing the judo and being with his dad, but one of the other children there had called him 'bad names'. When asked if he'd told his dad, Nathan shook his head.

Leading practice
In discussion later with Catherine it was decided that the keyworker needed to make time for a conversation with Nathan's parents. In the meantime, Catherine suggested she used one of the persona dolls at circle time that day. The keyworker chose the traveller doll, Anya, whose long red hair and colourful clothes were always commented upon by the children. She had been introduced to the group some time ago by a teacher who supported traveller children and who was very knowledgeable

about their lives and customs. The keyworker told the group that Anya was particularly sad because, after she had moved to a new area with her parents, she had been excited about going to her new school, but when she arrived the children had been unkind to her and called her names because she looked different, with her long red hair and colourful traditional clothes. The keyworker passed Anya around the group, asking them to say something kind to make her less sad. She observed Nathan as he watched intently as each child talked to the doll. When it came to his turn, he told Anya she was 'beautiful' and kissed her red hair. The keyworker told them Anya was feeling a lot better, then asked what Anya should do about the children who had been unkind. 'Tell the teachers . . . tell her mummy and daddy . . . tell them to stop making her sad . . . or her daddy will come and shout at them.' The last bit of advice had come from Nathan, who seemed more energised than he had been for weeks. Some of the children decided they were going to draw or paint a picture especially for Anya to cheer her up. Nathan drew a super-hero holding Anya's hand.

Reflection

● *How well do you feel Catherine and the keyworker handled Nathan's situation?*

● *What other action might they have taken?*

● *What advice would you give to the keyworker, when meeting with Nathan's parents over this issue?*

Task Discuss the above with your colleagues and peers. If you have little experience of dealing with such situations, try to find an opportunity to ask more experienced staff to discuss some past examples of their practice in this area with you.

What constitutes effective practice in the identification and support of children whose development, progress and well-being is affected by changes or difficulties in their personal circumstances? What strategies do we need to establish and implement, where necessary, specialist support?

In order for this standard to be demonstrated effectively, the practitioner needs to have a positive and trusting relationship as well as sound knowledge of individual children. Through ongoing observations and formative assessment the practitioner will come to know the uniqueness of each child and the personal factors that may help or inhibit that child's development, 'tuning in' to the child's particular needs. Observations that focus not only on developing cognitive, linguistic, creative and physical abilities, but on the child's levels of well-being and involvement can reveal underlying tensions or difficulties the child may be experiencing as a result of changes in their personal circumstances. Practitioners need to be aware of the complexity of what constitutes a modern-day 'family'. The issue around divorce, with the resulting need to accommodate step-parents, step-brothers and -sisters in extended family situations, or becoming a one-parent family; the trauma linked to separation or bereavement; the emotional upheaval that can accompany the birth of a sibling or a mother's post-natal depression or the long-term illness or disability of a family member are some examples of this complexity. Research into the effect of such trauma and transitions on young children highlights the importance of extended care and support networks. Young children will not be able to articulate the difficulties such changes and transitions involve and may respond with uncharacteristic behaviours. It is the practitioner's responsibility to provide a calm and supportive environment for a child having to deal with such change, encouraging the child to express their fears and frustrations, through, for example, the use of empathy dolls/puppets and stories. Parents/carers who are themselves experiencing some of the trauma of the above changes may not want to talk or communicate, and may well be in need of help, advice and support themselves. It is an essential part of the good practice that *Every Child Matters* (DFES 2003) promotes, for practitioners to work in partnership with parents/carers, establishing trusting relationships that support the child and his/her family not only in the everyday sense, but through difficult periods and transitions. If such a relationship is created initially, the practitioner is in a position to help and support both the child and the family, by listening and then helping them where necessary to receive appropriate specialist help. In leading practice, the EYP needs to ensure that practitioners know how best to offer help and support, but also the appropriate boundaries in such sensitive situations (see Chapter 4).

The longitudinal EPPE research (2003) supports effective working with parents, pointing to the excellence of those centres that work in unison with parents, and the positive outcomes for children and parents that were the result of such open partnerships. Bronfenbrenner's 'Human Ecology' theory (1979) clearly supports the interdependent and interactive nature of the relationship between home environment and school (see Chapter 2). The REPEY (Siraj-Blatchford *et al.* 2002) and KEEP reports (DFES 2005a) reinforce this message too, as does the continuing research and work undertaken with parents/carers at Pen Green's Children Centre (**http://www.pengreen.org/**).

Having established an open, honest and trusting rapport with parents can aid the practitioner where concerns about an individual child's development emerge. Working with children from birth to 5 years may well mean it is the practitioner/keyworker who is the first to voice such concerns. Discussion of these initial concerns with parents can help provide a holistic picture of a child's behaviour within the setting and in their home environment. It may be that parents/carers have been dealing with 'difficult' behaviour from a child without saying anything to staff, in the hope that maturation would solve the issues. In such a case the child with behavioural difficulties can be helped, through the creation of consistency in terms of clear boundaries being reinforced both in the setting and, with parents' cooperation, at home. Individual behavioural and educational plans can be created with input from parents, the keyworker and SENCO, to support children in the setting and at home, with parents having a clearer understanding of their role. All this can be achieved if an effective partnership with parents/carers exists, where the parents trust the perspectives of practitioners but also feel they are listened to. If parents are involved in their child's learning journey, they will be more willing to accept advice and any specialist help that is suggested, rather than possibly raising barriers, being in denial and resisting the support and advice offered.

The EYP needs to ensure that colleagues are informed about any particular transitions that can influence a child's holistic development, and are knowledgeable about the processes involved in applying Early Years Action or Early Years Action Plus (see **http://www.bbc.co.uk/schools/parents/life/sen/statements/sen_whatnext.shtml**) to a child's needs. Leading Practitioners must understand and have confidence in seeking out appropriate specialist help; in some instances this might involve the use of the Common Assessment Framework (CAF) (see Chapter 5). Most importantly, the setting needs to offer a calm, caring environment that supports children and their families in achieving the most positive outcome possible.

Focus on practice

David, a tall, energetic, 4½-year-old child from a white working-class family, and Amin, a delicate, 4-year-old Asian child, both of whom had attended their local early years setting since they were 3, recently became friends. They were not in the same group, but as soon as the outdoor provision was opened each morning they spent their time together. At first glance, it seemed to some of the practitioners who were making observations of the children in their play that Amin was the leader and David the follower in their games. It was David, however, who was the first to pinch and hit one of the children with SEN, and Amin who followed his example. The first incidence went unrecorded, as the child with SEN could not vocalise, and the adults on duty were otherwise engaged. It wasn't until the mother of a child on the autistic spectrum complained about the red marks on her daughter's arms that staff became extra vigilant. David was seen to kick out at a child with partial sight, when the child's support worker was temporarily occupied tying another child's shoe lace. David was asked to say sorry, but he refused and was taken inside to sit down until he felt able to apologise. Amin, who had not been seen to be directly involved, was allowed to continue to play uninterrupted. After a short interval he went inside to David's group, where he and David played quietly together with the cars and road mat. The incident was forgotten and David wasn't made to apologise. This 'bullying' of the children with SEN went on for some weeks before practitioners, during a casual conversation at a staff meeting, picked up that a pattern of behaviour was emerging with the two boys and the setting's special needs children.

Identifying good practice
An investigation of both boys' profiles by the Lead Practitioner, Janet, showed that the profiles were not up to date. Further conversations with their keyworkers revealed nothing to suggest reasons for the boys' behaviour, so both the boys' parents were asked to come in independently to discuss matters. It was revealed during the meeting with Amin's parent (only his mother attended; her English was poor and

she was obviously embarrassed and reluctant to talk), with the help of a bilingual support assistant, that she was three months pregnant but had not wanted to say anything yet, as a previous pregnancy had miscarried at 16 weeks. She did admit, however, that Amin knew about the baby as he had had to change rooms to prepare for the new arrival. During her meeting, David's mother told Janet that David had been trying to pinch and hurt his baby sister, now 5 months old. His mother had not mentioned it, as she was hoping he would 'grow out of it'. Janet explained sensitively that, although the boys' behaviour had not been in any way acceptable, some insight had now been gained as to the possible causes of it. Both boys in their own ways were suffering from low self-esteem and low self-worth, which often happened during and after the arrival of a sibling.

Leading practice

Janet told the parents that the boys would be closely monitored but would also be praised and rewarded for any good behaviour they demonstrated. She asked that the parents try to show them as much affection as they could in order to bolster their child's self-esteem. After her conversations with both parents, Janet talked to the boys' keyworkers, who complained that it was difficult to keep up with the amount of 'paper work' now required of them, and that admin duties already cut into what could be used as consultation time with parents/carers. Janet decided to consult with the head of the setting about accommodating periods for the up-keep of profiles within the existing timetable. She also wanted to raise at a staff meeting the difficulties some staff were having in finding time to interact effectively with parents/carers, with a view to finding solutions to closer working with parents.

There was a noticeable improvement in Amin's behaviour within a very short space of time. The home corner in his group was changed into a baby clinic and lots of focus and discussion, stories and rhymes were taking place around the importance of having a new brother or sister. One of the 'casualties' of this improvement in Amin's behaviour was his brief friendship with David. David continued to be aggressive to other children, but somewhat indiscriminately now. He was being sent in from outdoor play for aggressive behaviour during nearly every session. His keyworker asked for another meeting with his mother, but a reply arrived saying she was too tied up with the needs of the baby. In discussion with Janet, it was decided to ask if a home visit would be possible. This was agreed, but, when David's keyworker and a nursery assistant visited, David's mother seemed exhausted and unwell. On their return, both the keyworker and nursery assistant expressed concern – the phrases 'a bit depressed' and 'tired all the time' had been used more than once as David's mother had tried to explain and apologise for the unwashed clothes and neglected housework, adding that David's father encouraged his son's 'manly' (aggressive) behaviour, which was frequently aimed towards her and his baby sister. After further discussion with Janet and the head of the setting, it was agreed that the help of a community family support worker would be enlisted. This proved successful, for after a few visits it was established that David's mother was suffering from severe post-natal depression. She subsequently received treatment and the family received the support it needed, a consequence of which was the gradual lessening of David's aggressive behaviour.

Reflection

- *Do you feel that this situation was dealt with effectively by the Lead Professional?*
- *How do you feel the boys' keyworkers fulfilled their roles, (a) initially and (b) subsequently?*
- *Do you feel the setting's behaviour policies were being implemented effectively?*
- *What is your opinion of communication between staff in the setting?*
- *How do you feel the setting responded to the needs of a family requiring extra support?*

Task Discuss the above and any other issues this scenario raises for you with colleagues/peers. Again, if you do not have a long experience of practice and dealing with such issues, try to discuss this with a colleague who can give you some examples from their past practice.

How do we develop practice to ensure that effective and sensitive communication with children from birth to the end of the Foundation Stage is achieved? How can the EYP lead and support practice in listening to, valuing and respecting what children say?

In order to develop meaningful and effective communication with children, we need, as with other areas of development, to have a sound knowledge and understanding of the theories and research that underpin children's acquisition of language. Chomsky's idea (1965) that infants are born 'pre-wired' may be one aspect of language acquisition, while Bruner (1983) and other more recent researchers would argue that language is essentially embedded in the social and emotional environment of infants' lives (see Chapter 2). It is important for the practitioner working with very young children to be aware of the unheard 'voices' of infants, who may not talk until their second year. As practitioners we need to realise that the first three years contribute substantially to children's acquisition of language and therefore their ability to become skilful communicators. The early forms, models and experiences of language to which they are exposed will affect their ability to communicate as they develop (Bernstein 1976, Tough 1974). We need to recognise, for example, and support the protoconversations between adults and babies, in anticipating turn-taking, a social skill that will be very important as they grow socially. We need to appreciate the pleasure a 1-year-old child expresses while listening to and making sounds; often they mimic the sounds significant adults around them express. Vygotsky (1978) suggests this is more than simple mimicry, that it is necessary to create something new within the process of imitation. We need to assist and encourage the personal vocabulary a child at 20 months might begin to develop, 'tuning in' to their attempts at communicating with us. Praise, repeat and extend the emergence of one- and two-word utterances at around 18 months that can contain such sophisticated messages. Celebrate the beginnings of diversity, as children start to communicate in their home language, for the languages children speak are all closely linked to their sense of identity and self-esteem. Listening respectfully and sensitively to their attempts at communication, at whatever age/stage, helps children define their sense of self and raises their sense of well-being.

Stern (1985) reinforces the importance of playful communication with babies and infants during daily routines, such as nappy changing, washing, the 'snuggling in' before sleep. In this way the practitioner reinforces the behaviour that mothers might intuitively engage in, treating their babies and infants 'as the people they are about to become by working in their zone of proximal development' (Stern 1985, p.43). As practitioners we need to understand also the physical maturity necessary for children to articulate sounds we, as adults, can understand. Whitehead (1996, p.13) suggests: 'By the age of four the physical maturity of the nervous system and the finer muscle control over the mouth, throat and tongue, and even the presence of teeth, make the young child's pronunciation of languages very much closer to the adult forms . . .'

Listening, then, is a vital skill for the practitioner to develop and a skill also to be encouraged in children themselves. The practice guidance for the EYFS (DFE 2012), in the Development Matters section on 'Language for Communication', gives examples of progressive developmental stages with advice on how these can be supported and promoted to meet the individual child's needs. In the 30–50 months developmental stage, for example, 'effective practice' revolves around choosing stories for children with repeated actions and replies, reinforcing the earlier turn-taking. As Meek (2000, p.203) points out, 'children, discovering language and playing with it, meet its physical nature before its sense'. Hence it is important for the practitioner to share in the delight of rhythms and rhyme with children. The knowledgeable practitioner will also recognise in young children the ability to express through many other means what Magaluzzi calls 'the hundred languages of children' (Thornton and Brunton 2006). So, in promoting and supporting effective practice, we help children develop their ability to communicate and we listen. We listen because:

- children are entitled to have their views and experiences respected – they are people too!
- it informs us of children's real interests and concerns and how they feel about themselves, which in turn makes practitioners more reflective
- it is a vital part of establishing trusting, respectful relationships
- it makes practitioners sensitive to the diverse ways children perceive the world around them and their home communities
- it extends our knowledge of children as unique individuals
- it models for children the need to listen to others
- it helps us provide an environment in which all children feel confident and self-assured, safe in the knowledge that their thoughts, feelings and ideas will be taken seriously.

Focus on practice

Kylie's voice

Kylie lived in a constantly noisy environment. A home visit revealed a spacious and clean environment with laminate floors and minimal furniture. A wide-screen television, its volume quite high, was the focus of the room. In the corner there was an aquarium with piranha fish in it. A large sofa, on which Kylie's teenage brother lounged, watching the television, two chairs and a glass coffee table and a display cabinet comprised the rest of the furniture. No toys or books were visible. The sounds of loud music filtered down from upstairs. French windows opened out on to a square of grass bordered by bushes. Under one was wedged a half-inflated football. A bicycle with stabilisers was propped against the nearside fence. A dog on a lead in the neighbouring garden ran up and down the length of the garden barking.

Conversation was difficult above the noise, but the family members seemed comfortable with it, raising their voices to be heard. When told by his mother to bring down Kylie's toys, her brother returned from upstairs with a plastic washing basket containing an assortment of Barbie dolls, a board book, some comics, felt-tipped pens, crayons and paper. Kylie began to draw radiating lines across the pad of paper while the adults talked. When asked a question Kylie would nod or shake her head. Her mother explained that she was always this 'shy' in front of strangers, usually you 'couldn't shut her up'. There was obviously a big age difference between Kylie and her brother, and her mother said she was pleased Kylie had been given a place in nursery, to help her make friends with children her own age, as there were no other young children in the neighbouring houses.

During Kylie's initial visits with her mother to the setting, or if work intervened and her 17-year-old brother would accompany her, Kylie remained silent. She watched the other children intently, and when approached would seek out her brother or mother and sit on their lap. She investigated the areas of continuous provision and the interactive displays within the room, as long as her mother or brother were close by. Staff suggested Kylie would need time to settle in and her mother agreed to make arrangements with work to enable this to happen at the beginning of the new school year in September. Unfortunately, when September arrived, Kylie's mother was not able to stay with her through a gradual settling-in period, as her employer would not agree to her having sufficient time off work. However, Kylie's brother, who was unemployed, was happy to bring Kylie to the setting and stay. He tried to encourage his sister to access the provision in his deep loud voice, which stopped a number of other children in their tracks, initially, but they soon adjusted to having him among them. Her brother would often model what Kylie should be doing with the dough, sand, water and paints, as well as 'play fighting' with some of the young boys, until asked to stop by the staff. Kylie would access the activities and basic provision, but, as soon as her brother moved, she moved with him. After two weeks, her brother arrived one morning and announced he would have to leave Kylie with staff, as he had got a job. Kylie clung on to her brother as long as possible. When he finally left, she didn't cry, but sat with her thumb in her mouth on a floor cushion in the book corner, pushing away staff and other children if they attempted to engage or comfort her. Her keyworker made valiant attempts to draw Kylie out of her obvious sadness, but she remained silent and implacable for the rest of the week. The following week, her mother rang to say Kylie had caught a bad cold and would not be attending until she was better. The task of bringing Kylie to the setting was then given over to her grandmother, who was also caring for her other daughter's young baby and toddler, and was unable to stay. The keyworker noticed that Kylie's grandmother both asked and answered questions on Kylie's behalf, as her older brother had done. Kylie continued to spend her time in the relative quiet of the book corner, which had been made into a 'reading den' with its canopy and comfortable cushions. By this time, the other children had stopped attempting to include her in their play.

Identifying good practice

Being a resourced setting meant that a number of children with particular needs accessed all the rooms, accompanied by either the setting SENCO or a support worker. Ben, a child with autistic tendencies, also enjoyed the calm of the 'reading den'. Gradually, he and his support worker and Kylie, through the use of the Picture Exchange Communication System (PECS) (**http://www.pecs.org.uk**), developed their own signing system to communicate. Kylie's keyworker was concerned that this might delay Kylie's attempts to speak, and discussed her concerns with the Leading Practitioner. The Leading Practitioner suggested that, as long as language was being used in conjunction with the PECS to stimulate Kylie's communication skills, it should be continued for the time being, as Kylie seemed to be gaining security from it. Kylie began to use her voice a short time later, during a role-play session with Ben and his support worker in the home corner. Observing from a distance, her keyworker watched as Kylie repeated the words of encouragement that Ben's support worker was saying, while Ben engaged in the pretend play of making a meal for Kylie and his support worker to taste.

Leading practice

Later that day, when Ben had finished his half-day's attendance, Kylie's keyworker introduced her to an empathy doll, 'Susie', who had 'fallen on the way to school and hurt her knee'. While Kylie 'nursed' the doll, quietly speaking words of comfort, her keyworker read the story of *On the Way Home* (Murphy 1982). After reading the story through, the keyworker then asked Susie what she liked about the story and, in a soft voice, Kylie answered for the doll, moving its head and hands, while the keyworker listened attentively. Kylie's attachment to Susie was such that her keyworker decided to let Kylie take the doll home (having read the home visit report on the lack of toys). She asked Kylie to help her pack a bag for Susie, listening carefully to Kylie's suggestions about what the doll might need to go 'on holiday' to her house, noting, too, that Kylie was having some difficulty in pronouncing soft 's' sounds at the beginning and end of words. When other children attempted to join in with help and suggestions, Kylie backed away, but encouraged by her keyworker, who told the other children that this was a special task for Kylie, she resumed packing the doll's bag, her self-esteem restored at being given a 'special' task. When Kylie's grandmother came to collect her, the keyworker began to explain, but was soon listening to Kylie giving her own reasons for the doll's 'holiday' and what she and Susie were going to do. Her keyworker suggested that, when Kylie brought Susie back, they might like to tell everyone about the exciting time they'd had.

In discussion with the Lead Practitioner about the success of using the empathy doll, it was decided that this could be extended, involving sending the doll home on 'holiday' with a number of children. Kylie's keyworker also mentioned the slight difficulty Kylie displayed with articulation and it was agreed the situation should be monitored, and sound story sacks used both in the setting and at home.

Reflection

- *How well do you feel staff at the setting responded to Kylie's needs in settling her in to her new surroundings? How might this have been done differently?*
- *What are your feelings on the use of signing as an additional means of communication? Do you consider the keyworker's concerns were valid?*
- *How effective do you feel the use of the empathy doll was in this particular situation? In what other situations might it be used?*
- *Do you feel Kylie was listened to and her wishes respected?*
- *Have you experienced similar situations where new children have elected to remain silent? What strategies have you used successfully to encourage the child's communication skills?*

Task Reflect on how successful you have been in engaging with families who may have differing priorities, which makes partnership difficult to achieve. If you have not been in practice very long, try to observe a more experienced colleague in such an interaction with a family, and write your reflections on this in your journal. If you can then share these and discuss them with your colleague, this might help both of you to reflect further on the situation.

Conclusion

What effective strategies can we develop that reflect our knowledge and understanding of how children learn and develop and our commitment to ensuring each child achieves his/her full potential? How do we create fair, respectful and supportive relationships while achieving such effective practice?

An effective Lead Practitioner, as is shown in this chapter, needs to have sound knowledge of how children develop and learn, and be aware of current emergent theory, research and initiatives. Armed with such knowledge and understanding we should be able to provide effective support for both children and families. Children do not grow in a vacuum. It is hoped that, from reading this and previous chapters, the importance of knowing the individual child and their family has been emphasised. The high expectations we have of children need to be established from the beginning, based on sound prior knowledge of the dynamics within the child's family and the interests and experiences of the child him/herself. Expectations built round some external model of achievement, which bear little relation to those experiences and interests, may well build in failure and a low sense of self-esteem. What constitutes 'full potential' should be related to each child's individual needs, rather than to some standardised 'norm'. The personalised learning through which a child achieves this potential should reflect, respect and value the diversity of their life experiences. By modelling respect and value for and of each child, you will raise that child's self-esteem and create the beginnings of a positive, trusting relationship that will enrich both adult and child. From such a safe, supportive base, with their confidence high, children will be motivated to engage with any appropriate challenges they are set. From the practitioner's perspective, the necessity for continuous formative observation and assessment of children should be self-evident. Through such essential information gathering, each child's learning journey can be supported successfully and possible concerns highlighted and acted upon.

Sharing such knowledge with parents/carers as the child's first educators is another essential aspect. Even if the response is not as supportive or positive as you would wish, most parents want the best for their children; it is within the translation of this wish that frustrations and misunderstandings can occur. We cannot be 'precious' or obtuse about sharing our particular knowledge and understanding of the child. Current research and practice underpins, time and again, how vital that relationship with parents/carers is for the child's development and learning. High expectations need to be understood and shared if they are to be achieved, and possible stereotypes or misconceptions about each child's abilities challenged. Realistic expectations based on prior knowledge, respect for and commitment to each individual child's needs and a working partnership with parents/carers will help create an environment where children will feel supported and respected, and as a result achieve their potential.

What effective behaviour management strategies can we create to support and promote the development of positive social, emotional, behavioural, attitudes and independence in children?

Again, as a potential EYP, the practitioner must be informed about current thinking in child development, for example the recent studies in brain research, cortisol studies, the theory of mind, and emotional competency (see above and Chapter 2), which are enriching our understanding of the complex mechanisms that inform the development of babies and young children. With such knowledge, we can create more effective strategies for helping a child understand and develop control over their own feelings as well as developing their awareness of the feelings and needs of others.

We need, as practitioners, to accept that children's behaviours will affect our own responses, producing negative as well as positive thoughts and feelings. We must counteract prejudice and stereotyping that can trigger a number of negative behaviours, while accepting that we may have our own personal prejudices, by modelling positive behaviour and establishing fair and consistent rules and boundaries.

Again we need to share these with parents/carers, in order to provide consistency across environments, as well as ensuring a 'whole setting' approach to implementing agreed behaviour policies that are age/stage appropriate.

Much contemporary research reinforces the need for young children to acknowledge their feelings and try with adult help to resolve conflicts, through experiences that might challenge their own perceptions of events, developing that all-important ability to empathise with another's view or expectations. The SEAL programme (DFES 2005b) provides

Pearson Education Ltd/Malcolm Harris.

comprehensive materials and examples of how to help young children feel good about themselves. From a positive sense of self they are then able to build positive relationships with others. The use of empathy dolls can help practitioners deal with unacceptable behaviours while still valuing the child as an individual. The environment itself can help promote sharing and turn-taking if well structured and resourced. An over-planned day can result in conflict and negative behaviours as children feel 'trapped' by unnecessary routines and structures that are more for the benefit of staff or external agencies. Involving children in the rules-making process, encouraging them to become self-monitoring and self-reflective, creates a less conflict-centred approach. Rewards can play an important role, as well as positive feedback and praise from adults, as long as it is specific rather than given indiscriminately. The care of a class 'pet', if possible, encourages young children to take responsibility for their own and others' behaviour. Many concrete examples of behaviour strategies can be given, but practitioners need to remember that effective strategies must reflect particular circumstances and the differing and complex individual needs of each child in their care.

Further reading

Bruce, T. (2004) 'Play matters', in L. Abbott and A. Langston (eds) *Birth to Three Matters: Supporting the framework of effective practice.* Maidenhead: Open University Press.

Edwards, C.P., Gandini, L. and Forman, G. (1998) *The Hundred Languages of Children: The Reggio Emilia approach – advanced reflections.* New York: Ablex Publishing Co.

Moyles, J. (ed.) (2005) *The Excellence of Play.* Maidenhead: Open University Press.

Nutbrown, C. (2006) *Threads of Thinking: Young children learning and the role of early education.* London: Paul Chapman.

Smith, P.K., Cowie, H. and Blades, M. (2003) *Understanding Children's Development.* Oxford: Blackwell.

Tizard, B. and Hughes, M. (1984) *Young Children Learning: Talking and thinking at home and at school.* London: Fontana.

Wood, E. and Attfield, J. (2005) *Play, Learning and the Early Childhood Curriculum,* (2nd edn). London: Paul Chapman.

Websites

http://www.ecm.gov.uk/multiageencyworking/

http://www.education.gov.uk/publications

http://www.everychildmatters.gov.uk/deliveringservices/caf/

http://www.foundationyears.org.uk

http://www.kategreenaway.ik.org/

http://www.pecs.com/

http://www.pengreen.org/

http://www.persona-doll-training.org

http://www.standards.dfes.gov.uk/primary/publications/banda/seal/

http://www.surestart.gov.uk

References

Barnes, P. (2001) *Personal, Social and Emotional Development of Children.* Oxford: Oxford University Press.

Bernstein, B. (1976) *Class, Codes and Control.* New York: Schocker Books.

Bronfenbrenner, U. (1979) *The Ecology of Human Development: Experiments by nature and design.* Cambridge, MA: Harvard University Press.

Bruner, J. (1983) *Child's Talk. Learning to Use Language.* Oxford: Oxford University Press.

Cadwell, L. (2003) *The Reggio Approach: Bringing learning to life.* Columbia University, NY: Teachers College Press.

Callcentre (2009) Picture Exchange Communication System. Available at: http://callcentre.education.ed.ac.uk/SCN/Level_A_SCA/Using_Symbols_SCB/Hot_PECS_News_HTA/hot_pecs_news_hta.html. Accessed on 18 February 2009.

Chomsky, N. (1965) *Aspects of the Theory of Syntax.* Cambridge, MA: MIT Press.

Denham, S.A. (1998) *Emotional Development in Young Children.* New York: The Guildford Press.

DFE (2012) *Early Years Foundation Stage.* Nottingham: DFE Publications.

DFES (2003) *Every Child Matters,* Green Paper. London: The Stationery Office.

DFES (2005a) *Key Elements of Effective Practice (KEEP).* 1021-2005G. Nottingham: DCSF Publications.

DFES (2005b) Excellence and enjoyment: Social and emotional aspects of learning. Available at: http://www.standards.dfes.gov.uk/primary/publications/banda/seal/pns_seal137805_guidance.pdf. Accessed on 31 December 2008.

DFES (2005c) *Common Assessment Framework.* Nottingham: DFES Publications.

DFES (2007) *Primary National Strategy: Creating the picture.* London: HMSO.

Dunn, J. (1993) *Young Children's Close Relationships: Beyond attachment.* Newbury, CA: Sage Publications.

Freud, S. (1965) *Normalcy and Pathology in Childhood: Assessments of development.* New York: International University Press.

Goldschmied, E. and Jackson, S. (1994) *People Under Three: Young children and day care.* New York: Routledge.

Goleman, D.P. (1995) *Emotional Intelligence: Why it can matter more than IQ for character, health and lifelong achievement.* New York: Bantam Books.

Gopnick, A., Meltzoff, A. and Kuhl, P. (1999) *How Babies Think: The science of childhood*. London: Weidenfeld & Nicolson.

Grenier, J., Elfer, P., Manning Morton, J., Wilson, D. and Dearnley, K. (2008) Guidance: the key person in reception classes and small nursery setting. Available at: http://juliangrenier.blogspot.co.uk/2011/09/key-person-in-reception-classes-and.html.

Harris, P.L. (1989) *Children and Emotion*. New York: Cambridge University Press.

Hutt, S.J., Tyler, S., Hutt, C. and Christopherson, H. (1989) *Play, Exploration and Learning: A natural history of the pre-school*. London: Routledge.

Laevers, F. (1994) *The Leuven Involvement Scale for Young Children*. Leuven, Belgium: Centre for Experiential Education.

Maccoby, E. (1980) *Social Development: Psychological growth and the parent-child relationship*. New York: Harcourt.

Meek, M. (1985) '*Play and Paradoxes*', in G. Wells and J. Nicholls (eds) *Language and Learning: An international perspective*. London: Falmer Press.

Meek, M. (2000) 'Transitional transformations', in E. Bearne and V. Watson (eds) *Where Texts and Children Meet*. London: Routledge.

Murphy, J. (1982) *On The Way Home*. London: Macmillan Publishing.

Ofsted (2005) *Managing Challenging Behaviour*. Ref 2363. London: HMSO.

Pascal, C. and Bertram, A.D. (1997) *Effective Early Learning: Case studies of improvement*. London: Hodder & Stoughton.

Schweinhart, L.J. (2003) *Benefits, Costs and Exploration of the High/Scope Perry Preschool Project*. Ypsilanti, MI: High/Scope Research Foundation.

Siraj-Blatchford, I. and Clarke, P. (2000) *Identity, Diversity and Language in Early Years*. Buckingham: Oxford University Press.

Siraj-Blatchford, I., Sylva, K., Mutock, S., Gilden, R. and Bell, D. (2002) *Researching Effective Pedagogy in the Early Years*. RB 356. London: DFES Publications.

Smith, P., Cowie, H. and Blades, M. (2003) *Understanding Children's Development*. Oxford: Blackwell.

Stern, D.N. (1985) *The Interpersonal World of the Infant*. New York: Basic Books.

Sylva, K., Melhuish, E., Sammons, P., Siraj-Blatchford, I., Taggart, B. and Elliot, K. (2003) *The Effective Provision of Pre-School Education (EPPE) Project: Findings from the pre-school period*. London: Institute of Education.

Thornton, L. and Brunton, P. (2006) *Understanding the Reggio Approach*. London: David Fulton.

Tough, J. (1974) 'Children's use of language', *Education Review*, 26(3), pp.116–79.

Vygotsky, L. (1978) *Mind in Society*. Cambridge, MA: Harvard.

Webster-Stratton, C. (2000) *How to Promote Children's Social and Emotional Competence*. London: Paul Chapman/Sage Publications.

Whitehead, M. (1996) *The Development of Language and Literacy*. London: Paul Chapman.

7

Transforming the environment for play and learning

Wendy Holland

Chapter overview

The Standard addressed in this chapter is:

6. Plan provision taking account of the individual needs of every child.

Relating to the above Standard, the following key questions will be addressed:

- What strategies can be developed to support the establishment of secure, stimulating and purposeful indoor and outdoor learning environments through planned and appropriate adult-initiated and child-led experiences?
- How can we ensure children are provided with flexible routines that meet individual needs, in a well-resourced environment that takes account of diversity and encourages inclusive practice and provision?
- How can we develop practice to ensure a stimulating environment that guarantees high-quality provision?

Introduction

This chapter will have as its focus those Standards that exemplify effective practice in leading and supporting the management of the child's learning environment, where the 'environment' is viewed in an holistic sense, to include the child's emotional and social well-being, as well as cognitive and physical development. It will discuss the practitioner's role in establishing and sustaining a safe, secure, purposeful learning environment, both indoors and outdoors; an environment that fosters the child's sense of well-being and natural curiosity, and where the child's ideas and contributions are valued. The necessity for appropriate and flexible routines which incorporate a balance of child-led and adult-initiated experiences and opportunities will be discussed, as well as the need for routines that allow children time to follow their interests and support particular individual needs. Routines also need to be created that are flexible enough to reflect the different kinds of access to and time spent in the setting by individual children, thus promoting the very necessary sense of continuity for the child between home, the setting, and possible other provision the child attends. The practitioner's responsibility for ensuring the environment is developmentally appropriate and, where necessary, specially adapted resources that reflect diversity and promote inclusive practice will be focused upon, as well as the practitioner's statutory accountability to all stakeholders for the delivery and maintenance of high-quality provision.

Theoretical underpinning, relevant research findings and new initiatives that highlight effective practice for these particular standards will, as in previous chapters, be discussed, as well as further reading to support more detailed analysis of the issues considered.

What strategies can be developed to support the establishment of secure, stimulating and purposeful indoor and outdoor learning environments through planned and appropriate adult-initiated and child-led experiences?

In order to develop effective strategies we need, initially, to look at the theory and current research that have been explored in previous chapters that underpin new government initiatives in Early Years through the Every Child Matters agenda to explore and expand the child's learning environment. With this point in mind, consider the following practice example.

Focus on practice

Babies at play

Rachel, the relatively new manager of a private daycare setting, housed in a large Victorian detached property, discussed with her Lead Practitioner, Alice, how best to improve the outdoor provision. Rachel has been in post for only two years and during that time has concentrated on improving the indoor provision and resources. The large but neglected outdoor area had been next on her agenda; however, with the statutory implementation of the EYFS she felt it was necessary to make changes sooner rather than later. The babies and young children attending the setting currently accessed the outdoors by being taken on regular trips to a nearby park and play area, as well as spending a limited amount of time with tricycles, scooters and prams on a small tarmac area at the front of the building. Alice felt some changes could be made relatively cheaply, as she had a number of contacts locally who could supply larger equipment such as tyres and milk crates, and suggested to Rachel that one of the trees in the grounds of the house could be made into a sitting log with sections cut for use as stepping stones. She also discussed re-organising the staffing rota, in order that outdoor play could be accessed more regularly. At a staff meeting, Alice discussed the proposed rota changes for outdoor provision, whereby one member of staff would be involved in a focused activity, while another practitioner monitored the children's play generally, with some flexibility if the numbers of children accessing the outdoors increased. Alice also suggested that the staff in each room took it in turns to plan for a whole week's outdoor activities. Some of the staff were resistant to the suggested changes. One practitioner, Mary, in particular, voiced concerns about the health and safety of the children, especially in parts of the garden that were overgrown; she also felt, along with other members of staff, that the weather was not always suitable for children to be outside. She added that the shed, situated round the side of the house, where the larger equipment was stored, was a long way to drag/carry the existing equipment and, if more heavy equipment was to be brought in, it would lengthen the setting-up and tidying-away time and might possibly lead to staff injuries. Generally, staff felt the existing arrangements, i.e. visiting the local park and play area, worked well enough.

Identifying good practice

Alice reminded staff of the new focus between indoor and outdoor provision that good practice demands in the EYFS. She suggested that some of the older children could help with tidying away equipment and felt the new arrangements should be trialled for a short period. The overgrown areas were fenced off temporarily and Alice modelled good practice by planning and implementing the first two weeks' outdoor activities. After each group had been responsible for one week's outdoor provision, staff met to discuss how they felt the new arrangements had gone. Some practitioners still had reservations, particularly if the weather was poor, and children had not come to the setting adequately dressed for it. Without some kind of covered area, attempting to mark-make or use small-world resources had proved difficult. The new staffing rota had also been hard to implement when members of staff had been absent.

Leading practice

Alice agreed that a covered area would improve things, but also reminded staff that it was not expected that the outdoors would exactly 'mirror' indoor provision, and that planning should include alternatives for differing weather conditions. She took the staff's comments back to Rachel and after discussion it was agreed that the outdoor provision needed more investment. The redevelopment would be staged, but the staff would begin to make changes to their practice to embrace the emphasis on more free-flow indoor/outdoor play. Alice suggested all-weather clothing should be purchased for the children, and it was also agreed that she and another member of staff would attend training on planning and resourcing outdoor provision currently being run by the local authority. The member of staff, Mary, who had shown most resistance to the proposed changes, was asked by Alice to attend the training with her.

After the training, Alice discussed with Rachel how best to tackle the outdoor provision, then she and Mary, who had finished the training more committed to outdoor provision, fed back to the whole staff. With Rachel's agreement, the following recommendations were made:

- Soft surfacing should be laid for a new climbing frame and separate slide.
- The area around the trees and shrubbery should be pruned back and cleared and plants inspected for 'safety', but left for such uses as a den-making area, treasure hunt trail and digging and planting activities.

- A veranda at the side of the play area should be made safe and roofed to provide cover in wet weather.

- A new shed should be situated next to the play area for storing equipment. Alice said this could be made multifunctional, by painting one wall of the shed with blackboard paint to encourage mark-making, and instruments hung on another wall to encourage musical activities outdoors.

Alice and Mary, through discussion and the use of a video from their training course, showed how clear and careful planning of outdoor provision could support the potential for children's learning and development in line with the principles of the EYFS.

Reflections

- *How do you feel Alice handled the changes proposed for the outdoor provision?*
- *Did the staff have reasonable cause for concern, or were they just being resistant to change?*
- *Should Alice have given time for more discussion with staff on the expectations for outdoor provision laid down by the EYFS practice guidance?*
- *Did Alice model good practice long enough for staff to adapt their practice?*
- *Did she give sufficient guidance on the new planning?*
- *Should staff have had more input on the proposed changes for the outdoor provision?*

Task **Consider these questions with colleagues (a) before reading the chapter below and (b) after reading it. Discuss to what extent it has informed your views.**

Active learning

The Early Years Foundation Stage Guidance (2012) advances the importance of seeing babies and young children as **active learners**. *Development Matters* (DFE 2012) describes the characteristics of effective learning as 'playing and exploring, active learning, creative and thinking critically'. This emphasises the need for practitioners to encourage this natural curiosity and drive to discover the world by creating 'enabling environments'. Such environments help children to actively build meaning, make connections and construct new ideas about themselves, other people and the physical world around

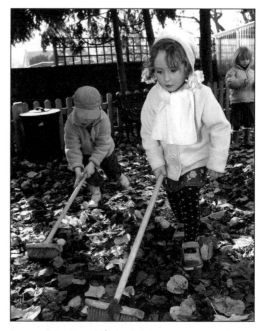

Pearson Education Ltd/Jules Selmes.

them (see Piaget's theories on 'assimilation' and 'accommodation' in Chapter 2). Athey (1990) refers to such attempts by children to make sense of their environment as 'schema', and the Reggio Emilia approach also refers to the environment as the 'third teacher' (see Chapter 6). The EYFS guidance considers that effective environments 'enable' children to engage in the creating and refining of such schema. Through the repeated activities of different schemas, children are able to act like scientists and/or researchers, discovering patterns, connections and links between a wide variety of phenomena; such active learning may well be 'interactive, messy, boisterous and often physical' (DCSF 2007, p.2). This view of the child as an inherently *active* learner should underpin practitioners' attempts to personalise and individualise their provision.

Personalised learning

Practitioners need to be aware of the different ways in which young children access the learning experiences that an early years setting provides. Knowledge of the child's learning at home can help the practitioner to create more personalised provision. Carr (2001) suggests that a child's learning disposition may help or hinder their ability to access the resources and experiences provided. For the young child to want to explore his/her environment, the practitioner needs to ensure the experiences and activities the environment presents are meaningful to that child. The ability to choose, to make decisions is also an important factor in the child's active learning, as it promotes autonomy. Where provision is limited or not developmentally appropriate, children will quickly lose interest. The match between a child's interests and the experiences made available can best be achieved through close observation and assessment of the child, and the development of meaningful partnerships with parents and carers (see Chapters 5, 6 and 8). The personalised learning journey and the effective practice it promotes have many benefits. The child's interest is sustained and their learning developed. The practitioner's knowledge of what the child can do and what the next steps should be are also developed, and, if shared with parents and carers, creates a secure cycle of learning between setting and home. The trust that this creates helps the discussion, where necessary, of any particular needs or concerns either the practitioner or parent may have.

Creating a trusting relationship in this way impacts upon the child's emotional development, for an 'enabling' environment should not be just about cognitive and physical growth. Emotional competency and a sense of well-being are important factors, as Laevers (1994) suggests, in the extent to which a child will engage with their learning environment. A low sense of esteem has been linked by research (Pascal *et al.* 1995) to low levels of involvement and 'surface' learning.

The importance of play

The EYFS promotes play as the medium through which young children naturally learn.

Observing children playing might lead one to assume that play is any or all of the following: a social learning device; a cognitive learning device; a physical learning device; fun and freedom; therapy; occupation while adults are busy.

(DCSF (2007) Effective practice: Play and Exploration, p.1)

A play environment, however free and unstructured it might appear, needs to be appropriately and adequately resourced and planned for. The effective practitioner should ensure that children have choice, not only in which activity/experience they decide to engage, but whether to do so on their own, with their peers or with adults. Sufficient space and time are vital prerequisites in an enabling environment where a range of activities should

Pearson Education Ltd.

be on offer, some of which may be planned and led by adults, based on their knowledge of children's current interests, learning styles and stages of development. Such a rich, enabling environment, where practitioners allow children to dictate the pace and length of focus, and sensitively and subtly intervene and support, provides a safe, secure dispositional milieu, in which children can develop and learn. Each Early Years setting will have its own unique milieu, presenting to children a particular view of what it means to be an active learner in that particular environment. Effective practice needs to try to establish a place where children will develop and learn in their own unique ways. The flexibility of such a play environment encourages the development of: 'playful minds . . . the most suitable approach to future life in our fluid, multi-media, global society' (David and Powell 2005, cited in DCSF 2007: Play and Exploration, p.1). Future research may indeed support the idea that learning through play helps children achieve specific Every Child Matters (ECM) (DFES 2003a) outcomes; what contemporary research has already established is that children's play can be complex and multilayered. It helps young children solve problems and gain a degree of control in their ability to absorb new knowledge and create meaning (see Jarvis 2007).

The role of the adult

Longitudinal research such as EPPE (2008, ongoing) and REPEY (Siraj-Blatchford *et al.* 2002) emphasises the importance of the adult's role when engaging with children. Practitioners who allow children to direct their own play spontaneously, knowing when to join in and when not to interrupt the flow of children's play and exploration, are enacting that vital 'scaffolding' of children's learning proposed by Bruner (1983). They are also displaying a trust and belief in children's abilities, reflecting the approach used in the pre-schools in the Reggio Emilia region of Northern Italy, where the child is seen as the investigator/explorer of his/her environment and the practitioners as facilitators and co-researchers with the child (see Chapter 6). If the practitioner acknowledges this need to learn from and with the child and communicates this new knowledge and understanding to parents and carers, an holistic and individually unique learning environment can be created (see Pen Green 2008, online). The EPPE report (2003) identified 'centres of excellence' where a mixture of child-initiated, adult-extended and adult-led activities/experiences prevailed. Through such strategies as 'sustained shared thinking' (REPEY 2002), it has been shown that the practitioner can extend a child's language and ideas, encouraging the child to perhaps reflect on previous actions/learning and thus promoting 'metacognition' (thinking about thinking). This ability of the child to reflect on their own experiences and prior knowledge and to self-regulate behaviour when interacting with peers is essential for the child's growth and development in all areas. The research also confirmed the centrality of play in a child's early learning journey.

The effective practitioner realises that different contexts can promote different kinds of play and learning, and will provide for both the ephemeral interests children may have and areas of more continuous focus. Settings must provide for what Hutt *et al.* (1989) describes as exploratory, inquisitive play ('epistemic') as well as creative, playful play ('ludic'), and recognise the differing responses required. Practitioners should avoid over-hasty intervention, particularly in epistemic play; trying to communicate verbally with a child might cut across some private world of concentration and thought that should not be disturbed. The effective practitioner understands that children sometimes need to have their own space, a space that is protected from their peers and adults.

Contemporary research into play itself (see Jarvis and George 2008) highlights issues in today's society with regard to children's more limited access to play in their physical environment. It is suggested that neighbourhood play has decreased due to higher levels of traffic and the perceived 'stranger danger' threat. Playtime in some schools has been reduced, making less time available for the all-important skills of negotiation, compromise and social debate to develop, all of which are underpinned by play (see Brock *et al.* 2008). The institutionalisation of very young children into private and voluntary daycare where access to outdoor provision might be limited, and the use of ICT games which can create isolated and solitary indoor play, all point to the possibility that the environment provided by an Early Years setting might be the only form of outdoor play experience to which a child has regular access.

Outdoor play

The EYFS (DFE 2012, online) clearly reinforces the need for 'play opportunities in indoor, outdoor and in out-of-setting contexts, which enable children to develop and learn'. Outdoor provision needs to have the same depth and breadth of engagement by practitioners as indoor provision. Children play and express themselves differently outdoors and, if practitioners are to create environments that harness the uniqueness of each child, outdoor provision needs to be planned so that children are inspired, challenged and intrigued, providing an environment just as 'enabling', with as much thought and planning as the indoor environment. The movement-based learning that is involved in children's schemas such as transporting, connecting, trajectory and rotation is often well fitted to outdoor provision where the space to move and explore safely can be supported. With provision that is flexible and versatile, too, children can re-create and change their environment imaginatively, taking ownership of their play milieu. However, research indicates (Pen Green Conference 2004, online), that, although the evidence of children engaging in schema-based play (see Chapter 5) is more common in outdoor environments, adults tend not to support or extend children's explorations of them to the same degree as schema-based play observed within indoor environments. As Learning Through Landscapes (2008, online) suggests, the practitioner's role here is crucial; they need to demonstrate knowledge, enthusiasm and commitment to ensure the best possible use is made of the outdoor provision. Centres should aim to offer and resource a wide range of holistic experiences for children outdoors, including areas where play is active, boisterous and noisy, and others that are calm and allow children space and time to reflect. Bilton (2005) suggests that boys particularly express themselves more effectively outdoors.

> If I have not yet learned to love Darth Vader, I have at least made some useful discoveries while watching him at play. As I interrupt less, it becomes clear that boys' play is serious drama, not morbid mischief. Its rhythms and images are often discordant to me, but I must try to make sense of a style that, after all, belongs to half the population of the classroom.

(Paley 1984, p.xii)

White (2008) suggests there are six major ingredients that provide a rich and satisfying outdoor experience for young children:

- natural materials;
- growing and the living world;
- water;
- physical play and movement;
- imagination and creativity;
- construction.

All of the above are central to the **Forest School** approach to outdoor provision, developed in Denmark in the 1950s, which is now gaining recognition within the UK. Many benefits have been demonstrated through this approach. It addresses the 'nature deficit' that many children may experience in today's society and encourages self-initiated learning with children engaged in

Pearson Education Ltd/Jules Selmes.

experiencing a variety of skills like den-building, treasure trails, bushcraft, environmental art planting and growing produce, as well as adult-supervised activities such as building woodland fires, cooking and learning to work with knives. Children with language difficulties particularly seem to benefit, as research suggests children make significantly more utterances when outdoors; through improved communication they also develop their emotional literacy. This more kinaesthetic and flexible approach to learning experiences develops children's ideas and respect and appreciation for the natural environment (Cook 2008).

Creative partnerships

Not all settings are in a position to set up a forest school, requiring as it does appropriate and available land, and considerable financial support. An alternative could be found through **Creative Partnerships,** which have now been established by a number of Local Authorities in England as a result of the Every Child Matters agenda. Some Early Years services are involved in helping settings access environmental projects as part of this partnership. They are also helping to establish practice along the lines of the Reggio Emilia approach (see Chapter 6), with local artists taking up residence in a setting for a period of time to help foster a more creative approach to Early Years practice (Canterbury Children's Centre 2006). The benefits of such creative partnerships with their focus on children's creativity are many:

- Children gain in confidence.
- They learn new skills that are not simply 'task-related'.
- They grow in emotional intelligence through learning to communicate their feelings and ideas to their peers.
- They have increased awareness of difference and diversity.
- They learn to collaborate and work as part of a team.
- The environment is seen as an effective 'third teacher'.
- There is a depth of interaction as a result of children's being given time and space to pursue their interests.
- The emphasis is clearly on process and not on outcomes.
- Children are encouraged to make judgements, become absorbed and be persistent.

Having an artist 'in residence' has an impact upon staff performance as well as that of the children. Adults need to feel 'delight and curiosity in discovering artistic opportunities . . . the more the child feels the pleasure of the practitioner, the more willing they are to let their own pleasure show' (Théâtre de la Guimbarde, in Dower 2004). There is a need from the beginning of the partnership to establish, for example, that the artist is sympathetic to the setting in terms of its ethos and principles regarding children's learning and development as well as having an ability to communicate with and listen to children effectively. Practitioners and artists need to reflect by sharing their perceptions on what is or is not working within a particular project and why. Adults also need to reflect upon how much they themselves are learning from such creative experiences, demonstrating Vygotsky's observation that 'teachers' and 'learners' often construct learning together, again reflecting the 'Reggio' approach. However, production of 'documentation' in such creative enterprises can be difficult. Practitioners therefore need to find ways to capture important moments in a child's learning which may be transitory. Again, the practice of individual learning diaries for each child, as championed by the EYFS, could be one way of assuring that those moments are not lost.

Having an artist in residence, as well as introducing new skills and experiences – a potter's wheel, creating sculptures, drawing and painting with unusual media, can also help practitioners look afresh at the kinds of activities that regularly occur in an early years setting. **Storytelling** by children themselves, with props they have made, encourages listening skills in the audience and speaking skills in the storyteller. As well as helping a child's creativity, stories can also give us insights into influences and anxieties or actual events which the child is trying to make sense of. The creative use of **movement**, which involves all the senses – hearing, vision, taste, smell and touch, can lead to the extension of verbal and non-verbal means of communicating for a child. Such movement aids expression, balance, flexibility, strength and confidence in developing relationships. Research has shown how essential movement itself is for children's growth and development. Greenland (2000) suggested that human beings did not just live in their heads but, as playful physical beings, in their whole bodies, while research suggests babies and young children are biologically driven to seek the physical experience that will most benefit their particular stage of development. Lindon (2001) suggests that children's powers of concentration are disrupted rather than aided by the requirement that the child sit still for long periods.

Using **photographs** to record a process or achievement, or to confirm an acquired skill, are often the perspectives brought to photography by adults, rather than seeing it as an art form in itself. Children, however, do not necessarily need a permanent record. A camera can provide the child with autonomy; they choose what they wish to photograph. I observed children on a visit to the park to feed the ducks taking photographs of the patterns left by their trainers in the mud, not the ducks they were going to feed! Photographs can be used to help communication with parents, support metacognition in children by recalling their previous experiences, and, if there is no common language, photographs can be a clear aid to communicating meaningfully.

The spontaneous expression of children's imagination through a range of different media, helped by an artist's perspective, demonstrates the innate human drive to explore, develop concepts and solve problems that all children have: 'through their imagination children can move from the present into the past and the future, to what might be and beyond' (Duffy 1998). Children thrive in an environment that fosters **connections rather than separations**. Good Early Years practice does not force young children to pursue knowledge on separate paths. Making mistakes and trying again should also be built into the process, with no pressures to produce a perfect result. Only through such first-hand experience can increasing competence and the confidence to accept new challenges be developed. The same starting point will and should have different outcomes for individual children, if practitioners apply the principles of good practice developed within the EYFS guidance. Using mixed age groups of 3- and 4-year-olds can work well, too, in creative enterprises. Working with an artist, it was found that the 4-year-olds were able to concentrate for longer periods of time when fully engaged in their work and this could be seen to impact on the concentration of the 3-year-olds in the group (Canterbury Children's Centre 2006).

Focus on practice

An artist in residence

Jane, the head of a local authority setting, had managed to secure funding for working with local artists. The Lead Practitioner, Cathy, had spent time in a Reggio setting in Italy during the previous year and was now trying to implement some of that experience into the setting's daily practice, with varied degrees of success. One of the principles Cathy was keen to address was the Reggio approach to allowing children to investigate processes, as she had felt for some time that the setting was putting too much emphasis on the children producing similar artefacts, often for the consumption of parents. One practitioner, Helen, clearly disagreed that the process in which children were involved was more important than product, her argument being that producing an end-product showed application and dedication.

Cathy was very enthusiastic about the thought of working with an artist for a two-week period. Themes that the setting were currently focusing upon were Light and Dark (reflecting the time of the year) and colours, again reflecting the changing colours in the world around them. Due to other commitments, Sue, the artist, was only able to visit the setting for a brief look round before beginning her time there. During a short conversation with Sue as she gave her a tour of the setting, Cathy discussed the current themes as they went around the different rooms, hoping to establish what kinds of focus Sue was intending to pursue, so that short-term planning could reflect this. Sue, however, was reluctant to commit to anything specific, and talked generally about wanting the experience with the children to be organic.

During the first week, Sue initially focused on showing the children how to create a simple weaving frame from wood and string, and then demonstrated the principles of weaving with strips of ribbon and material. The older children, especially a group of 4-year-old boys, enjoyed using the hammers, saws and tools to create the weaving 'looms', but quickly lost interest in the weaving process itself. The older girls persisted, creating loose, interesting patterns from two or three lines of weaving with various materials. Eager to have 'evidence' of the artist's involvement with the children, Helen emphasised how important it was for them to 'finish' their work. A small 'factory' developed with Sue and Helen mounting a display of the children's efforts at weaving.

Identifying good practice

On seeing this, Cathy spoke with both Sue and Helen, separately. She reminded Helen, yet again, that it was the process of weaving that should be the focus and not the product. With Sue, she thanked her for her contribution, talked about how the weaving activity had helped some of the children with their fine motor skills as well as extending knowledge in other areas of learning like the turn-taking and conversation that had taken place with the 'communal' piece of weaving Sue had initiated. Lastly, she commented on the need to focus on process rather than product. Sue looked confused, stating that she had thought from what Helen had said it had been a necessary part of her work with the children to encourage this. After some discussion and clarification, Sue and Cathy agreed a focus for the following week, both feeling much happier.

In the final week, Sue introduced special inks for the children to use on sheets of acetate, using daylight and a light box to explore the colours the children had created. One child, Joseph, who was generally shy about communicating with his peers, became fascinated by how the colours could be layered over each other to produce another colour. He became quite animated about the colours he'd create.

'Magic, it's magic', he'd say, proudly showing anyone who would look at how the process worked.

Leading practice

At a staff meeting the next week, Cathy asked for observations from staff about how they had found the experience. Most of the staff had found the experience beneficial, that Sue had been very supportive and full of suggestions, saying they would look more creatively now at how they used resources, and that the presence of a 'creative' mind in their midst had stimulated creativity within the children. Even Helen admitted that 'process' without any obvious 'product' was important, as evidenced by Joseph's reaction to mixing colours. One member of staff did worry that the children who had made the most 'noise' when it came to choosing what to do had dictated the way a session had gone, suggesting that, next time, perhaps choosing the composition of a group working with the artist might be better.

Task

- List in order of importance the number of ways Cathy might have improved the outcomes of Sue's time in the setting.
- Consider whether Cathy dealt effectively with the situation created by Helen.
- How would you deal with the suggestion by staff about choosing the composition of groups of children working with artists?
- Discuss the above with colleagues, comparing lists and possible solutions.

How can we ensure that children are provided with flexible routines that meet individual needs, in a well-resourced environment that takes account of diversity and encourages inclusive practice and provision?

In order to be truly inclusive and accommodate diversity, a setting's routines need to be flexible. Creating a balance between the safety and comfort provided by a regular routine and the need to meet individual children's needs is what effective practitioners must strive for. There is a statutory requirement for practitioners within the EYFS to provide holistic and inclusive provision for young children, which is underpinned by the ECM agenda and recent legislation, for example the Race Relations (Amendment) Act 2000, the Special Education Needs and Disability Act (SENDA) 2001, the revised Code of Practice 2002, the Children Act 2004 and the Childcare Act 2006 (see Chapter 4). The EYFS highlights the relationship with the 'wider community' in all its diversity that effective settings develop and engage in.

One of the ways in which a setting can demonstrate its commitment to its local community is by organising its daily and weekly routines to accommodate some of the particular needs of the families within that community. Through the creation of schedules and routines that are responsive to babies and young children's needs, and flexible enough to take into account the needs of parents/ carers, effective settings promote children's learning and development as well as building positive partnerships with families. The effective practitioner will understand the rationale for differentiation, when it comes to a child who, for example, attends more than one setting or with extended attendance may need a different period of rest. The effective practitioner, too, will understand the need for routines established for babies new to the setting to ideally reflect home patterns for sleeping and feeding. Children with issues around bladder control, specific medical conditions and SEN will require a more flexible approach. This will naturally affect the daily and weekly planning undertaken by practitioners, especially keyworkers, to ensure that individual needs are catered for.

Transitions

In more general terms, effective practice also needs to allow children time to come to terms with periods of transition from home into a pre-school setting or into mainstream school, ideally with a period of 'settling in' characterised by flexible planning that is sensitive to children's and parents' needs. Allowing children sufficient time to follow their interests should also be reflected in the day-to-day routines of the setting. If the day is broken up too often or routines are so rigid they stop children from becoming engrossed in activities and engaging in deeper levels of thinking, they become counterproductive. Again it is the balance between the safety and reassurance that comes from knowing what happens next for a child, and the time and freedom to engage in the kind of 'epistemic' investigative play that a child's curiosity feeds on, as well as the more imaginative, creative 'ludic' play, both of which promote deeper levels of thinking and learning (Hutt *et al.* 1989). The need for such flexibility now embedded in the EYFS framework (DFE 2012) has to be understood and supported by all staff for it to be effective. The Lead Practitioner will obviously model good practice, but may need to address the issue of more flexible routines in order that all staff understand the benefits for children and families. Looking at children as individuals and planning to meet their interests and needs, while ensuring overall development and progression within the areas of learning and development, calls for creative planning on the part of the whole team. If the keyworker has established a good working relationship with parents/carers and discusses children's interests and preferences (some of which will be ephemeral, while others will be more embedded), planning to meet individual needs should be easier and the very important continuity between the setting and home created.

Focus on practice

Staff in the baby room of a Children's Centre complained to the Lead Practitioner, Joy, about the routine laid down for nappy changing. In the present routine, nappy changing took place over a relatively short period of time for all the babies. This had initially been decided as a result of the low numbers of babies attending the centre. However, the number had increased slightly, as well as the number of toddlers now attending the setting, although staffing levels had yet to be increased. This had put pressure on the existing practitioners, not only in having to change more children, but they now had to queue for changing facilities that had previously been sufficient for their needs.

Identifying good practice

Over the next week, Joy observed the nappy-changing routine and could see that both babies and infants were distressed as well as practitioners. The pressures of time and lack of facilities were turning what should have been a relaxed, enjoyable experience into one that was fraught and hastily executed. After discussing the issues with staff, Joy expressed the opinion that the routine should change to reflect the individual needs of babies and infants; ideally, the babies' routines should reflect as far as possible the routines of home, in line with EYFS guidance. All the practitioners agreed this would be the better option, but pointed out that this change would affect the rest of the daily routines, for feeding, sleeping and if, for example, a practitioner was involved in an activity or observation. After looking again at the daily routines, Joy agreed that more staff were needed to support a more individual approach to the babies' and infants' needs. As numbers in the toddler room were at present quite low, she would speak with the manager about more flexible use of existing staff until new staff were appointed. In the meantime, she asked practitioners to support each other as much as possible when it came to organising observations and activities for children's profiles.

Leading practice

As a result of her discussion with the manager, Joy was asked to look at the routines in the 3–5 room. One area which took up staff time was the preparation and serving of snacks at a particular time each morning. Joy had previously worked at a setting where a rolling snack routine had been in place. She discussed with staff the possibility of making

Pearson Education Ltd/Jules Selmes.

such a change, citing her own positive experience. Rolling snack could involve the children in helping to prepare it, an activity with great potential for learning as well as acquiring skills. Rolling snack also met the requirement of meeting individual needs, where children accessed the snack when they wanted it, not at a specific pre-determined time. It also, as had been the case in her former setting, helped children who came to the setting without having eaten breakfast or those children 'at risk', who could access food throughout the day if needed. Joy also pointed out other benefits; for example, it encouraged children's learning and development within other areas of learning such as conversation, making choices and turn-taking.

Some staff were hesitant, raising health and safety issues, but Joy pointed out that, if snack preparation was seen as an activity in itself, it released members of staff from the duty of preparing snacks for all the children, and changed it into an activity they could share with the children – a much more productive use of their time. Again staff stated this change to the routine would affect the rest of the day; often snack time had released those practitioners not directly involved, providing time for other duties, such as catching up on observations and children's profiles. Joy agreed it was difficult to find time within the working day, but time was already put aside for preparation and planning. She suggested the 'rolling snack' be given a trial run for the following four weeks, and then reviewed.

Reflections

- *How do you feel Joy responded to the issue over the nappy-changing routine?*
- *Was the solution she proposed fair and workable?*
- *Do you feel she should have involved staff more?*
- *In being asked to look at staffing and routines by the Manager, do you feel Joy's suggestions for a 'rolling snack' would help alleviate staffing difficulties in the setting?*
- *Do you consider Joy introduced the idea of changes to the snack routine in a positive way?*

● *Should she have involved staff more?*

● *If you had been in Joy's position, what might your proposals to help solve the issues have been?*

Task Discuss the above with colleagues and compare your solutions.

Acknowledging the diverse needs of the wider community has been shown by longitudinal research such as EPPE (2008, ongoing) to enhance children's sense of well-being as evidenced in the development of their cognitive, emotional and social intelligence. The Early Years Transition and Special Educational Needs (EYT-SEN) research project commissioned by the DFES (2003b) also found that nurseries and integrated/combined centres that supported the local community had a positive effect on the achievement of all children generally and those children with, or 'at risk' of, SEN in particular.

Diversity

In relating to Standard 6, the practitioner needs to take into account the above issues of acknowledging diversity and promoting inclusive practice (see Chapter 4). By focusing on the uniqueness of each child and their interests, the effective practitioner can create an environment whose resources reflect the diversity of cultures and beliefs of the wider community – ensuring, through artefacts, books, activities and experiences that are shared with parents/carers, children will feel they, their cultures and beliefs are celebrated and valued. Providing labels and print in the environment written in children's home languages will help children come to understand the importance of print, and will also make parents/carers feel more welcome. Dual-language books that are commercially available or made by the children and shared with their peers and family also promote a sense of self-esteem. World music and stories in different languages available on audio tapes for children to access and share, multicultural dolls, puppets, clothing representative of several cultures available in role-play areas, foods from different cultural cuisines, prepared and available at the snack table for children to taste and discuss, as well as the celebration of special festivals, are all examples that settings using good diversity practice adopt.

For children with Special Educational Needs (SEN), materials and space need to be adapted wherever possible, so they have equal access to indoor and outdoor provision safely. Tracking rails and tactile symbols can help the visually impaired child negotiate the indoor environment with more autonomy. Outdoor provision, using the senses of touch, smell and sound, perhaps through the building of a sensory garden, would support inclusive experiences. The use of an extensive range of communication systems in a setting including PECS (www.pecs.com), Makaton, British Sign Language and Baby Sign (www.underfives.co.uk/signs.htm) helps hearing-impaired children and children on the autistic spectrum to feel included.

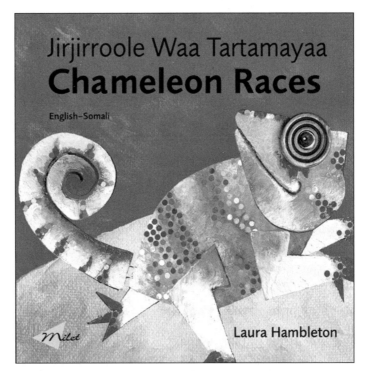

Source: From Chameleon Races/English-Somali by Laura Hambleton
(Milet Publishing 2005). Copyright: Laura Hambleton & Milet Publishing.

Simple, practical additions like ramps or widened door openings give wheelchair-bound children easy access to indoor/outdoor provision. The Index for Inclusion by Booth and Ainscow (2002), for example, provides a clear checklist for settings to help them examine and expand their inclusive provision and practice.

 Focus on Practice

Accessing outdoor play

The baby and toddler room staff at a newly built children's centre complained to the Lead Practitioner, Jenny, about the difficulty of accessing the outdoor space, due to design 'problems'. A number of issues around 'architectural features' had emerged over the weeks since the setting opened and this was one more. Staff had found that a raised ledge supporting the doors to the outdoor provision was proving difficult to negotiate safely for children who were crawling or beginning to walk. Staff felt this was stopping the majority of children accessing the outdoor area. They also felt the area itself, while, having some good resources (large sandbox, tactile crawling track and small-scale climbing equipment on a soft surface), was not a particularly safe environment for babies and infants, containing as it did high concrete planters at each corner of the space.

Identifying good practice

After observing the children's behaviour, Jenny then discussed the situation with the centre manager who agreed that the planters would be fenced off as a safety precaution. Jenny met with staff to consider ideas on how the room could be adapted to help children access outdoor provision in line with EYFS guidance. One member of staff, Brenda, suggested that a low-level, customised ramp could be placed over the ledge during the time the doors were open. Jenny felt that would help the children who were walking, but suggested something softer was needed for those babies who were crawling and eager to be outside.

Leading practice

Jenny led the discussion on how this might be achieved, with staff finally agreeing on the use of foam blocks covered in blankets being laid over the offending ledge. Both the ramp and foam blocks were a success and this encouraged Jenny to discuss with staff the planning for outdoors. The planning in place had been 'patchy' due to limited access and lack of a 'rota' for identifying responsibilities in this area. This was addressed in line with EYFS principles on meeting children's individual interests and needs.

Reflections

- *Do you feel Jenny supported the staff's concerns effectively?*
- *Do you consider the solutions arrived at in enabling the babies' and toddlers' access to outdoor provision appropriate and adequate?*
- *Should Jenny have been more proactive if she was aware outdoor provision had been 'patchy'?*
- *Have you been in a situation where 'architectural features' have been an issue when trying to provide high-quality provision and practice? If so, how did you deal with them?*

Task Discuss this issue with peers and colleagues, especially if you have not yet had experience in such situations. Note their comments in your journal, and consider where such problems might arise in your own setting, and how you might deal with them.

How can we develop practice to ensure a stimulating environment that guarantees high-quality provision

In attempting to meet the Standards underpinning this question, the EYP needs to show visible evidence of high-quality inclusive practice and provision, where the environment is viewed as an effective, enabling 'third teacher', supporting the cognitive, physical, emotional and social needs of children. The statutory requirements of the EYFS underpin each child's learning journey towards the **Early Learning Goals** and these need to be met and clearly demonstrated. The EYP is responsible for modelling and leading good practice in observing, assessing, planning and recording children's progress (see Chapter 5). Reporting this process to the stakeholders, most significantly the children themselves and their parents/carers, is an important part of practitioners' **accountability** for high-quality provision. The EYP is also accountable, through the progress of their own professional development and performance management, to senior staff and management, as well as external bodies. This accountability can be demonstrated in a number of ways. Practice that promotes and supports the vision or mission statement of the setting can be evidenced through the physical environment and routines that continuously demonstrate good practice, and through policies that are revised on a regular basis to take into account changes in legislation and government initiatives.

The EYP needs to highlight any specific training that staff may require to understand and embrace change and so ensure they are given the opportunity to improve their own professional development. This in turn should have a positive impact on the standard of provision in a setting. The EYP needs to take into account and act on feedback from parents/carers, through the use of, for example, suggestion boxes, regular discussion or noticeboards. This not only promotes a good working partnership, but also demonstrates flexibility and respect for stakeholders' views in the process of maintaining high-quality provision. Management, through performance review, can help the EYP to reflect on practice and provision and make any necessary changes. Drawing up improvement or action plans that are SMART (Specific, Measurable, Achievable, Realistic and Time-bound), as a result of such feedback and reflection, will support and encourage reflective practice among staff. Again, the detail of such action plans need to be demonstrably open and accessible to stakeholders. Informing parents/carers through displaying such plans in the setting or through news letters or reports promotes transparency.

Conclusion

What strategies can be developed to support the establishment of secure, stimulating and purposeful indoor and outdoor learning environments through planned and appropriate adult-initiated and child-led experiences?

We have seen in this chapter how theories of development and learning that underpin good, effective practice are evidenced in the latest initiatives of the ECM agenda and the EYFS practice guidance. The young 'scientist/explorer' central to Piaget's vision of how children develop has now become the 'active learner' described in the principles of the EYFS. The role of the adult in supporting, sustaining and resourcing children's development echoes the work of Vygotsky and Bruner, demonstrating the crucial role the knowledgeable adult has to play in a child's learning journey. Being knowledgeable not only relates to content but also to context. The knowledgeable adult must understand sensitively how to engage a child in sustained shared thinking and must also recognise when not to intrude upon that deep-level learning that the solitary learner needs to investigate undisturbed. The 'enabling' environment that practitioners need to create in order for children to develop and grow effectively is reminiscent of the 'third teacher' approach grounded in the practice of Reggio Emilia pre-schools (see Chapter 6), an approach that sees trust and equality in relationships begin to develop, where practitioner and child go on a journey of discovery and research together. The need to personalise learning, to see children as holistic individuals, is now supported by numerous longitudinal studies and research into effective Early Years practice, as well as reflecting the five outcomes of ECM (DFES 2003a). There is also the requirement to create secure environments where:

- Children's sense of well-being is nurtured and protected.
- The milieu is shown to support meaningful links with home in order to aid those potentially difficult moments of transition.
- Experiences are provided that are stimulating, intriguing and challenging, both indoors and outdoors.

All these factors have been shown to be integral to the most effective environments for the child's emotional, cognitive, social and physical growth and development. In such environments children can engage in epistemic and ludic play – play that is never undervalued by the phrase 'just playing', but seen as the multilayered, complex problem-solving activity that it is. Play is now embedded in the principles and philosophy of good Early Years practice, as evidenced by the EYFS guidance. The opportunities for play in today's early years settings need to reflect the knowledge we now have with regard to the child's developing brain (see Chapter 2). Movement feeds the synapses in a child's brain, and the new emphasis on outdoor provision and the opportunities it affords physical development reflects this knowledge and understanding. It also reflects a realisation that today's children may suffer a 'nature deficit', as a result of Western post-industrial cultural mores and practice. Local Authority funding to improve outdoor provision, the launch of Forest School projects and creative partnerships are all attempts to redress the balance, to provide all children, whatever their individual needs, with secure, stimulating and purposeful indoor and outdoor learning environments.

How can we ensure children are provided with flexible routines that meet individual needs, in a well-resourced environment that takes account of diversity and encourages inclusive practice and provision?

Flexibility is difficult to plan for but the necessity to accommodate children's individual needs is now grounded in legislation supporting the rights of the child and underpins the principles and practice of the EYFS. Routines need to be flexible enough to take into account those all-important links between home and the setting, whether it be the feeding and sleeping patterns of babies and infants reflecting the patterns and practice of home, or attempting to embed children's interests, however transitory, into short- and medium-term planning. How to plan for the unexpected is a skill the effective practitioner needs to acquire and, when children's interests take hold, planning and routines need to be flexible enough to accommodate them. The mix of child-led and adult-led activities and experiences this process can create is shown repeatedly by research to be the best way of supporting children's learning and development. Planning and routines also need to support children at particularly vulnerable times such as the transition from pre-school to mainstream settings, or at times when their personal circumstances are temporarily difficult, for example the arrival of a new sibling, or the ill-health of a parent, or a death in the family.

When organising and resourcing the environment, the effective practitioner needs to take into account the free flow of play between indoor and outdoor provision. They have to ensure that all children have equal access to such provision and that the resources reflect the diversity of the wider community. If physical changes to buildings are required for children with particular disabilities, then, within reason, this must be swiftly undertaken in order to ensure that practice is inclusive. In supporting diversity, practitioners may need to examine their own beliefs and values to ensure that stereotyping does not take place. Treating all children equally does not mean treating them 'the same'. The values and beliefs of the wider community need to be embraced and, where there are difficulties and tensions, these need to be worked at for the children's sake. Difference and the richness diverse cultures can bring to a setting should be celebrated if an environment is to be truly inclusive.

How can we develop practice to ensure a stimulating environment that guarantees high-quality provision?

Upholding the mission statement or vision for a setting depends on fundamental principles being agreed by all staff. In that way the delivery of high-quality provision can be maintained and sustained. The effective practitioner needs to be self-reflective and encourage such reflection in other staff. The willingness to undergo training in new skills or make changes to established practices needs to be modelled and other staff supported during such periods of change. Policies need to be up to date, expressing current thinking and legislation, in order for high-quality provision to be maintained. Being accountable to stakeholders, particularly children and their parents/carers, is a clear responsibility for the effective practitioner. Children and their parents/carers should have a voice in relation to the practice and provision of a setting, and their views acknowledged, taken seriously and acted upon. We are also accountable to such external bodies as the Local Authority and Ofsted. This is another area of responsibility, and the ability to respond to such inspections with positive action plans for improvement is a necessary skill that needs to be developed. Being able to maintain the identity, defend, reflect upon and sustain the delivery of high provision means that the effective practitioner is forward looking and never complacent about their practice and provision.

Further reading

Athey, C. (1990) *Extending Thought In Young Children: A parent-teacher partnership.* London: Paul Chapman.

Bilton, H. (2005) *Outdoor Provision in the Early Years.* London: David Fulton.

Canterbury Children's Centre (2006) Searching for meaning. Available at: **http://www .canterburycc.co.uk/meaning.php**. Accessed on 4 January 2009.

Hutt, S.J. *et al.* (1989) *Play, Exploration and Learning: A natural history of the pre-school.* London: Routledge.

Websites

British Sign Language and Baby Sign: **http://www.underfives.co.uk/signs**.
EPPE: eppe.ioe.ac.uk/eppe/eppintro.com

Pen Green: http://www.pengreen.org

Picture Exchange System (PECS): http://www.pecs.com.

References

Athey, C. (1990) *Extending Thought In Young Children: A parent–teacher partnership.* London: Paul Chapman.

Bilton, H. (2005) *Outdoor Provision in the Early Years.* London: David Fulton.

Booth, T. and Ainscow, M. (2002) *The Index for Inclusion* (2nd edn). Developing Learning and Participation in Schools, Bristol: CSIE.

Brock, A., Dodds, S., Jarvis, P. and Olusoga, Y. (2008) *Perspectives on Play.* Harlow: Pearson Education.

Bruner, J. (1983) *Child's Talk: Learning to use language.* New York: Norton.

Canterbury Children's Centre (2006) Searching for Meaning. Available at: http://www.canterburycc.co.uk/meaning.php. Accessed on 4 January 2009.

Carr, M. (2001) *Assessment in Early Childhood Settings: Learning stories.* London: Paul Chapman.

Cook, J. (2008) 'Setting up a Forest School', *The Teacher,* November, p.43.

David, T. and Powell, S. (2005) 'Play in the early years: the influence of cultural difference', in J. Moyles (ed.) *The Excellence of Play.* Maidenhead: Open University Press.

DCSF (2007) *Early Years Foundation Stage Practice Guidance.* Nottingham: DCSF Publications.

DFE (2012) *Early Years Foundation Stage.* Cheshire: DFE Publications.

DFES (2003a) Every Child Matters. Green Paper. London: The Stationery Office.

DFES (2003b) The Early Years Transition and Special Needs (EYTSEN) Project. London: The Stationery office.

Dower, R.C. (2004) *International Creative Practice in Early Years settings.* London: Arts Council England.

Duffy, B. (1998) *Supporting Creativity and Imagination in Early Years.* Burkingham: Oxford University Press.

Greenland, P. (2000) *Hopping Home Backwards: Body intelligence and movement play.* Leeds: Jabado Publications.

Hutt, S.J. *et al.* (1989) *Play, Exploration and Learning: A natural history of the pre-school.* London: Routledge.

Jarvis, P. (2007) 'Monsters, magic and Mr. Psycho: Rough and tumble play in the early years of primary school, a biocultural approach', *Early Years, An International Journal of Research and Development,* 27(2), pp.171–88.

Jarvis, P. and George, J. (2008) 'Play, learning for life: The vital role of play in human development', in A. Brock, S. Dodds, P. Jarvis and Y. Olusoga (eds) *Perspectives on Play.* Harlow: Pearson Education.

Laevers, F. (1994) *The Leuven Involvement Scale for Young Children.* Belgium: Centre for Experiential Education.

Learning Through Landscapes (2008). Available at: http://www.ltl.org.uk/. Accessed on 15 February 2009.

Lindon, J. (2001) 'Striding ahead', *Nursery World,* November, pp.12–13.

Lindon, J. (2008) *Understanding Child Development: Linking theory and practice* (2nd edn). London: Hodder Arnold.

Paley, V. (1984) *Boys and Girls: Superheroes in the doll corner.* Chicago, IL: University of Chicago Press.

Pascal, C. *et al.* (1995) *Evaluating and Developing Quality in Early Childhood Settings: A professional development programme.* Worcester: Worcester College of Higher Education.

Siraj-Blatchford, I., Sylva, K., Mutock, S., Gilden, R. and Bell, D. (2002) *Researching Effective Pedagogy in the Early Years.* RB 356. London: DFES Publications.

Vygotsky, I. (1978) *Mind in Society.* Cambridge, MA: Harvard.

White, J. (2008) *Playing and Learning Outdoors.* London: Routledge.

8

Partnership and leadership in Early Years

Wendy Holland, Jane George and Pam Jarvis

Chapter overview

The Standards addressed in this chapter are:

2. Work directly with children and in partnership with their families to facilitate learning and support development.

7. Fulfil wider professional responsibilities by promoting positive partnership working to support the child.

8. Lead practice and foster a culture of continuous improvement.

Relating to the above Standards, the following key questions will be addressed:

- What strategies are needed to ensure that effective working partnerships with children and their families are valued and embedded in practice in order to promote children's well-being, learning and development?

- In what ways can the EYP lead practice to ensure that multi-agency team working is understood, valued and used effectively in supporting children's particular needs, both among professionals within the setting and external agencies?

The Family in Time

The family of the past	The family of the present	The family of the future
Was a traditional/extended family in the pre-industrial and early industrial period (to the early twentieth century)	The liberation of women, including the rejection of full-time housework and childcare for paid work has brought about the development of the 'symmetrical family' where parents of both genders take equal roles (theoretically, but don't forget the female 'triple shift', i.e., paid work/housework/childcare)	*This obviously has to be based on logical prediction*:
Was a 'unit of production' in the pre-industrial period – working life was carried out in or nearby the home, often with the whole family 'pitching in'		A continuing rise in 'alternative' family lifestyles
		Growing flexibility in gender partnerships focused upon shared child-raising, often outside formal marriage
Was a family of many brothers and sisters – parents had several children, but expected to lose one or two due to higher infant mortality (see typical large Victorian family picture above). From the mid-twentieth century onwards, contraception and better health care reduced the amount of children born, but increased life expectancy	There was a liberalisation of divorce laws in the Divorce Act (1969) followed by a growing divorce rate 1970-1990, and a subsequent rise in the amount of single parent, single parent + grandparent(s) and reconstituted or blended families	Emerging roles for older people, as the lifespan extends and people remain healthy and active for longer These may possibly be associated with provision of care for grandchildren/great grandchildren while parents are working
	There is a growing rate of children born outside formal marriage (1980-present), and falling marriage rates	Expansion of artificial fertility techniques and associated legislation may eventually allow completely 'test-tube' babies via the use of artificial wombs, and stem cell fertility techniques may additionally allow same-sex couples to genetically co-parent their own child
Marriage was for life, but the typical life-span was shorter than today	There has been a rise in alternative family lifestyles (e.g., gay families, friendship group 'families')	
The industrial revolution (1800-1850) brought the change of 'going out to work' for the adults of the family	The typical family tree structure of the modern family is 'beanpole' like, with many single and two child families but longer lived members (see five generation 'beanpole' family picture above)	As the 'baby-boomers' born 1945-1965 retire, society will have to decide how to fund their pensions from a shrinking workforce, and as such baby-boomers reach the end of their lives, the British working population will start to fall ... Immigration of people born from 1980 onwards and their offspring may help to re-balance society in this respect
After the Second World War (1945 onwards) many families moved to new, single family-sized houses in the suburbs and the cultural stereotype of the nuclear family with the 'instrumental' commuter father and 'expressive' housewife mother became the 'norm'	Fertility techniques have been piloted that allow women to consider older first time child-bearing	
	More people are remaining single and childless, meaning that we have both an aging and falling population	It is as yet uncertain how the 'credit crunch' may impact on families in the long term

Photos: Alamy/ClassicStock (l); Corbis/Gary Houlder (c); Alamy/JUPITER IMAGES/Banana Stock (r).

Introduction

In this chapter we are going to address the various ways in which Early Years Professionals can develop effective working relationships with other adults in order to ensure that outcomes for children are enhanced and improved. In particular we will consider how EYPs can work effectively in partnership with parents and carers (an aspect of the EYP's role which has been emphasised in the revised EYFS Framework, DFES 2012a); work with staff from other professional groups and backgrounds as well as develop positive working relationships within their own teams. The skills, knowledge and values which support the achievement of these Standards will be considered as well as how recent research supports effective practice.

Focus on practice

Josh's family

Josh, a 3-year-old, whose family had recently moved into the area, began attending a private daycare setting, set in a reasonably affluent urban area of a city. His key worker, Eve, noticed how his mother, Fran, who brought him in the mornings, seemed very reserved and reluctant to engage in conversation, making her younger child, a 10-month-old daughter, the excuse for a quick departure. By contrast, his father, who collected Josh in the evenings, was talkative and generally pleasant, often apologising for being a little late. Josh appeared to settle into his new surroundings quite quickly, and formative observations soon began to show he had good communication skills and a facility for problem solving.

Identifying good practice

One morning, determined to share an observation with Fran, Eve attempted to draw her into conversation, but the younger child was crying and Eve quickly saw that Fran was on the verge of tears herself. Josh was also not as happy to leave his mother this particular morning, so Eve tried to distract him with his favourite activity of constructing with the large hollow blocks. She mentioned the incident to the setting EYP, Pat, who suggested a meeting with Fran, at a less hectic time than the morning 'meet and greet'. Eve thought she might mention this to Josh's father when he called to collect him that evening, but he was even later than usual, so late that Eve had been on the point of phoning Josh's home contact number. She had intended to remind Josh's father of the setting's closing time, but he'd been so apologetic and thankful, Eve had let the matter go.

In a casual conversation in the staff room, Eve mentioned to Pat how Josh's behaviour was beginning to change. The young boy's concentration, which had been remarkably good initially, was noticeably weaker, and he separated from Fran, whom she described as 'moody' and 'unpredictable', with increasing reluctance, adding 'she's so different from Josh's father'. Pat asked if Eve had managed to set up a meeting with Josh's mother, to which Eve replied she had tried twice and each time Fran had not attended and made excuses afterwards. From other brief comments, Pat was beginning to worry about Eve's 'preferential' treatment of Josh's father. She suggested that as something was definitely having an effect on Josh, it might be beneficial for Eve and herself to meet with both Josh's parents. Eve immediately defended the father, saying, as he ran his own company single-handed, it was difficult enough for him to find time to collect his son, let alone come to meetings, whereas Fran 'had all day'. Things were brought to a head one morning when Josh kicked out at another child and then tried to bite him. A meeting with his parents was arranged, but only Fran arrived. The meeting revealed several important facts that had not appeared on the admissions proforma or in initial discussions with Josh's parents. Eve and Pat learned that the family had moved to the area to be nearer Fran's family, so that she could return part-time to her job as a radiographer, but this had been put on hold as Fran had been experiencing prolonged 'constant tiredness' after the birth of her daughter, something she had not experienced with Josh. She felt Josh had picked up on this and was becoming a 'difficult' child at home. Although her sister was doing her best to help out with the children, she too was finding Josh's behaviour very demanding. Fran, who had seemed distressed and at times near to tears during the meeting, expressed real concern over the fact that Josh's behaviour was now 'public'. She had put it down to them moving away from the only place he'd known as 'home'. Pat reassured her that was possibly one reason for it, plus the additional stress of attending a new setting that all children experienced. She asked if Fran had seen her GP about the tiredness, but Fran replied that the family had only just become registered locally and had been trying to self-medicate with 'tonics'. She didn't feel she could 'trouble' a doctor with simple tiredness. At the suggestion another agency might be able to provide temporary help (a family support worker), Fran was adamant that her own family was all the support she needed. When asked by Eve, what her husband felt, Fran shrugged, 'he thinks I'll feel better when I'm back at work, - it's me - I need to pull myself together'. Pat proposed that with a three old and an infant, there was little wonder she was tired, and suggested no- one would think she was 'wasting time' if she mentioned it at the family clinic the next time she attended. Pat proposed that the setting would continue to observe Josh and keep her informed of any new developments and that Fran and Eve could start a 'home/school diary' through which they could better communicate, given that mornings could be particularly 'hectic'. It was also agreed that there would be a meeting in a month's time 'to discuss how the whole family were getting along'.

Leading practice

After the meeting, Pat asked Eve how she now felt about the situation with Josh and his parents. When Eve began to suggest that Fran had a lot going for her, lovely home, supportive sister, great husband who supported her – it wasn't as though she had to go to work, Pat stopped her, saying she had a real concern that Fran was possibly suffering from some kind of depression and might need professional help. She also asked Eve to reflect on her relationship with both parents and ask herself why she was ready to forgive Josh's father his continual lateness, which had at times been extremely inconvenient for staff, but did not make a similar allowance for Fran's behaviour?

Eve did reflect and realised she had been biased in her approach. She made extra efforts with Fran, particularly on mornings when she appeared at the setting exhausted and strained, and did eventually speak with Josh's father about the inconvenience to staff that his continual lateness caused. When Eve tried to talk to him about Josh's behaviour, he became evasive, saying that was an 'area' his wife dealt with and he didn't want to interfere, adding he felt sure Eve was doing a great job with Josh. Fran heeded Pat's words and went to see her GP, who diagnosed and began to treat her for mild post-natal depression. Josh's behaviour gradually settled and his sense of well-being and involvement began to increase. Fran began to appear less exhausted and was more willing to stay and talk with Eve about Josh's achievements, as well as communicating through the home/school diary. After Josh had been at the setting for six months, Fran found part-time work as a radiographer and introduced her sister, who would be collecting Josh in the afternoons, to Eve. Fran voiced her concerns that Josh's behaviour might 'dip' as a result of her returning to work part time, but Eve reassured her that even if Josh did react negatively to the changes in his routine, together, they could support him through it.

Eve informed Pat of the change in circumstances, when presenting the changed paper work for collecting Josh. Pat 'positioned' herself unobtrusively in the 'meet and greet' area of Josh's room occasionally and noticed a real difference in Fran's demeanour, something over the following weeks she was pleased to hear Eve comment on positively herself.

Reflections

- *How would you have dealt with Eve's rather 'one-sided' attitude to Josh's parents? Here you could also reflect on gender issues, and consider if we are more likely to expect more from mothers than fathers, and the potential unfairness this raises.*

- *How might you continue to work with Fran if she completely refused to follow your suggestions to seek further professional help for her illness, and appeared to be increasingly depressed, to the point that you began to have concerns that the children's well-being may be at risk?*

- *What if Eve had not responded to Pat's suggestions in such a positive fashion? How do you think Pat should have moved on to manage the situation further?*

Task Discuss this scenario with your colleagues and peers. After consideration are you aware of having implicitly 'different rules' for mother and fathers in our settings(s)? If so, how might you remedy this? Discuss with colleagues how you feel the above scenario relates to the Standards focused upon in this chapter.

What strategies are needed to ensure that effective working partnerships with children and their families are valued and embedded in practice in order to promote children's well-being, learning and development?

Stable, healthy families are at the heart of strong societies. It is within the family environment that an individual's physical, emotional and psychological development occurs. It is from our family that we learn unconditional love, we understand right from wrong, and we gain empathy, respect and self-regulation.

(Centre for Social Justice 2010, p.6)

The above quote suggests that the family is central and familiar, but 'the family' can have several meanings (for example see 'The family in time' above). In fact we could be said to live in several 'families'; the nuclear family, the extended family and the ancestral family to name a few, all of which impact upon a child's development. The EYP needs to be aware of the possible forms 'the family' might take when trying to meet the needs of individual children. The practitioner could be dealing with a relatively new mother who is unsure of her own parenting skills, wary of the 'public' nature of the setting and feeling she is being judged on these emerging skills, a young father who has been given the job to take the baby to the setting and is desperate to get on his way, or possibly even a grandmother bamboozled and/or annoyed because 'it wasn't done like that in my day'. Many caring adults feel threatened by institutional contexts, by the agendas they feel are set by practitioners without sufficient consultation, and the incomprehensible jargon used between professionals. This sense of insecurity is sometimes aggravated by the media 'hype' which criticises parents for allowing their children unedited access to the internet, for working too many hours, for being lone parents or divorced … the list is long. Practitioners need to be wary of being influenced by media headlines that may lead them to blame carers for being too busy, stressed, disorganised, defensive or having poor relationships with their children, and try instead to empathise and see life from the carer's perspective.

Reflection *One of the authors of this chapter found the detailed handover of her grandchild from the setting quite strange at first. Her children had only attended a church hall playschool prior to being admitted to school in the late 1980s/early 1990s, where arriving and departing had been a far more casual process. After the 'culture shock', however, she now avidly reads the daily report on her grandson and talks to him about it on the way home. The author finds this a positive process, presenting her with a number of opportunities to reconnect with her grandson. However, some carers may find the whole reporting system worryingly intrusive or threatening if their knowledge of children's services principally depend on reports in the tabloid press.*

Task Discuss how you explain to adults new to the setting about the daily processes involved. Do you consider your entire community of practice, which is likely to include parents, other family members, unrelated carers (e.g. child minders) and the perception of your setting that they take with them into the wider community?

Consider also how the daily record sheet may be received by carers of children having difficulties settling into your setting, who are going 'through a phase' or who may be presenting with developmental issues/delays. The author who started this reflection remembers being mortified on once being told that her 17-month-old grandson had been 'smacking' the other children, although in the end it presented an education opportunity when she bought a book for him entitled *No Hitting!* In some families, the response may have been different; practitioners do need to consider the impact and influence of their communications. This relates to the leadership ability to think beyond the immediate situation.

The leading practitioner needs to establish the setting's policies while building a trusting partnership with parents and other relevant adults providing care for the child. All practitioners also need to be aware of the impact of environmental factors on how a family functions (see Bronfenbrenner's view of the bi-directional influences on a child and their family helps show the complexity of such influences in Chapter 2). Obvious factors such as employment, health, housing will impact on the functioning of every family within the setting's neighbourhood. Ghate and Hazel *et al.* (2002) describe the characteristics of families who may be 'at risk' as a result of 'poor' environments, 'poor' in this sense meaning not just poverty but also environments that do not have 'optimal parenting' conditions. While acknowledging that not all materially poor families live in poor environments, they suggest there is a strong link between 'geography' and 'deprivation'. The Coalition Government have focused provision in the Early Years principally towards the *child in the family* and to offer support to the most deprived families in society (see Chapter 4).

The multiplicity of factors involved shows the implausibility of trying to formulate one policy that will work to create a 'partnership' with all families. Early dialogue is essential and needs to be maintained. Such dialogue also has to be meaningful for both practitioners and families. It should empower families by providing accessible and non-threatening information, advice, support and training. It should raise awareness about facilities and services through user-friendly media; how, for example, will adults with limited reading skills feel if most information is only available in printed form?

> The best services in the world will not necessarily enhance parents' ability to cope unless they are perceived as helpful and acceptable . . . to ensure that parents feel in control of the type of support they receive and the way in which it is delivered.
>
> (Ghate and Hazel *et al.* 2002, p.262)

These authors go on to suggest that problems arise when parents no longer feel 'in charge' of their children, in the sense that they are in some way handing them to someone else who will take over their care. In order to feel secure, they need to feel that there is a partnership in which the parents are the 'senior' carers.

Focus on practice

Focus on Families?

In an announcement from the DFE: *Focus on families - new drive to help troubled families* presented on **http://www.education.gov.uk/inthenews/inthenews/ a0070284/focus-on-families-new-drive-to-help-troubled-families**, on 10 December 2010, the Coalition Government propose:

➡

As a first stage of this new drive to help troubled families turn their lives around, the government:

● Will give local authorities new freedoms to pool budgets to help provide more joined up solutions for troubled families

● Will provide new money to a number of local authorities through the Early Intervention Grant for trialling innovative new approaches to help families with problems . . .

Children's Minister Sarah Teather said:

One way we are doing this is by reforming Sure Start so it is better at supporting the most disadvantaged families. Another is by giving local communities the freedom to use budgets flexibly and redesign services, so that they can deliver family intervention and relationship support unique to the needs of their local area. I look forward to seeing the results of this new approach.

Identifying good practice

If you work in a children's centre while the Coalition Government are in office, it is likely that you will find yourself working with several if not many families who are being offered various services through this scheme.

Task Work with your colleagues and/or fellow candidates to put together a 'wordle' on the ideas that first spring to your mind when you hear the term 'troubled families'. What you need to do is to list the first ten words or phrases that come to mind working alone, and then pool what you have written. Enter the resulting data into this website: http://www.wordle.net/ making sure to enter repeated words or phrases the correct amount of times (if descriptions are almost identical, alter them slightly to make them absolutely identical). What you will then be presented with is a set of well-presented generic ideas about such families that the group in question hold. Consider the resulting document, and reflect together how it might make *you* feel to come from a family that has been labelled as 'troubled'.

Leading practice

'"Where's your Mama gone? Where's your Mama gone?" Used to sing that to the kids when Monica f***ed off, never a dry eye in the house, all shot off upstairs howling they did'.

This is a quote from the hit TV series *Shameless*, from the principal protagonist, single father 'Frank Gallagher'. The programme relies on stereotyping a 'troubled family' within a range of humorous situations and interactions, and is likely to have informed some of the ideas that your more junior staff carry around with them when they think about the concept. How would you, largely in modelling good practice, help them to see past this type of 'popular culture' response?

Support for parenting

Research has demonstrated convincingly that parental involvement makes a huge difference to children's achievements (EPPE 2004). The role of all carers involved with children under the age of 5 should be supporting all parents to become the best parents they can be, and not to replace the parent in any way. The impact of parental involvement can also have tangible benefits for parents, early education settings and the wider community through the creation of a 'triangle of care' between parent, child and practitioner. In this section we will consider how the EYP can support the development of parental involvement in their child's learning and development in the setting and beyond. We will do this by examining some examples of good practice in relation to parental involvement, including the work of the Pen Green Centre (PGC) in Corby, the Parents Early Years and Learning (PEAL) Project and the *Birth to School Study: a Longitudinal Evaluation of the Peers Early Education Partnership* (Evangelou *et al.* 2005). We will also be referring to 'Positive relationships' from the EYFS framework (DFES 2012a) with regard to its focus on parents as partners. International evidence found in the approach taken by the pre-schools in the Reggio Emilia district of Northern Italy, and the impact of such programmes as Head Start and High/Scope in the USA (see Chapter 2) on creating successful partnerships with parents will also be discussed.

In creating open, and trusting partnerships with parents, EYPs need to be able to reflect on their own values and beliefs in relation to parental involvement. As the DFE suggests in its 'Know how' guide to the statutory EYFS Progress Check at Two (DFES 2012b), some practitioners, in attempting to build partnerships with parents, may find certain parenting styles fit more closely with their own views, and they clearly need to reflect on this potential for bias. Experience of building relationships within diverse family situations where the practitioner may be from a different culture to the family, for example, can have an enriching effect on practitioners' perspectives and values. EYPs need to be prepared to move beyond traditional deficit approaches, which appear to suggest that the professional's principal role is to compensate for some kind of inadequacy on the part of the parent, again do be beware of operating within a 'disadvantage' culture. Such a 'deficit' model can lead to the creation of a partnership where the parent/carer is 'passive', which may eventually lead to resentment, if they feel that their role has been usurped by the professional. Reay (1998) suggests that this 'deficit' view can be particularly problematic in practitioners' perceptions of the abilities and interests of working-class parents, in relation to their child's development and education. She further suggests that although both working-class and middle-class mothers invest time, effort, money, thought and emotion into their children's development and education, the difference that emerges tends to be the *effectiveness* with which middle-class mothers are able to access, shape and facilitate their child's care and education due to their greater 'cultural capital' (Bourdieu 1977). Finch (1984, p.15) in her study of inner city playgroups describes how, '... middle class outsiders step in to take over playgroups which working class mothers cannot "manage" on their own. This fits neatly into the process of educating working class women in "proper" childcare practice.' Such perceptions can often understandably be perceived by parents to be patronising and/or tokenistic.

Bruce and Meggitt (2006, p.648) propose that parents are 'the first and most enduring carers and educators of their children'. It is clear that the home environment remains critical to young children's development and learning, whatever the quality of the professional setting. As such, the effective practitioner needs to understand each child's background and early experiences through both acknowledging the child *within the family* and incorporating the child's early experiences in learning activities. The surest way to achieve this, as suggested at the beginning of this chapter, is through the development of an open, honest and authentically respectful relationship with the child's parents and other carers. True parental involvement needs to reflect a model of empowerment (Whalley 2007). This model seeks to promote a parent's sense of being an active participant and co-educator in their child's learning and development rather than a passive recipient of information from professionals; this reciprocal relationship also enables the professional to become an active learner. This approach underpins the work at the Pen Green Centre (PGC) where a similar model is used to enable parents to develop skills in critical reflection so that new knowledge and understanding can be co-constructed with their children and with the professionals employed in settings. The PGC opened in 1983 in Corby in response to social and economic decline in the area resulting in poor outcomes for children and their families. It developed a strong vision of a service which would 'honour the needs of young children and celebrate their existence. It would also support families however they were constituted within the community' (Whalley 2007, p.3). While PGC has been involved in many different types of parental involvement programmes since 1983, the Parents Involvement in their Children's Learning Training Programme (PICL) (Whalley 2007) warrants further investigation here.

Focus on practice

PICL

Although it may be impossible for all EYPs to replicate the work of PICL in its entirety, an understanding of the approach could offer a way forward for many practitioners. The PICL programme seeks to support parents to develop knowledge, skill and understanding of their child's learning and development using a group work model. Concepts such as 'involvement', 'well-being' 'adult style' and 'schemas' are examined. Parents are also supported to develop skills in using video in order to record observations of their children at home. Parents and staff share video footage and written observations in order that the parent/carer and the practitioner can engage together in planning for the child's learning and development, both in the home and at the nursery. The PICL programme has demonstrated parents from any cultural or social economic background can be actively and meaningfully engaged in supporting their children's leaning and development. See **http://www.pengreen.org** for more information about PICL and 'Centres of Energy'.

Task Access the PGC website using the link above. Consider how you might apply the approaches described in your own setting considering the concepts of 'involvement', 'well-being' 'adult style' and 'schemas'. How might you use the PGC approach to strengthen your relationships with children and their families? What opportunities might there be for you to work in this way with children and families, modelling this practice for your colleagues, possibly creating and supporting training for your team on some of these ideas.

The focus on 'partnership working between practitioners and with parents and/or carers' in the EYFS (2012), and the development of such projects as Parents, Early Years and Learning (PEAL), Peers Early Education Partnership (PEEP) and its longitudinal evaluation, Birth to School Study (BTSS) (Evangelou *et al.* 2005) should alert EYPs to the previous and present governments' ongoing commitment to extending and improving the practitioner's ability to involve parents meaningfully in the education of their children.

PEAL (see http://www.peal.org.uk/) is a consortium project run by the National Children's Bureau (NCB), Coram (formerly the Thomas Coram Foundation for Children) and the London Borough of Camden, who have collectively developed a training programme for practitioners to help them work with families to ensure that parents are appropriately involved in their children's early learning. PEAL advocates the following elements as central to partnership working with parents:

- Authentic relationships
- Communication and partnership
- The exploration of what is effective practice in the early years.

PEAL supports practitioners in beginning the process of involving parents; this includes establishing the setting's values in relation to parental involvement, opportunities for parental involvement and helping the practitioner to reflect upon any skill or knowledge gaps they may have in relation to working with parents in this way. PICL is one of the tools a practitioner might use to begin the partnership process.

Parental involvement has been at the heart of the collective Early Years experience of children within the European context for centuries, initially informally, and then by the formation of cooperative groups in the post-Second World War period until the present. The first pre-schools in Reggio Emilia, for example, were founded by parents and a range of opportunities for involvement continue to be offered to parents. 'Parent participation enables a communication network that leads to fuller and more reciprocal knowledge as well as to a more effective search for the best educational methods, contexts and values' (Malaguzzi in Pen 1997, p.28).

> The central focus is on the relationship between children and adults. The [school] . . . should be seen not as a single system, but as . . . a system of relationships and communication among children, teachers and parents . . . a living organism that pulses, changes, transforms, grows and matures.
>
> (Rinaldi 2005, p.85)

In the Reggio Emilia approach (Malaguzzi in Penn 1997) induction programmes for new parents ensure that parents are familiar with the layout of the building, the staff and, most importantly, that they understand the values, principles and philosophies which will shape their children's early learning experiences. Parental participation is nurtured through a range of methods to stimulate parent's interests and enable them to connect with the work of the setting. A day book, for example, uses photos to capture the children's significant experiences during the day. Extensive communication round the 'documentation' of children's learning and development is also an area where parents help by giving input and suggestions for future planning. They, alongside the teachers, are seen as co-researchers with their children and facilitators of their own children's learning journeys.

Programmes such as Early Head Start (see **http://www.literacytrust.org.uk/socialinclusion/earlyyears/headstartresearch.html** for more information) and High/Scope in the USA (see **http://www.highscope.org/**) again reinforce the vital importance of the active participation of parents in children's learning and development, particularly in communities judged to be economically and socially disadvantaged.

The EYFS (2012) has integrated many of the ideas outlined above into its framework, reinforcing the need for parental involvement to be seen as a fundamental element of effective Early Years practice that needs to be developed. Many settings use and see the value of home visits (see Chapter 6) as the beginning of this vital partnership between parents and practitioners. The introduction of the Progress Check at Two, which involves close cooperation and dialogue between a child's key worker and their family, could also be seen as a partnership 'in action'. For this Progress Check, through observations, photographs or other means of recording a child's learning journey in the setting, as well as any information and insights from the parents, the practitioner has to assess the child against the three Prime Areas of Learning and Development and their Early Learning Goals. The child's parents are then invited in for a discussion of their child's progress, and any concerns at this point are discussed with a view to possible intervention, for example, support with speech and language from a trained professional. The examples given in the 'Know how' guide (DFE 2012), stress the importance of the parents' contribution, and the need for an open and transparent discussion. Some critics of the Progress Check at such an early age suggest, however, this could be seen as 'pathologising' disadvantaged families (Brock and Rankin 2011). One of the reasons given for this early check on development by settings is to facilitate the progress check performed by health visitors on 2-year-olds, the thinking being that together both checks would provide a holistic picture of a child's progress in all areas, with any necessary interventions highlighted. The case studies given as examples in the DFE document clearly show, however, the need for real sensitivity when discussing possible interventions.

Focus on practice

The Progress Check

Julie, a young key worker in a Children's Centre attached to a local authority primary school, had said very little during the staff training on the Progress Check for 2-year-olds; it seemed reasonably straightforward. A child was assessed against the *Development Matters* document for 22–36 months (see http://www.early-education.org .uk/sites/default/files/Development%20Matters%20FINAL%20PRINT%20 AMENDED.pdf) and then this was shared with the parents. Julie knew she could always ask Simon, a more experienced practitioner who was studying for EYPS, if she needed any advice or help. The first Progress Check Julie attempted on Susie, a well-adjusted, child, who was 'exceeding' expectations, went well. Julie had taken lots of photographs of Susie's development during the child's six months at the centre and she often spoke with Susie's mum when she came to collect her daughter, so the chat they had over the Progress Check had not been difficult. The subsequent report had been relatively easy to write, although she did ask Simon to look at it before she gave it to Susie's mum. There were some issues, however, around the next of her key children due for the check. Amy, aged 2 years, 2 months was the youngest of four children, her sisters being aged 8, 10 and 14. Amy's mother, was single, in her mid-40s, and not easy to talk to. During the three months Amy had been attending the setting, her mother was usually in a hurry, as she'd told Julie on numerous occasions, because she was 'holding down two jobs'. The older sisters had all attended the setting prior to Julie's arrival there, the younger two were now at the attached local primary school, and according to their mother, were all doing really well. This made it all the harder for Julie to discuss issues of concern she had around Amy's lack of expressive language. Amy seemed to understand, but she rarely spoke, and would often push other children away if they tried to engage with her. Julie had looked at the descriptors in *Development Matters* and felt that Amy's progress was captured by the descriptors in the 16–22 month band.

Identifying good practice

When Julie finally managed to arrange a meeting with Amy's mother, she met great resistance to the suggestion that Amy was 'behind' in her language. 'All the girls have been the same, they took their time talking, then I couldn't shut them up!' Julie tried to sound a little more determined, about the benefits of getting early 'help' for Amy, but she could see that Amy's mother was adamant there was nothing wrong with her daughter's speech, insisting, 'She understands everything me and her sisters say to her.' Julie began to feel awkward and unsure, but in keeping with the concept of the parent as the 'first best educator' she realised that she did need to genuinely listen to parents' opinions and show her willingness to act upon them. As such, it was agreed that Amy should have more time to 'develop her language skills', and that Julie would meet again with Amy's mother in six weeks' time.

Leading practice

When Julie relayed the incident to Simon, he agreed to observe Amy, using a time sampling method, and discuss the results with her. Simon found that Amy loved the home corner, picking up the toy phone and talking into it, with the occasional word clearly stated, or walking round using a toy mobile phone pressed to her ear, as if listening, then babbling in response. In adult-led activities or at small group times, however, Amy generally remained silent, happy to attempt to copy hand movements in action rhymes and songs, but when asked a direct question, would respond by pointing her finger, or shaking her head, only occasionally giving a one word reply.

Simon's final time slot of the day took in the arrival of Amy's mother. This particular day, Amy's 8-year-old sister had come too. She immediately picked Amy up, and started talking at her, rather than to her, not waiting for any verbal response from the child. Simon's impression was that she saw Amy very much as an animated 'dolly'. Amy smiled and pointed to the home corner. This was all the excuse her 8-year-old sister needed to go in and play, and the way she organised Amy's play reminded Simon of a stage magician and his 'glamorous assistant'. Simon saw that Amy's needs were being almost immediately anticipated, and the babbling when it did happen, was immediately understood and acted upon, clearly to Amy's satisfaction.

Meeting up with Julie later that day, Simon talked about what he had observed, and how some of the causes for Amy's 'silence' were now clearer. Her sister had obviously been doing her talking for Amy, accepting her pointing or head shaking as sufficient language. Amy's babble, too was not being repeated back in a more recognised form, but accepted, as the family understood more clearly than 'strangers' just what the babbling meant. It was also clear that Amy did indeed understand what was being said to her, when her sister said, 'let's see what you've painted today', the 2-year-old tugged her sister's arm, leading her to where the day's 'art work' was laid out for parents/carers to collect.

Simon suggested that Julie might benefit from revisiting some of the latest research on young children's language that underpinned the Progress Check, to aid her confidence when speaking to Amy's mother again about the purpose of the check. He also suggested that Julie talked about Amy's favourite books at nursery, with a view to loaning some to Amy for her mother or possibly her two older sisters to read with her. He also advised Julie to discuss with Amy's mother how Amy loved playing in the role play area with the phones. Simon also added that the setting was investing in some 'speak easy' microphones that recorded children's voices, which he felt Amy would love playing with. It would also give Julie the chance to really listen to Amy's 'babble'. Simon finally gently added that perhaps more photographic evidence could be put in the child's Learning Journey.

Julie followed Simon's advice, ruefully admitting to herself that the 'evidence' in it was a little sparse. At first Amy's mother was cool with her, but Julie gradually regained some of the trust she felt she had lost by her mishandling of the situation initially. Having done several other Progress Checks, she was also beginning to feel more confident in answering parents' questions, and justifying the need for the check, detailing the many benefits that might follow.

By the time Julie was able to set up another meeting with Amy's mother, several things had happened. Simon's prediction that Amy would love the 'speak easy' microphone, proved to be right. The child's face had been a delight to see (one Julie caught on camera) at the sound of her own voice, which encouraged her to 'talk' more frequently. Julie, also found herself 'tuning in' to the child's 'babble', distinguishing Amy's attempts at single words. Over recent weeks, she had begun to celebrate the changes in Amy's speech with her mother, who still seemed a little defensive and guarded. When the meeting began, this time, Amy's mother proudly announced they'd bought a Karaoke machine for her eldest daughter's birthday, saying that they couldn't stop Amy 'singing' into it, adding, 'she talks much better when she's singing'. Julie seized the moment to suggest that, singing songs with Amy that she knew from nursery would be really helpful, and offered to print some out for the family to use with Amy at home.

During the Progress Check this time, Julie was careful to emphasise all the positives about Amy's development, including improvements in the child's language. There were also many more photographs and comments in Amy's Learning Journey for them to discuss, with Julie pointing out how the family's efforts to help Amy 'talk' had led to some real improvements. She couched the offer of support for Amy's speech, in the same way, suggesting this was just another means of helping Amy to be understood by everyone. Her mother's response this time was less negative, though still guarded.

When Julie shared this with Simon, he congratulated her on getting Amy's mother 'on side', adding that he felt sure the positive results from any interventions would soon show. He asked Julie what she had learned from the experience. The young practitioner agreed the key thing was to develop a good trusting relationship with the parents, through constantly celebrating each child's small steps in development, as well as providing clear 'evidence' in the Learning Journey, and encouraging contributions from families, while being sensitive and very positive during the Progress Check itself, especially if you have concerns about a child. She added that while doing the checks had reinforced what she had known, that no two families are the same, she needed to take more account of this diversity. She did add, however, that the timing of the check could be problematic, depending upon how long the child had been in the setting.

Simon was pleased with Julie's response, adding that the diversity found in families attending the setting was not as obvious as some he had worked in. Differences in child-rearing between individual families, he reflected, regardless of ethnicity and 'culture' were often subtle but hugely influential. Julie had clearly considered this and adjusted her practice.

Acknowledging some truth in Julie's final remark, Simon decided whether some further training of staff was needed. He also determined to clarify for himself how much flexibility in the timing of the check was available, and that to some degree depended upon closer working with local health visitors.

Simon began his next training session with an overview of the EYFS (2012). He emphasised the following points:

● Explanation of how the guidelines explore the many issues, challenges and dilemmas involved, and provides advice that relates to how the practitioner needs to reflect upon and ensure their approach is both inclusive and anti-discriminatory.

● The emphasis on practitioners attempting to understand the specific needs of parents, gaining knowledge and understanding of particular lifestyles or beliefs and establishing some common ground around child-rearing practices through thoughtful and meaningful communication.

Task Discuss and critically evaluate Julie's practice in this scenario. Reflect on Simon's support, and discuss what might you have done differently. Reflect too, on how the practice issues in this setting might be taken forward.

Examples of reasons for delaying the check include: family difficulties that can impact on a child, such as bereavement, separation or the arrival of a new sibling, recent health issues, and children going through transitions.

Another aspect of the revised EYFS (2012) is the concept of 'school readiness', which suggests that while 'purposeful play' is the method through which the very young learn, by the time a child is in their Reception year, their experience should be that of more adult-led learning, in preparation for the 'formal' environment of the Year 1 classroom. Some critics of the 'school readiness' concept point out that summer-born children will be disadvantaged, having their 'play' time considerably shortened. They also challenge the very notion that children aged 4 and 5 years need to be introduced to 'formal education', and often cite examples of practice from our European neighbours such as Finland, where children are not introduced to formal education until the age of 7 years, whose cohorts still perform significantly better in international league tables than England:

> Finnish pre-school teachers placed less emphasis on reading and writing than the Year 1 teachers in England; yet, by the time they are 15, Finnish pupils are outperforming their English counterparts . . . by a considerable margin in reading literacy and by smaller margins in mathematical and scientific literacy.
>
> (Ofsted 2003, p.2)

A possible difficulty for the practitioner could now be in having to promote the real benefits of child-initiated play for younger children to parents, while justifying its absence in the Reception year.

Focus on practice

Justifying play

Lily, a UPP, in a private daycare setting, felt crestfallen as she finished tidying the room at the end of a particularly busy day. The reason for her low-self esteem was a brief conversation she had just had with Joseph's mother, 'All you lot do with the children is play, he can't write his name yet. What do I pay you for?' Lily had looked over at 3-year-old Joseph who'd taken his chance, while the adults were talking, to play in the sand tray with some of the small world people creating a world of battles and secret places. She began patiently to explain as she had on several occasions to his mother, how important child-led play was for Joe, but his mother cut her short, promising to 'take this up' with the deputy manager. Lily knew that the deputy would have sympathy with Joseph's mother's opinion, to some degree, as would a few of the staff. The issue of child-led and adult-led play was something she had 'battled' with when she first began working at the setting.

Identifying good practice

The new manager had what Lily considered to be a more open-minded approach, and after a few months, when staff training for the EYFS 2012 began, allowed Lily to speak on the respective benefits of child-led and adult-led play, 'as you'll be up to date with the research'.

She'd been nervous, but managed to engage staff through a selective use of videos of child-led and adult-led activities, then getting staff to experience model-making freely, then with an adult leading them. Some refused to engage, but were less vocal about it all being 'a bit silly and pointless', when Lily showed the power point on recent research into the positive effects of play, interspersing it with clips from Swedish and Finnish settings, of 'forest schools', as well as 'centres of excellence' in the UK where a balance of child-led and adult-led play was normal practice.

Leading practice

She finished to a silent room, after she had showed the OECD 'league tables' where the UK were significantly lower down than other European countries in terms of their children's abilities in numeracy and literacy. The final slide contained the findings of the latest UNICEF report (2007), that put England bottom of this particular league table, for children's well-being. Apparently English children were the most unhappy and had the lowest self-esteem. 'You'll notice at the top of both league tables are countries that encourage children to engage in playful experience until at least their sixth birthday, when more formal education begins.' The manager thanked Lily for her input and asked for questions. When none were forthcoming, with several staff looking at their watches, the manager suggested practitioners went away and thought about it, but as staff were leaving, Lily heard several negative comments, 'It's alright for them, they've got "forests" on their doorstep', 'they haven't got pushy parents'. 'It doesn't work here.' 'These children need to be challenged.'

ReflectionThe 'pushy parents' remark made Lily reflect. It was true, parents were very interested in their child's development, something that Lily had welcomed at first, it being so different from the other settings she had experienced. But the longer she worked here, the more she began to feel that parents were 'setting the agenda'. Many of the children would be going on to private schools. She had hoped that the new manager would resist suggestions to formalise practice before the children were 'ready'. So she went to see her, trying to ward off any negative comments from the deputy manager. Lily suggested that it might be good for parents to be given some input on the benefits of learning through play, and that she would be pleased to help organise such an event. She also suggested, acknowledging that it might 'cost' in terms of staffing, that some members of staff might visit a 'centre *of excellence' for themselves. The manager agreed with the suggestion about informing parents, and to Lily's delight said that she and a number of other setting managers would be visiting Pen Green in the near future, and she was considering the setting become an 'outpost', 'a centre of energy'. Without having to express her concerns about some members of staff, her manager thought a visit to a neighbouring 'prep school', whose staff she knew personally, and who knew the value of play, balancing their practice between child-led and adult-led play, would perhaps be more beneficial. Lily could see the appropriateness of this suggestion. It was often the 'projected' pressure of 'preparing' very young children for formal education too soon that led to some staff constantly 'leading' and 'prescribing' children's play in the setting.*

Lily felt she had achieved something, after her meeting. The parents and staff would be exposed to different but very effective practice, and her manager continued to show her openness to new ideas about the value of children's play and sharing this with parents.

Task Discuss with colleagues the above scenario. How would you have reacted in Lily's situation. Do you feel Lily's situation is commonplace? How might settings using this balanced approach respond to the government directives on 'school readiness'?

Examination of research findings that identify and exemplify current good practice may help support practitioners in developing their own partnerships with parents, for, as Siraj-Blatchford and Manni (2006) suggest, good practice, effective pedagogy and strong partnerships with parents/carers must be complementary if a child's learning and development is to be rich and empowering. Discussions with other professionals both within and beyond their settings may also support the development of successful ideas and practices. The practitioner's own understanding of what parental involvement is and how it can be achieved, needs, however, to be grounded in the specific needs of their own setting and the families that attend it through ongoing dialogue with all stakeholders.

> **In what ways can the EYP lead practice to ensure that multi-agency team working is understood, valued and used effectively in supporting children's particular needs, both among professionals within the setting and external agencies?**

In looking at the EYPS Standards, we need to have a clear understanding of the EYP's leadership role both within and beyond the boundaries of their settings.

Leadership of multi-team working within the setting

Caution needs to be used when considering theories around team building, team working and team management, as most of these derive from a business perspective; see Rodd (2007). Early Years setting leaders have traditionally been expected to adapt their role on a daily basis, moving between the direct care and education of children to leading practice and being a member of a team, to leading and line-managing the team. The demarcation lines between being a team colleague and a leader are blurred to say the least. However, expectations with regard to roles in Early Years practice are continuing to grow. Given the Coalition Government's specific investment in Early Years, and their focus on 'payment by results'; all leaders of practice need to be aware that there is an on-going emphasis on accountability, alongside expectations of excellent practice within settings. So in a time of increasingly ambitious expectations, we need to investigate what is meant by *leadership* in terms of the EYP's role and how it is different from a traditional model which has tended to be much more about the *management* of a setting and its staff.

Whalley (2005) suggests that effective leadership within the context of Early Years settings demonstrates the ability to:

- Enhance the learning and development potential of 0–5 year olds
- Encourage, enable and empower parents in their roles as parents and primary educators
- Develop and enhance the skills and knowledge and understanding of staff, including other leaders and potential leaders to enable them to work in ways that are:
  - Reflective, thus informing practice
  - Not professionally and/or personally 'role precious'
  - Recognising the need to work across professional boundaries for the benefit of children and families
  - Innovative
  - Evidencing a commitment to ongoing professional development, of themselves and others.

(Whalley 2005, p.10)

An EYP can demonstrate all of the above without necessarily line managing any members of staff within a setting. Research indicates that there is no single behaviour, trait or style which defines 'good' leadership behaviour. Goleman (2000, p.5) specifies six leadership styles:

- The *Coercive* leader demands compliance;
- The *Authoritative* leader mobilises people towards a vision;
- The *Affiliative* leader creates an appropriate emotional climate;
- The *Democratic* leader builds consensus through participation;

- The *Pace-setting* leader expects excellence and self-direction;
- The *Coaching* leader develops people for the future.

He adds:

> According to the data, the authoritative leadership style has the most positive effect on climate, but three others — affiliative, democratic, and coaching — follow close behind. That said, the research indicates that no style should be relied on exclusively, and all have at least short-term uses.
>
> Goleman (2000, p.5)

Reflection *One of the authors of this chapter leads a team in a Further and Higher Education College. She reflects: You aspire to be a particular type of leader when you are able to work within the boundaries of your 'ideal self'; however, you do have to adapt your style to suit*

- *The individual(s) you are working with at any given time*
- *The actual situation/task you are trying to manage*
- *The culture of the organisation in which you are all working*
- *The relationship that exists between yourself and the people or person you are trying to work with at the time*
- *Other people involved in the situation, for example, children, parents, wider community.*

She says 'whilst I aim to be a pace-setting, affiliative, democratic leader who coaches future leaders, circumstances sometimes force me to become an authoritative, coercive leader, which I find very uncomfortable.'

Task Consider what type of leader you are/wish to become and record your thoughts on this in your journal. Revisit this at regular intervals when these arise through your critical incident analysis (see Chapter 1). Additionally, consider the situations which move you from your ideal style to see if there is a pattern and/or trigger. Might there be any ways that you can guard against this?

Goleman goes on to propose that the most successful leaders have strengths in the following emotional intelligence competencies:

- Self-awareness
- Self-regulation
- Motivation
- Empathy
- Social skill.

And that these are equally important in leadership activities. He concludes, in agreement with the points in the reflection box above:

Each (style of leadership) makes use of the key components of emotional intelligence in different combinations. The best leaders don't know just one style of leadership; they're skilled at several, and have the flexibility to switch between styles as the circumstances dictate.

(Goleman 2000, p.1)

Siraj-Blatchford and Manni (2006, p.12) in their ELEYS (Effective Leadership in the Early Years Study) urge the need for caution against the straightforward application of research findings to leadership in Early Years settings. Many such findings come from research based in Primary and Secondary schools where 'outstanding leadership' has been unequivocally linked to 'improving organisational performance and raising achievement'. Children's centres, daycare settings and nursery schools are rather different organisations in which these authors propose that the role of leader is correspondingly likely to be subtly different, identifying 'categories of effective leadership practice', regardless of specific setting, that were indicated by the findings of the REPEY case studies (Siraj-Blatchford and Manni 2006):

- Identifying and articulating a collective vision; especially with regard to pedagogy and curriculum.
- Ensuring shared understandings, meanings and goals: building common purposes.
- Effective communication: providing a level of transparency in regard to expectations, practices and processes.
- Encouraging reflection: which acts as an impetus for change and the motivation for ongoing learning and development.
- Commitment to ongoing, professional development: supporting staff to become more critically reflective in their practice.
- Monitoring and assessing practice: through collaborative dialogue and action research.
- Building a learning community and team culture: establishing a community of learners.
- Encouraging and facilitating parent and community partnerships: promoting achievement for all young children.
- Distributed leadership.

(Siraj Blatchford and Manni 2006, pp.26–7)

Task Access the ELEYS report at http://acecqa.gov.au/storage/eleys_study. pdf. Work with your setting colleagues to consider to what extent your setting embodies the bullet points presented by the authors above, and where improvements could be made. Ideas and documents from an exercise of this nature would be strong candidates for inclusion in the evidence that you present for validation.

Southworth (1998) suggested that leaders need to recognise the complexity of their role and understand that settings are dynamic rather than static organisations, which are continually evolving (see the quote from one of the authors above about her experience of leadership). There is also a need to recognise that contexts differ at every level; for example, they differ between individual children, families, local communities, socio-economic classes and cultures. Added to this is the ebb and flow of staff morale and energy levels, the arrival of new staff and students and the departure of others are just some of the factors to which settings need to continually adjust and make room for new energies, opportunities and challenges. The need for a Leading Practitioner to act as a combination of leader, supporter and innovator of good practice is today more necessary than ever. How this role will vary to some degree within each setting, is what Siraj-Blatchford and Manni (2006, p.26) refer to as 'contextual literacy'. They add to this that leaders in Early Years settings need to have a strong commitment to collaboration (which may feed into 'distributed leadership', see list above) and improvement of learning outcomes. The EYP role, with its emphasis on *leadership* rather than management was created to fill this niche.

Teamwork

Having looked at research and practice in terms of the EYP's leadership role generally, we now need, in order to address the original question, to look at the EYP's role in establishing team confidence in and value of multi-agency working. In order to do this effectively, we need to look at the concept of teamwork. Margaret Edgington (2004, p.54), provides us with examples of the types of teams we might find in many Early Years settings:

- The *cosy* team are a close-knit 'inward-looking' group of practitioners with well-established patterns of working, which they feel are effective. They are, therefore, resistant to change, especially if it is suggested by a new member of the team. In practice they will probably ignore, sometimes quite obviously, any suggested changes.

- The *turbulent* team are outwardly accepting of any suggested changes, making little comment at team meetings, but subversive in their comments when out of earshot. Such 'undercurrents' of disagreement are often picked up by visiting students to the setting. Members of this kind of team will subtly ignore any suggested change.

- The *rigorous and challenging* team live up to their name, being committed to change and reviews of practice, sometimes as a means of improving their own continuing personal development (CPD). Usually quite knowledgeable about the latest reviews, they engage in debate, embracing any changes that eventually have the agreement of other staff.

(Edgington 2004, p.54)

From the above descriptions it can be seen that in attempting to lead such teams, the EYP would require very different and considered approaches in order to fully engage them (see the personal comment above from one of the authors on this point).

In the variety and complexity of Early Years settings from pre-school playgroups, children's centres, private daycare, foundation units, nursery schools and primary school nursery and Reception classes there are varied and complex 'teams' that reflect particular hierarchies in terms of roles and responsibilities. Rodd (2007) proposes that teamwork should involve the subordination of individual needs so that team members are able to fully engage in joining coordinated activity in a concerted attempt to reach common goals, and that this is particularly important in early childhood services where a united effort is more likely to succeed in the complex arena which centres around children, families, their relationships and their feelings.

Task Visit http://www.businessballs.com. You will find that it offers a huge selection of team-building activities and team-building games that you can browse completely free of charge.

If you are interested in personality analysis, you may also find the online test on http://www.humanmetrics.com/cgi-win/JTypes2.asp of interest, and you can find a deeper analysis of the Myers-Briggs 'types' on http://www.geocities.com/lifexplore/mbtypes.htm also completely free of charge.

Do remember, however, that personality theories are just that – theories, and that human beings are individuals, not 'types'. The only way to really work out how people respond to various situations is to get to know them.

Action research

Action research is a particular type of research methodology that developed over the last half of the twentieth century in education and health practitioner education. The basic method involves measuring a particular area of practice, enacting a change and measuring the impact of the change. This can be enacted on a 'loop' until the practitioner is convinced that the practice has been developed to an acceptable standard.

Figure 8.1 A diagrammatic view of action research

Source: Opie, C. and Jarvis, P. (2012) Introduction to Methodology, in P. Jarvis, S. Newman, W. Holland and J. George (eds) *Research in Early Years: a step by step guide*, p.61, © Pearson Education Ltd 2012.

Reflection *Veteran practitioner-researcher Angela Anning proposes that the following should be deeply considered before embarking on a practitioner research project:*

- *The paramount importance of confidentiality in observing, listening to and reporting on the behaviours of young children and their parents.*

- *The need to understand the sensitive nature of using cameras and when deciding what to write in field notes.*

- *The need to be very sensitive to the ways in which researchers attempt to engage in dialogue with very young children and in interview processes with Early Years workers.*

- *The impossibility of getting fully informed consent to be a research participant from a child under the age of 7.*

- *The need to reflect on potential conflicts between a professional role serving the needs of children, families and communities and the researcher's role in 'objectifying' the objects of enquiry.*

- *The potential for the research processes to influence/change relationships with colleagues. (For example, what if they express an opinion that is highly antithetical to your own? What if they exercise their right to withdraw from your research?)*

- *Are practitioners always able to be non-judgemental about practice in their setting? (For example, when assessing a rota system that has previously caused the researcher a lot of personal inconvenience.)*

- *What will be the results of honestly sharing your findings with your colleagues? Might this sometimes create issues within the setting, in certain circumstances?*

Anning warns: 'the brutal fact is that your position as a professional gives you power over your community; but is it justifiable to use this power as a researcher as well, without serious thought and preparation?' (Anning et al. 2010, p.190).

Question

Have you carried out any research projects alongside your EYPS training pathway, or did you do so on a first degree? Did you take into account the points that Anning makes above? Reflect on this in your journal, and then consider how you might bring these ideas into your own ongoing research activities and in supporting students and/ or colleagues in your setting who are engaging in research for various qualifications.

This drive towards effective multi-agency working, Frost suggests needs to be balanced with the development of practice within individual professions and settings:

Efforts to improve children's services systems should focus on positive organisational climates rather than on increasing inter-organisational services co-ordination. This is important because many large-scale efforts to improve children's services systems have focused on inter-organisational co-ordination with little success and none to date have focused on organisational climate.

(Frost 2005, p.21)

If such an organisational climate is to be empowering and effective it needs to reflect some or all of the categories suggested by Siraj-Blatchford and Manni (2006) in their ELEYS project report (see above).

> **Task** How can leadership impact on organisational climate and vice versa? Continue the evaluation of leadership in your setting that you started above. Which aspects do you think you would find most and least easy to develop within the organisational climate in which you work? Consider other settings in which you have worked/been on placement where the situation would be quite different, and how the balances of easy/difficult with regard to specific aspects would change.
>
> You may choose to carry this out as a private exercise in your journal or share with colleagues, whichever may seem most appropriate in your current situation.

The importance of the team

You can use theories around the identification of specific roles within a team as an effective team-building tool: they can help to reinforce your understanding of the fact that everyone is bringing something to the team, and that you all need each other if you are to be successful. A good team leader will work to individual strengths and preferences. Although preferred roles are relatively unchanging over time, most people can happily perform two or three roles, sometimes simultaneously, particularly important in small settings.

Alongside having the right mix of roles and personalities, teams also need other pieces of a complex situational 'jigsaw' to fall into place. We cannot assume however that individuals will recognise that they are expected to be working *together*; therefore the EYP may need to allow reflection time for team members to recognise their interdependence as well as their independence.

This deals with the 'inside' team, but EYPs are also frequently called upon to work with professionals outside the remit of the individual setting in looser 'team' constructions. The next section deals with such 'multi-agency working'.

Multi-agency working with external professionals

For some settings, such as children's centres, contact with other professionals is more easily facilitated, as external professionals are more visible within the varied life of the centre than, for example, in schools, where they may work in side rooms or individual classrooms on an infrequent basis. For some settings, accessing external agencies can be somewhat problematic, as a result of limited resources and heavy workloads.

This vision of effective multi-agency working is underpinned at statutory level by the Childcare Act (2006). Edgington (2004, p.2) maintains that early childhood practitioners have always worked within a multi-disciplinary context because, 'services for children and families have been developed by professionals holding a range of qualifications within the disciplines of education, social work and health, and are (variously) funded by and organised by the local authority, by private enterprise or by the voluntary sector'.

However, simply having or being exposed to a range of professional expertise does not equate to integrated working, nor can we simply assume that those professionals work in collaborative ways to achieve shared outcomes for children and families. As we noted earlier, the Childcare Act (2006) (see Chapter 4) and associated legislative frameworks now put a duty on Early Years services, education, social and health services in particular to work in synthesis.

Challenges

The challenges to effective integrated team working are not to be underestimated; they involve bringing together staff from a range of cultural and social backgrounds, and frequently involve overcoming professional and/or cultural practice barriers to work towards common goals, maximising the benefits to children and families. Professions tend to create 'communities of practice' (Lave and Wenger 1991) in which certain ways of doing things and expressing ideas using specialist language may exclude others. Profession-specific language used in the workplace may be unfamiliar to those from a different profession, for example teachers use acronyms such as SATs (Standard Assessment Tasks), EBD (Emotional/Behavioural Disorder) etc. which may not be familiar to health workers, whereas the Emergency Services phonetic alphabet (e.g., Alpha, Bravo, Charlie, Delta etc.) may be everyday parlance to health workers, but not at all familiar to teachers. Hence it can be sometimes difficult for practitioners from different professions to work together seamlessly. These are not inconsequential issues and they need to be addressed sensitively if we are to be successful in multi-agency working to the benefit of children and families.

Evidence from the studies of Wigfall and Moss (2001) suggest that there are common barriers to effective team-working:

- Loss of individual professional identity
- Competitiveness
- Poor communication, leading to feelings of isolation and resentment
- Lack of shared vision and shared understanding of desired outcomes.

These factors are often underpinned by poor management and weak organisational structures and/or the use of inappropriate leadership styles.

Focus on practice

Majid's transition

Majid, had just turned 3½ years old when he arrived at his new setting, a nursery class attached to a children's centre. He and his parents had moved because of his father's new job; a move from Birmingham where there had been extended family, to a strange city, with few friends. Majid's mother spoke little English, relying on his father to interpret in most situations. He'd been unable to be there during the home visit, so the nursery had sent Nabeela, a bilingual teaching assistant, with Rachel, a GPP, soon to experience her EYP final assessment. The house had boxes in each room, waiting to be unpacked, and Majid was swinging from the curtains, as his mother nervously told him to stop. He was finally distracted by the teaching assistant as she unpacked a basket of toys, and called him over.

Identifying good practice

Rachel, with the help of Nabeela, managed to find out Majid's interests, as well as the necessary information about dietary requirements, home routines, his health and well-being, and if he had had his two-year Progress Check. His mother looked unsure at the last question, but then nodded. With Nabeela's help his mother explained she was making allowances for Maijd's behaviour as there had been a lot of sudden changes, but she expected he would settle down before he began nursery. As Majid had only offered single words in response to Nabeela's questions while they played, Rachel asked if Majid was confident in using his home language. His mother used her hands to express 'a little bit', adding what Nabeela, translated as 'difficulty in saying some words'.

After the visit, Rachel prepared all the documents in readiness for Majid's arrival at nursery. She had made sure there were some of Majid's favourite resources available (dinosaurs and trains) on the day of his first visit. To the surprise of his mother, he seemed to settle well, and after two weeks was happy to see his mother wave goodbye. Rachel tried to make a point of having Nabeela on hand to interpret at home time, and had asked his mother for family sayings and names for everyday routines in his home language, so he could see these displayed around the setting. As Rachel began to observe Majid, she realised he was being quietly aggressive to some of the other children, nipping them or pushing past them to get to a toy he wanted, and he rarely reacted when his name was called. Rachel became concerned when Majid didn't respond to Nabeela's gentle requests for him to have 'kind hands', and as he rarely turned at the mention of his name, began to wonder about his hearing. His language had shown no real improvement, he still spoke only in his home language, and that infrequently.

Leading practice

Before calling in Majid's parents, Rachel asked the Speech and Language Therapist, who visited the setting regularly to support a number of children who had been identified through the Progress Check at 2, if she would observe Majid, adding she couldn't find any paperwork to support his being checked at two years.

After observing Majid, she felt he was having difficulty articulating words, as a result of his open-mouthed breathing, often caused by congestion in the nose and sinuses. This had led over time to him being 'flat tongued', and he needed a period of referral to correct this. She left some simple activities for Rachel to carry out with Majid, such as helping him sip through a straw and learning to breathe with closed lips, and blowing his nose. She also suggested his congestion might be affecting his hearing. When Rachel mentioned this to his mother, she appeared

➡

quite alarmed, nodded quickly and took Majid home mid-conversation. The next morning, Majid's father arrived with him, wanting to know why his son had been seen by some specialist without his consent, adding that there was nothing wrong with his young son. With Nabeela's help, Rachel tried to explain why she had asked for Majid to be informally observed, and that any official referral would naturally have to be agreed with his parents. That seemed to mollify his father, who remained adamant that his son did not need to see any 'specialists', adding it was Rachel's job to teach Majid English.

Rachel discussed the situation with her nursery's manager, who suggested she and Rachel, together with the Speech and Language Teacher should meet with Majid's parents. It took several proposed meetings before Majid's parents turned up, during which time Majid's language had not improved significantly, and his behaviour had worsened. His father's body language spoke his disapproval, but after listening to the professionals, his manner softened and he finally agreed, not only to speech and language interventions but to a hearing test being carried out, to see if Majid's 'constant colds' were having some impact on his hearing. After this meeting, Rachel's manager made formal referrals to both the Speech and Language and Hearing Impairment teams. His speech and language support came through quite quickly, but there was a delay with Majid's hearing test. His Speech and Language teacher offered to speak with the local peripatetic teacher for hearing, in support of the nursery's referral. It took several more phone calls by the nursery manager before Majid was finally seen. The result of the hearing test showed some depression in hearing in his right ear that would need to be monitored and might require minor surgery if it didn't improve.

Reflection *Discuss with colleagues the strengths and weaknesses of the above scenario. How would you as an EYP have reacted to Rachel's dilemma? What does this tell you about multi-agency working?*

Conclusion

This chapter set out to address those Standards which underpin the EYP's role in effecting a wide range of working partnerships that can enhance the learning and development of children through multi-agency practice. Focus has also been placed on the role of the EYP as a *leader* rather than as a manager, modelling good practice and supporting teams within settings. Literature, theories and research initiatives that support these Standards have also been explored, and you have been asked to identify with and reflect upon practice evidence supplied through various scenarios. Two key questions were examined.

What strategies are needed to ensure that effective working partnerships with children and their families are valued and embedded in practice in order to promote children's well-being, learning and development?

In attempting to answer the above question, consideration of what 'the family' means in contemporary Britain and its impact on children's learning and development was discussed. The need for practitioners to reflect on their own values and beliefs in order to develop meaningful and inclusive partnerships that value the diversity of children and their families was shown to be underpinned by considerable research into working in partnership with parents/carers. This section established the need for practitioners to avoid a 'deficit' model of parents' abilities and instead recognise and celebrate them as being children's first educators.

The need for EYPs to lead and support practice in establishing authentic partnerships with parents means going beyond a surface structure that simply involves them in supporting various practitioner-instigated activities within the setting. Empowered parents should be involved in decision making and policy issues, and should be welcomed by practitioners as co-researchers and co-facilitators of their children's learning and development. It is the EYP's responsibility to lead staff away from the 'unilateral' relationships that can often exist between parents and a setting where information about children moves from staff to parents, and rarely in the opposite direction.

In what ways can the EYP lead practice to ensure that multi-agency team working is understood, valued and used effectively in supporting children's particular needs, both among professionals within the setting and external agencies?

The traditional roles of the leading practitioner within an Early Years environment were examined along with the need to develop the role of the EYP. Theories and research underpinning concepts around effective leadership were examined, for example, Goleman's (2000) ideas on the links between emotional intelligence and successful leadership. The findings of the Effective Leadership in the Early Years (ELEYS) project undertaken by Siraj-Blatchford and Manni (2006) were also considered. Finally, the complexity of creating a successful 'organisational climate' as suggested by Frost (2005), in the full range of contemporary Early Years settings, with all their diversity, was investigated. A final word from Whitaker offers a concise and realistic definition of the complexity of a leader's work:

> Leadership is concerned with creating the conditions in which all members of the organisation can give of their best in a climate of commitment and challenge. Leadership helps an organisation to work well.

> (Whitaker 1992, p.74)

In attempting to answer the above question, consideration was also given to how a team is defined, and the roles within it. There is a need for the EYP to be proactive in encouraging reflection on the part of staff so that they recognise their interdependence as well as their independence, and in ensuring that practitioners feel valued as individuals while working collaboratively. The EYP, as leading practitioner, also needs to agree with staff from the onset the setting's ethos with regard to relationships with parents and carers, and the value placed on the concept of 'the child within the family'. The practitioner must also sensitively support the staff within the setting to underpin the team's endeavour to address the individual and

233

holistic needs of each child, which will involve leading and supporting practice through multi-agency working, in particular, overcoming professional barriers to achieve a common aim, while simultaneously developing the day-to-day work of core specialist teams.

Further reading

Anning, A., Cottrell, D., Frost, N., Green, J. and Robinson, M. (2010) *Developing Multiprofessional Teamwork for Integrated Children's Services: Research, policy and practice* (2nd edn). Milton Keynes: Open University Press.

Brock, A. and Rankin, C. (eds) (2011) *Making it Work for the Child: Professionalism for the early years interdisciplinary team*. London: Continuum.

Frost, N. (2005) *Professionalism Partnership and Joined up Thinking in Frontline Children's Services*. Totnes: Research in Practice Series.

Johnson, S. (1998) *Who Moved my Cheese? An amazing way to deal with change in your work and in your life*. New York: Vermillion.

Rodd, J. (2007) *Leadership in Early Childhood* (3rd edn). Maidenhead: Open University Press.

Siraj-Blatchford, I. and Manni, L. (2006) *Effective Leadership in the Early Years Sector (ELEYS) Study*. Available at: **http://acecqa.gov.au/storage/eleys_study.pdf**. Accessed on 25th April 2012.

References

Anning, A., (2010) '"Research" in early years settings, a pause for thought'. *Early Years: An International Journal of Research and Development*. 30 (2): pp.189-91.

Anning, A. Cottrell, D. M., Frost, N., Green, J. and Robinson, M. (2010) *Developing Multiprofessional Teamwork for Integrated Children's Services: Research, policy and practice* (2nd edn). Maidenhead: Open University Press.

Belbin, M. (2004) Management Teams: Why they succeed or fail. London: Butterworth-Heinnemann.

Bourdieu, P. (1977) *'Cultural reproduction and social reproduction'* in J. Karabil and A. Hasse (eds) *Power and Ideology in Education*. New York: Oxford University Press, pp.487-511.

Brock, A. and Rankin, C. (eds) (2011) *Making it Work for the Child: Professionalism for the early years interdisciplinary team*. London: Continuum.

Bruce, T. and Meggitt C. (2006) *Childcare and Education*. Abingdon: Hodder Arnold.

Centre for Social Justice (2010) The Centre for Social Justice Green Paper on the Family. London: Centre for Social Justice

DFES (2012a) *Early Years Foundation Stage Statutory Framework*. Cheshire: DFE Publications.

DFES (2012b) *Early Years Foundation Stage Practice Guidance*. Cheshire, DFE Publications.

Edgington, M. (2004) *The Foundation Stage Teacher in Action*. London: Paul Chapman.

EPPE (2004) Available at: http://eppe.ioe.ac.uk/eppe/eppeintro.htm

Evangelou, M., Brooks, G., Smith, S., Jennings, D. and Roberts, F. (2005). *The Birth to School Study: A longitudinal evaluation of the Peers Early Education Partnership (PEEP) 1998-2005*. London: DfES.

Finch, J. (1984). *Education and Social Policy*. London: Longman.

Frost, N. (2005) *Professionalism Partnership and Joined up thinking in Frontline Children's Services.* Totnes: Research in Practice Series.

Ghate, D., Hazel, N. *et al.* (2002) *A National Study of Parents, Children and Discipline.* London: Policy Research Bureau.

Goleman (2000) Leadership that gets results. Available at: <http://academy.clevelandclinic.org/Portals/40/HBRLeadershipGetsResults.pdf>. Accessed on 25 April 2012.

Lave, J. and Wenger, E. (1991) *Situated Learning: Legitimate Peripheral Participation.* Cambridge: Cambridge University Press.

Malaguzzi, L. (1997) quoted in H. Penn, *Comparing Nurseries: Staff and Children in Italy, Spain and the UK.* London: Paul Chapman.

Ofsted (2003) *The Education of Six Year Olds in England, Denmark and Finland: An international comparative study.* London: Ofsted Publications Centre.

Opie, C. and Jarvis, P. (2012) Jarvis, P., 'Introduction to methodology', in P. Jarvis, S. Newman, W. Holland and J. George (eds) *Research in the Early Years: A step by step guide.* Harlow: Pearson Longman.

Raey, D. (1998) *Class Work: Mothers' involvement in their children's primary education.* London: University College Press.

Rinaldi, C. (2005) *In Dialogue with Reggio Emilia.* London: Routledge.

Rodd, J. (2007) *Leadership in Early Childhood* (3rd edn). Maidenhead: Open University Press.

Siraj-Blatchford, I. and Manni, L. (2006) *Effective Leadership in the Early Years Sector (ELEYS) Study.* Available at: http://acecqa.gov.au/storage/eleys_study.pdf. Accessed on 25 April 2012.

Southworth, G. (1998) *Leading Improving Primary Schools.* London: Falmer Press.

UNICEF (2007) An Overview of Child Well-Being in Rich Countries. Available at www.unicef-irc.org/publications/pdf/rc7_eng.pdf. Accessed on 23 August 2012.

Whalley, M. (2005) *Leadership and Management in the Early Years.* Pen Green: Pen Green Base.

Whalley, M. (2007) *Involving Parents in their Children's Learning.* London: Paul Chapman.

Whitaker, P. (1992) *Managing Change in Schools.* Milton Keynes: Open University Press.

Wigfall, V. and Moss, P. (2001) A study of a multi-agency childcare network. Available at www.jrf.org.uk/sites/files/jrf/391.pdf. Accessed on 23 August 2012.

Part 4

Becoming an Early Years Professional: validation and beyond

9

Managing your placement supervisor, mentor and your own continuing professional development

Poonam Cant

Chapter overview

The Standard addressed in this chapter is :

8. Lead practice and foster a culture of continuous improvement.

The text will consider key points and examples of work-based learning that relate to candidates on specific EYPS pathways. These key points are as follows:

- The role of a placement supervisor
- The role of a mentor
- Expectations of an EYPS candidate
- Managing the relationships with supervisors and mentors well
- Approach while in placement.

There is advice and guidance for candidates in paid work, and for those in placement, attempting EYPS at different stages of their career.

Florentyna's 'CPD'

Florentyna had just finished her Foundation Degree in Early Years, and during her application process to take the BA (Hons) top-up in Early Childhood Studies her interviewer asked her whether she wished to sign on additionally to the Early Years Professional UPP, as the setting was in a 'super output' area and she would qualify for a government-funded place. Florentyna discussed this with her supervisor at work who agreed that this would be a very good idea. In her subsequent conversation with the training centre, Florentyna was asked whether she had equivalent qualifications to GCSE English and Mathematics from the school and college qualifications that she had from Poland, where she had grown up. The training centre offered a service that would inform her of the English equivalents of these qualifications (via a UK agency called 'NARIC', see **http://www.naric.org .uk/**). When Florentyna's results came back, she discovered she had the equivalent of both GCSE Mathematics and English at grade C or above. Florentyna did, however, feel that she still needed to improve her spoken English skills. The course leader for the BA (Hons) Early Childhood Studies explained to Florentyna that this was the first stage of her 'CPD' – continuing professional development, which she would discuss with her tutors, mentors and placement supervisor throughout her BA (Hons) and EYPS training programme. Florentyna was subsequently referred to a higher-level English as a Foreign Language class for higher education students that she was able to access for no charge through her EYPS training centre.

Introduction

At this point, Florentyna's next questions would be likely to be: 'who will be my mentor?' and 'How will I be expected to work with them?' This chapter will attempt to provide basic answers to these questions. Candidates on placements are assigned a supervisor and mentor to help them during their placement. The supervisor is the candidate's direct line manager. Those who are in paid work like Florentyna will already have a supervisor, while those who enter work placement will be allocated to a supervisor on arrival. The mentor may be a more experienced colleague within the candidate's setting, or a qualified EYP who has been employed by the training provider to mentor the candidate. As such, the supervisor and mentor have slightly different roles but they share a common goal of preparing the candidate to be successful in gaining EYP status. They play a facilitation role to ensure that the candidate has appropriate experiences and opportunities and they also prompt and support the candidate in their professional development, which will include activities within the workplace and external training.

The role of a placement supervisor

The placement supervisor is responsible for professional decisions concerning the candidate's progress, performance and assessment. Within the setting they are likely to be team leaders and first line managers. As such, they familiarise the candidate with the setting, staff and policies and procedures. Once placement has begun, they take an interest in how the candidate is performing and delivering against agreed objectives and act as a facilitator to ensure the candidate attends meetings and team discussions of relevance and gains the experience needed.

The supervisor is likely to set the candidate specific tasks during placement and to subsequently direct and guide the candidate in the performance of these tasks. Supervisors do not usually perform the tasks themselves but the activities they undertake may model good practice and share responsibility. They are available to discuss the approach the candidates will adopt, and their conclusions and ideas. Supervisors also provide a managed environment where goals are set, meetings are scheduled, resources are allocated and deadlines are set. As the relationship develops, the supervisor is likely to provide personal support as well as feedback on progress. They will also help to write a professional development plan for the candidate once they have observed them in practice and identified areas for improvement.

The role of a mentor

Mentors are usually well-established practitioners with significant leadership experience. They are likely to be Early Years Professionals and will have therefore been through the assessment process and possibly be assessors themselves. They can help to clarify understanding of the Standards and the evidence required, but they must not give detailed advice relating to the content of validation tasks ,or coach the candidate in any way. They can also be helpful in supporting staff at the setting to understand the EYP assessment process, the tasks candidates are likely to get involved with, and the Standards against which they will be assessed.

The role of the mentor is to provide encouragement and to act as a sounding board. For example, sometimes a candidate may wish to discuss how to overcome difficulties in negotiating with staff in the setting in order to obtain the experience they need. Mentors support candidates to find solutions rather than solving problems for them. They also act as a facilitator to help candidates to identify gaps in their knowledge and to gain opportunities for any additional experience they may need. They may help the candidate to consider and seek options within or external to the setting.

Focus on practice

GEP candidate Janine is on placement in a children's centre and is aware that in order to meet the Standards she needs to build relationships with parents and be able to lead and support others in this aspect. As she is new to the setting and has little experience of working with under 5s, she discusses this with her supervisor. The deputy manager seems very reluctant to let Janine talk to parents directly. Janine does not know how to approach overcoming her reservations, so she discusses this with her mentor. The mentor prompts Janine to think about why the deputy manager may have concerns and then urges her to think of ways she can address them. Janine researches possible training and talks to other practitioners; she then decides that she should approach the manager again but this time with a plan and justification. She clarifies her understanding of the Standards she aims to meet with her mentor, and she explains these to her supervisor. With a clearer understanding the supervisor decides to set Janine a project on improving working with parents within the setting. This not only involves consultation with staff, parents and other professionals but also enables Janine to improve her skills as she attends some formal training on working with parents. Janine and her supervisor agree that she will run workshops with staff and parents and cascade the training material she has produced to her colleagues.

Reflection *Janine has used her mentor for support to successfully overcome issues she has faced in getting her setting to support her in the activities she needs to undertake. The mentor has helped Janine to think about the solution herself and to structure her thoughts in the form of a plan and training. Providing her supervisor with a justification has helped towards a solution that not only develops Janine's professional understanding, but produces wider benefits to the setting. Janine will now be supported in working on a project which will prove invaluable for her EYP written tasks, tour visit and documentary evidence file, and possibly undespin a witness statement. The setting will improve the quality of its provision - a win-win situation.*

Expectations of an EYPS candidate

An Early Years Professional is defined as a highly skilled practitioner who raises the quality of provision in an Early Years setting. As such, whatever the training pathway, EYPS candidates in paid work and on placement will be expected to be 'self-starters'. The expectation will be that you have the potential to swiftly become a confident and knowledgeable practitioner with the ability to meet objectives, complete tasks and deliver results to a given deadline. You will be expected to provide leadership and support to change, shape and improve practice in the setting and make a real difference. The supervisor, staff in the setting and mentor will quite rightly have very high expectations of you, hence they will set challenging tasks and expect tangible results. If candidates feel that they cannot rise to this challenge, they also have to question how they will deal with the independence required to produce the materials and performance tasks worthy of a 'met' outcome at validation.

The supervisor is usually a very busy individual with a demanding job role and schedule. They will not have time to nurse you through a placement. They will expect you to highlight your own needs and have the ability to work out solutions for yourself, demonstrating an independent ability to overcome potential barriers. You will be expected to possess suitable time-management and project-management skills to deliver the tasks assigned to you. In other words, on a day-to-day basis, it is likely that they will expect you to manage yourself.

Work placement supervisors will expect you to have a high level of knowledge about the Early Years Foundation Stage (DFE 2012) and to quickly build a strong working knowledge of the setting's policies and procedures, what you are doing within these, and standard concepts of Early Years best practice (see, for example, the references to the Common Skills Framework in Chapter 2). However, in the early days, the supervisor should expect to have to coach GEP candidates in particular to relate all this to the day-to-day practice of the setting, as they develop practitioner skills and child development social policy knowledge.

You will be expected to work alongside regular staff at the placement, striving to achieve the aims of the setting hosting the placement, while continually reflecting on and trying to improve your own skills and your contribution to the placement. The supervisor will not expect to have to sort out basic issues around team working, as they will expect you to be mature and empathetic in your approach.

It can be very difficult for EYP GEP candidates to gain the respect and credibility of others, let alone 'lead and support' if they do not have much experience of working in an Early Years setting. To overcome this, such candidates should familiarise themselves with their colleagues and empathise with them as this is vital to their own success. All EYPS candidates, whatever their pathway, should strive to recognise that their needs and rights and those of others have equal importance, while those of the children are clearly the main focus of every care and education setting. You should adopt a style of communication that your colleagues are comfortable with, ensuring that you consult with all stakeholders, e.g. children, managers, other practitioners and parents. You should try to foresee problems and attempt to solve or overcome them before they become an issue. Most importantly you should show respect for yourself and others. If you can demonstrate that you work well with colleagues and children, the supervisor will be confident that you have the potential to lead and support change.

Focus on practice

Before GPP candidate Thomas, a primary school teacher, starts his placement he analyses gaps in his experiences, his strengths and weaknesses and identifies that he needs to gain experience of working with babies. He discusses this with his placement supervisor and they arrange a period of time where he works exclusively in the baby room. He discusses areas of provision that he is uncertain about, e.g. feeding, nappy changing etc., with his supervisor and she ensures that the room leader is aware of gaps in his experience. Together they formulate a step-by-step plan to ensure that he ➡

will steadily gain knowledge and experience. He establishes a good rapport with the staff in the baby room and takes time to understand how each person likes to work. He takes time to observe, as part of his training, and he offers to help where he sees staff are struggling. He makes himself familiar with the policies and procedures of the setting and the allocation of duties across the setting and in the baby room. He shadows each member of staff for a period of time to increase his awareness about their practice and the guidance offered by the setting. He asks detailed questions about the babies and their routines and the manner in which this information is gathered. He listens to staff and sensitively asks questions to increase his knowledge. While undergoing this process he notices that routines are not formally updated with parents. Rather than raising this with management he talks to staff first and realises that they are asking for the information and that it is recorded in the daily diary used to exchange information, but that there is no formal mechanism to update the routine board, which means the information can be out of date. He talks to staff, and volunteers to do this, with the result that they are grateful; they see the merit in doing it but feel they do not have time, so his input to the setting is perceived as highly positive by all concerned.

Reflection *Thomas has analysed his own professional development to identify gaps in his experience and discusses them with his supervisor, enabling her to facilitate the acquisition of the skills he requires. He uses different methods to familiarise himself with policies, procedures and practice within the setting. He takes time to get to know his colleagues and respects them by helping them, listening to them and consulting with them, which means that when he does wish to initiate change they are willing to listen and can see the merit in his actions. As the supervisor can see positive changes there will be increased confidence in his capabilities. One issue that may arise with GPP candidates who have substantial experience in classroom environments is that they may give an impression to baby room staff that their roles are somehow less 'important' than those of a classroom teacher, and that the development of babies is less complex than that of older children. This can be very frustrating for baby room placement hosts, given the huge amount of neuronal development in the period preceding the third birthday! However, Thomas has very carefully avoided this pitfall.*

Managing the relationship with supervisor and mentors well

You must manage the relationship successfully with your mentor and supervisor to ensure that the support and input needed are timely and secured. It is vital to remember that all parties share the same goal, which is for you to be successful in developing professionally and in achieving EYP status. Relationships should be managed well by all parties, as, while they are generally rewarding, there is the potential for frustrating elements to creep in that may build up to confrontation, see the example above. You should always make sure that you understand what the supervisor expects of you and that you make best use of the time allocated to you. You can help to meet this goal by trying to:

- Think for yourself by setting your own objectives, drafting plans, reflecting and analysing practice, and regularly discussing these with your supervisor and mentor, making revisions where agreed.

- Arrange formal meetings and remember to arrive well prepared and on time, as you are not the only demand on the supervisor/mentor's time.

- Plan for meetings to ensure that you use the time efficiently. If necessary, email information in advance, and summarise discussions to avoid misunderstanding and to highlight any issues.

- Be honest, as placements are a period of training and you are unlikely to get everything right first time. Even though discussing errors can be very uncomfortable, by keeping the supervisor and mentor informed you will gain their respect and also be able to discuss avoiding similar scenarios occurring again. Avoid blaming others for difficulties experienced – while you are unlikely to be to blame for all problems arising, you are unlikely to be completely blameless in all situations. Considering where you could have done things better is at the core of reflective practice and therefore constitutes a key point that informs CPD. If you are experiencing difficulties, the supervisor and mentor are there to help you. The worst scenario is that a lack of progress is interpreted as a lack of enthusiasm and effort.

- Keep a sense of perspective on any feedback that the supervisor/mentor gives you, as they are trying to improve your performance. You must use this as a learning process and actively ask for suggestions on how to improve. You should respect and follow the advice given, as the supervisor and mentor are more experienced, and the supervisor in particular knows the setting and its staff, children and parents better than you do. This means that a solution that may appear promising in the abstract may not be feasible within a particular setting at a particular point in time. GEP candidates especially should remember that 'perfect world' solutions are unlikely to be helpful in a 'real world' practice environment.

- Take the initiative by inviting feedback rather than waiting for the supervisor to offer it or criticise. You should ask questions that show that you are independent and can respond to feedback, e.g. Am I doing enough? Where can I improve?

- Discuss reflections and analyses to ensure that you are fully supported to identify development requirements or initiatives that need to be worked on.

- Show that you are enthusiastic and passionate about your work and the setting. By going the extra mile, you will gain the respect of others.

- Plan your work to ensure you have enough time and resources to meet deadlines, particularly those set by the supervisor.

Focus on practice

UPP pathway candidate Rohana identifies that she has little experience of working in the pre-school room. She also has no multi-professional working experience. Before she starts her EYP training she meets with her mentor and they agree to a brief ➡

meeting every other week with email contact when necessary. Before their first meeting Rohana identifies her personal aims and what she needs to do to meet the Standards. During their first meeting they discuss her personal objectives and gaps in her knowledge and experience. The discussion enables the mentor to identify possible tasks/projects that Rohana could lead, not only to close these gaps in her skill set but also to support more junior staff. Rohana takes notes of their discussion and next time they meet they agree two specific tasks and analyse whether or not they need resources, training and staff involvement. They also discuss timescales and 'deliverables'. Rohana emails a summary of the meeting to her mentor, also cc'ing her supervisor. While undertaking one task, Rohana realises she has upset a member of staff and makes her mentor and supervisor aware of this. During a phone conversation with her mentor, Rohana considers how she might repair this relationship. She subsequently discusses this with her supervisor and consequently accomplishes it successfully. She also researches training and resources and uses a progress report as the agenda for the following meetings. She ensures that she is prepared for each meeting and sets a clear agenda each time which covers progress to date and issues. She makes most meetings and, when she cannot, she takes the initiative in rearranging for a mutually convenient time. During one meeting Rohana seeks input on her progress, and learns that her supervisor would like her to change her method of communication from a newsletter to staff to a workshop so that she can get a more comprehensive input from all who work in the setting, and would like Rohana to help her with this.

Reflection *Rohana has identified her own objectives and has set up regular meetings. She takes time to read and familiarise herself with the Standards and has thought about what she needs to do to ensure she meets them. By being clear, she quickly gets agreement for her role. By taking the time to prepare and document their meetings, she is able to update her mentor on progress so that they are left with more time during the meeting to discuss her approach and outcomes of her work. As a result, Rohana develops professionally as she is receiving more qualitative input. Her honest approach and her quest for feedback enable her to adapt her work flexibly to suit the setting and get better results. The relationship between candidates, mentors and supervisors should ideally mirror a 'developing conversation', added to in short, productive chunks of dialogue, rather than long periods of non-contact followed by detailed feedback, in which it may emerge that one side or another has been labouring under a misunderstanding for quite some time. The candidate should never forget that they are at the centre of this relationship, and therefore must own the greatest responsibility in keeping it running smoothly.*

Approach while in placement

You should show an element of personal enterprise by seeking areas of opportunity where you can initiate change in order to drive continuous improvement. The setting supervisor will almost certainly have an idea of aspects of practice that are ripe for development and, given the constraints on their time, may be grateful for someone else to take the lead on these. You should work with the supervisor to identify skills or projects that are needed and which you can lead and be responsible for. These projects can provide excellent material for the written, documentary and tour elements of the EYPS assessment process as well as bringing significant benefits to the setting (see Chapter 10).

To ensure that you manage the supervisor and mentor well during your placement, you must take a structured approach to your work while completing tasks set by yourself, your mentor and your supervisor. To produce quality work that will bring positive change to the setting and that you can use for EYP assessment, you should regularly document your work and make ongoing reflections and analyses thereon to bring about improvement. The professional journal (see Chapter 1) is a very useful vehicle for this. If you do this well there will be significant benefits to the setting and you will gain an understanding of your immediate professional development and more long-term continuing professional development. The following simple guidelines may help you to structure your work.

1 Plan

You should start by using an objective approach to reflect on what you have done in the past and where you are now. You should list the skills and resources available and how they have been developed to allow you to establish strengths and weaknesses. Once you have done this you should align yourself with the professional challenges you are likely to face. Any skills gaps identified require an action in your development plan. If you are taking an academic qualification alongside your EYPS training, the Personal Development Planning or Personal Planning and Development module within this qualification should support you in this endeavour.

You should analyse what brings out your best performance and ensure that you operate on projects that use your skills to the greatest advantage, while facilitating a conducive environment. You should be aware of the views of others such as managers, colleagues and parents and what they have said about your performance, your strengths and areas for development, always considering if one of these could provide a strong witness testimony for you (see Chapter 10). You should consider where you would like to go in the future and then scrutinise your strengths and weaknesses, and find ways within the standards to address these.

You should spend adequate time thinking through your aims, objectives, options and actions, considering these in the light of a SWOT (Strengths, Weaknesses, Opportunities and Threats) analysis of your existing skills and the relevant workplace. You should set objectives, plan actions and manage time and resources effectively in order to achieve personal and organisational goals aiming for and attempting to achieve high standards. You may also find the use of Specific, Measurable, Attainable, Realistic and Time-based (SMART) targets helpful in this endeavour.

2 Research

You should take time to research and know the way the setting is organised and to become familiar with its policies and procedures. By understanding the mission statement and the aims and objectives of the setting, you can determine possible ways that you can help your supervisor achieve them by making a high-quality contribution. A sound knowledge of the Early Years Foundation Stage (2012), up-to-date knowledge of child development theory and relevant social policy, and concepts of best practice are essential (see Chapter 2), but in addition you should keep abreast of current thinking and critically evaluate options that may be relevant for implementation in the setting. You should develop your knowledge and skills by researching, analytically reviewing and discussing areas of provision; those who show true leadership potential are always developing their knowledge and skills and those of their colleagues, not seeking short cuts or 'quick fix' solutions.

3 Prepare

You should visualise your performance before you start, to enable you to foresee any issues and allow you to mitigate them. You should talk to other staff in the setting to enable you to consider the best way to go about your tasks. It may be advisable to shadow experienced practitioners for a period of time to gain the benefit of their knowledge and approach. You should take time to identify the skills, people, resources and time available and consider funding, training needs etc. and how they are going to be secured. A collaborative and mutually agreed approach is more likely to result in successful implementation than hasty, quick-fix, maverick 'solutions'.

Ensure that all options have been considered before a proposal for resources is put forward, as the nature of Early Years work means that there are considerable demands on resources. To get support for resources or training you need to help your supervisor by providing a justification. You need to 'sell' the proposal to those in authority by making it relevant to the project and show that it will make a measurable difference to practice by improving standards and/or quality. The mentor's role in this thinking process is also key, in that they can as a 'sounding board'. If a proposal enables additional or enhanced skills to be acquired then it is more likely to be supported.

The project plan should demonstrate considerable benefits to the children and the setting to ensure that you get support from all staff for the project. It is important to draft an action plan so that all work is clearly linked to achieving the objectives and to break the work into manageable steps and 'deliverables'.

Focus on practice

GPP candidate Rosy reviews the EYP Standards and identifies that her weakness is her ability to clearly demonstrate the 'Take responsibility for improving practice through appropriate professional development, for self and colleagues' aspect of Standard 8, as EYPS training is the first formal CPD she has taken in the past five years. She discusses this with her mentor and they analyse which areas are most likely to be needed for her role as a practitioner and for the projects Rosy is working on. They determine that the setting has invested in resources to promote the use of ICT but they are not being used by staff or the children as effectively as they could be. Rosy suggests to her supervisor that she undertake a project which focuses on use of ICT while working with children, developing both her own practice in this area and the practice of other staff. Rosy agrees to lead a project on identifying ICT equipment available and how to use it as part of their work with children. Rosy and her supervisor decide that Rosy will use Microsoft Word and Excel to plan the project, produce project updates, prepare guidance and training notes for staff. They include an objective of training in Microsoft office packages on her development plan; Excel and PowerPoint in particular. They consider the options and decide that rather than attending a formal training course Rosy will have access to the nursery administrator, who is skilled in this area, unlike Rosy who dislikes technology in general!

They subsequently agree the primary objective of the project is to train the staff to use ICT in their work with children, which has been somewhat lacking in the setting despite the proficiency of some of the younger staff with their smartphones! Rosy takes this away and produces a set of smaller steps, having consulted with other practitioners in the setting, before she starts any practical intervention. For example, they agree that one of the steps will be 'evaluating training options on products available for use in the setting' and include this in the plan. Rosy then agrees the resulting project 'deliverables' with her supervisor and they agree these will form the agenda for future meetings and updating on progress.

Reflection *By considering her own shortfalls and discussing them with her supervisor, Rosy realises that she shares this weakness with her colleagues. This results in her leading a mutually beneficial project for the setting. Clear objectives and 'deliverables' are set and Rosy uses ICT to keep the supervisor informed. This should lead to a good working relationship throughout the project and, provided the 'deliverables' are met, should lead to a satisfactory result. Rosy increases her confidence and is able to use her ICT project in her tasks to demonstrate how she has met the Standard. She has documentary evidence for her file in the form of project plan, minutes, training notes etc. She may be able to generate information for the tour and collect some witness testimonies from the basis of this activity.*

4 Perform

You should use your intuition and be confident in your own abilities, reinforced through practice and training; however, you should welcome feedback and suggestions for improvement. By breaking challenges down into smaller achievable steps or tasks, you should consider options at each stage and try to ensure that you have adequate time to think and reflect. You should have confidence in your own judgements, but you should discuss your analysis and approach with other staff in the setting to gain feedback. Wherever possible, you should consider innovative and creative practice and use your initiative to demonstrate your adaptability and problem solving. It will help the supervisor if they can rely on you to use acquired knowledge and work cooperatively with the staff in the setting, as this means the project will have longer lasting value.

5 Communication

You should communicate effectively throughout with the supervisor and all those with whom you interact, including (sometimes especially) those with whom you collaborate in a multi-agency fashion, using a wide range of appropriate methods. For example, you should use speech, writing, technology and behaviour effectively in order to present and exchange opinions, ideas and information. Effective communication will earn you significant respect within and outside the setting.

6 Teamwork

You should work with others in order to establish and achieve common goals. By forming effective working relationships with staff in the setting and getting them involved in projects you are more likely to be successful. You will be able to undertake a variety of roles, both collaborative or in a leadership role, if you are successful in forging good relationships.

You should cooperate by sharing ideas and encouraging others to contribute theirs. If you work in synergy with others and share responsibility through challenges, collectively you will deliver more and make more of an impact. You should identify the contribution of others honestly to your mentor and supervisor so that they also get recognition. You should try to anticipate potential for conflict and aim to remove it or mitigate it. By playing to people's strengths and as a reliable and trusted member of the team, you will be able to lead and support others. If you know and understand the specific team dynamics within a setting (see Chapter 8), you can build on this to develop your leadership qualities.

7 Reflect

You should take a step back and analyse your actions, causes and effects. The professional journal is an ideal vehicle for this purpose (see Chapter 1). You should consider:

- how effective your planning and preparation was
- your research and whether or not you could have implemented/may in future implement other methods
- your style of participation
- how you effectively obtained, recognised and validated the contribution of others
- what you observed and whether or not you tried to take an unbiased view when watching and listening, and to what extent this was successful
- your decisions, actions, strengths and needs for further development
- how well you analysed events, actions, responses and behaviour and whether or not you did this objectively
- the learning gained not only by yourself, but by colleagues, children, parents and relevant others
- building the learning gained into effective planning for the future.

Focus on practice

While working on placement, UEP candidate Jim observes that the children play well when the age groups are mixed. But within this setting, the children are normally segregated by age: babies, toddlers and pre-schoolers. After several conversations with both his mentor and his supervisor, he decides to work on a project looking at adopting a multi-age approach in the setting for specific activities. He also plans to use this as the basis for his practitioner research assignment for the BA in Early Years degree he is taking alongside his EYPS training. He receives a lot of negative criticism from the other practitioners, as they believe it is too difficult to facilitate group activities, but his supervisor has read many articles about the topic and is keen to introduce the concept to the nursery.

Jim and his supervisor decide to trial some activities with children from each age group to determine whether or not it is a feasible initiative. Having trialled a few different activities it becomes apparent that the multi-age approach is very successful for quite a few activities and that it was worth introducing this to the setting. To convince other staff, Jim produces a purpose-designed version of the report that he has written for his module assignment, which summarises the research he has conducted and his reflections upon the trials performed, their results and what was gained by each of the parties impacted, e.g. the children, staff and parents. He discusses this with his module tutor, mentor and supervisor, and makes some minor revisions based on their advice before sharing it with his colleagues. His reflective piece identifies some issues, but convinces the other practitioners of the merit of mixing age groups for certain activities and persuades them to trial it. The practitioners become willing to experiment with this approach, and it becomes part of their short-term planning. Jim becomes very interested in this area of practice, and decides to visit a setting that has fully adopted an integrated multi-age approach, to further his knowledge in this area.

Reflection *Jim has used his research and reflection on play to identify an opportunity to change and improve practice. His reflective practice allows him to identify issues which can be overcome, and is very useful in persuading others to embrace change. He produces a variety of purpose-designed training materials on this specific area of practice, using these to communicate his ideas to colleagues, and, in so doing, also helps them to develop their practice and that of the setting. When he achieves his EYPS he engages in CPD by becoming an expert within this area of practice, via collaboration with other settings, initially within his own location and then within a wider geographical area. Jim eventually moves on to study for a Masters of Early Years degree, which gives him the opportunity to collaborate with one of his Masters module tutors to write a journal article on the multi-age approach.*

8 Review

Effective mentors and supervisors will regularly ask the EYPS candidates with whom they are working the following questions:

- What did you want to achieve?
- What actually happened?
- What went well?
- What didn't go well?
- What would you do differently next time?
- Did you identify ways to sustain a commitment to development?
- Can you identify how you have changed and added value to the setting and to practice?
- Can you demonstrate that you have contributed to change which has benefitted the setting?

It is also extremely useful to use the professional journal to reflect on these points on an ongoing basis, so you have already reflected upon the answer to these questions before you are prompted to do so by your supervisor and/or mentor.

Focus on practice

Having completed half her time at placement, GEP candidate Freya decides to assess her skills by carrying out a review of people's perception of her as a practitioner. This is an innovative approach, never used before by the setting, but Freya has used it before in her previous career in marketing. She wishes to use the information she collects to enable her to review her progress and performance to date with her supervisor.

She decides to adopt a '360-degree' approach and solicit the views of her past work colleagues, other practitioners and managers both directly and indirectly involved with her day-to-day work, other professionals working in the children's centre, parents and the children. She also asks a colleague to take detailed observations on her personal practice and leadership skills.

Having collated all the information, Freya analyses all the points and, where possible, determines the reasons for views expressed. She identifies examples of good practice and areas for improvement for her supervisor. It was apparent that Freya was highly regarded within the setting but that the parents were not aware of her work and influence within the setting apart from the information from their children and their limited exposure to her as an individual. However, she realises that, using this approach, she has not managed to give a clear picture of the tangible results her work has delivered or the benefits of the changes to practice she has inspired. Nor does it reflect Freya's own concerns about her limited experience in leading a team discussion. She decides to list these and add them to the agenda for discussion.

Freya concludes with her supervisor that she must add a development objective to her personal plan, and that this will be leading a team debate. They also agree that she can take on more responsibility and get to know the parents by running a workshop for them on the EYFS (2012), which will feed into the work that volunteer parents carry out within the setting. This will bring benefits to the parents, the children, the staff and the setting. Freya and her supervisor agree to use the 360-degree approach at her next review as it has given them valuable information. Freya's supervisor will also recommend this approach to her other senior staff.

Reflection *Freya has used an innovative approach to assessing her skills but, recognising that it does not give a complete picture, she has used her initiative and collated more information for her meeting as this also raises development points. By using these methods Freya has made her supervisor's job much easier and has added some important development objectives for herself to ensure she continues to improve professionally.*

9 Continuing professional development (CPD)

Reflective practice will enable you to:

- develop intuition
- increase effectiveness of observation
- identify strengths and weaknesses
- avoid repeating mistakes
- avoid blame and encourage respect for delivering practice.

It is important for you to set yourself developmental objectives focused on your professional competence, either on your own or with your placement supervisor. Continuing professional development (CPD) is essential for Early Years Professionals to maintain, improve and broaden their knowledge and skills and develop qualities to enhance their professional life.

You should seek a wide variety of opportunities, not just academic/formal training courses (as we saw in the example of Jim), to improve your professional competence. You should plan to undertake a broad range of activities specifically chosen to better equip you professionally. Some ideas include:

- analysing and employing innovative practices
- attending workshops
- networking with other EYPs or other professionals working with children
- visiting other settings and shadowing professionals working in other settings or in other professions with children
- seeking professional accreditation or quality assurance and getting noticed for your professional expertise.

Conscious updating of professional knowledge can also be achieved by pursuing qualifications, attending seminars or courses and undertaking research. You should learn by continual reading, and reflecting on your own practice as well as shadowing that of others. Multi-agency working can also be highly instrumental in developing senior practitioner skills within the contemporary Early Years environment, and building most directly upon those skills that EYPs most specifically hone through their highly multi-agency focused professional training.

We hope that this chapter helps you to negotiate the complex web of skills and relationships that Early Years Professionals need to build to succeed in the multi-agency workplace of the future. The remaining chapters will look forward to the validation process, and listen to a wider range of voices from Early Years Professionals reflecting upon their thoughts about gaining Early Years Professional Status, and the range of professional roles that may be open to them in the children's workforce of the future.

Further reading

Cottrell, S. (2005) *Critical Thinking Skills: Developing effective analysis and argument.* London: Palgrave MacMillan.

Hobart, C. and Frankel, J. (2004) *A Practical Guide to Child Observation and Assessment.* London: Nelson Thornes.

Melhuish, E. (2006) 'Policy and research on preschool education and care in the UK', in E. Melhuish and K. Petrogiannis (eds) *Early Childhood Care and Education, International Perspectives.* Abingdon: Routledge.

Mitchell, H., Wild, M. and Swarbrick, N. (2007) *Early Childhood Studies Reflective Reader.* London: Learning Matters Ltd.

Northedge, A. (2005) *The Good Study Guide.* Milton Keynes: The Open University.

Redman, P. (2005) *Good Essay Writing (A Social Sciences Guide).* London: Sage.

Schon, D.A. (1983) *The Reflective Practitioner: How professionals think in Action.* New York: Basic Books.

Journals

Children Now

Early Years Educator

Educational Researcher

Nursery World

Reference

DFE (2012) The Early Years Foundation Stage. Available at:
http://media.education.gov.uk/assets/files/pdf/e/eyfs%20statutory%20framework%2020 12.pdf. Accessed on 26 April 2012.

10

Surviving validation

Pam Jarvis and Jane George

Chapter overview

This chapter will address key points and questions that you are most likely to be confronted with as you move through the validation process at the end of your training pathway. It will cover the generic aspects of EYPS validation, including the Development Review, preparing for the written tasks and preparing for the setting visit. Candidates should note that training providers work within geographically organised consortiums, and each consortium may choose to carry out the specified activities in different ways. This is a major change from the programme that ran between 2007 and 2011, where the processes for validation were nationally standardised. This chapter is therefore only a general guide, and you are urged to contact your provider if you have questions relating to the exact format of processes such as the specific structure of the written assignments/tasks (different centres may refer to them as one or the other), or a breakdown of the assessment visit processes.

Candidate reflections on validation (2007–11)

A very experienced leading practitioner reflected: At the time I probably hated it and thought God, this is a ridiculous exercise, but actually with the benefit of hindsight I can see that it was quite a valuable exercise . . . It was quite a good way of assessing people skills and their ability to tackle situations, and in fairness they are the type of situations that you do face, and they are difficult situations, so I think in hindsight it was a very good way of selecting people that were appropriate to get through the EYP process . . . It helps you to understand what you have done, where you have shown true leadership and possibly identify areas where you could improve, same with innovative practice, the biggest thing I got out of it was the reflective side, and I think that is a skill that doesn't come up earlier on in your education with child care. So I think it was a really valuable skill to take back and I think having done the EYP process now, I do engage in reflective practice a lot more.

➡

> *A practitioner on the 'long pathway' (the equivalent of the current UPP) re-*
> *flected:* One of the most nerve-wracking things I've ever done in my life. I was
> absolutely petrified . . . But yeah, I got through it . . . I suppose . . . it's up to you
> to go out, and if you really want that qualification and that status, you're going to
> have to go out and grab it, it's not going come on a plate.

The Development Review and the summative assessment process

What is it?

The process consists of briefing and preparation for assessment and the final assessment itself. Briefly, it comprises the formative Development Review followed by the summative written tasks and follow-up setting visit.

The preparation for, and completion of, the Development Review, the resulting Action Plan and the final assessment is common to all four Early Years Professional Status pathways. Whatever the length of the pathway, or structure of training programme, all candidates will be required to demonstrate their practice and leadership skills in working with babies, toddlers and young children through a range of formative and summative processes designed by the consortium who manage the EYPS delivery within the relevant region. The resulting programme will be delivered by the individual training provider.

When does it happen and how much of my time does it take?

Candidates move through the formative and summative assessment processes as they become increasingly ready for assessment against the Standards. This means that the timing of the briefings, Developmental Review, Action Plan and final assessment will vary from pathway to pathway. GPP candidates, who have most of the skills that they need to complete EYPS when they sign onto the programme will be expected to move from beginning to end in six months. UPP candidates, who are experienced practitioners but need to attain a minimum of 60 academic credits at level 6, and GEP candidates who have a full degree on admission to their training programme, but need to attain a significant amount of practice and leadership experience will normally have 12 months to complete. Most UEP candidates will also move through the programme in 12 months, but some providers may offer a longer period of training, which commences before candidates have completed the second year of their degree. Where this is the case, candidates will be warned that they have an *absolute maximum* of two years from signing on to the pathway to completion; there is no scope for an extension beyond this point. There may, however, be some possibility for short extensions for candidates on pathways lasting six months or a year; although this is only usually permitted when severe and unexpected problems crop up in the candidate's life outside their EYPS training programme. For example, serious illness of oneself or a close relative is likely to be looked upon sympathetically; asking time to be added to your EYPS pathway so that you can go on holiday or deal with the pressure of day-to-day work is not! Asking for time to be added to your pathway will normally require a formal application process to the consortium through the lead institution (not simply to your individual training provider), so we strongly advise you to consult with your training provider as soon as possible if you begin to seriously think that you may need an extension to your pathway.

How does the EYPS assessment process 'work'?

Early Years Professional Status validation process: the basic steps

NB *The specific way that these activities are designed and timed will vary from consortium to consortium.*

Step 1	1 day in training centre Exploration of the role of the EYP Detailed consideration of the Standards The Forward Agenda
Step 2	Candidate in Early Years setting (employment or placement) Exploration and initial self-review against the EYPS Standards Some training providers may do this through a 'personal development planning' (PDP) or 'professional planning and development (PPD) module that also gives you credit towards an academic qualification
Step 3	1 day in training centre Briefing on the written tasks
Step 4	Time in setting to consider how the written tasks will be approached, and to further develop opportunities to gain experience
Step 5	1 day in training centre: preparation for the Development Review
Step 6	Time in setting Preparation of formal self-analysis against the EYPS Standards. Materials sent by candidate to training centre for examination by the assessor who will conduct their Development Review
Step 7	The Development Review: candidates undertake a range of set tasks defined by the relevant EYPS training consortium and receive feedback from an assessor. Candidates must then use this feedback to draw up a formal action plan towards validation
Step 8	Prepare validation written tasks or assignments and reference these to the Standards
Step 9	1 day in training centre Review written tasks or assignments with peers Prepare for the setting visit by an assessor Finalise date for the setting visit
Step 10	Time in setting Put finishing touches on preparation, e.g., complete activities that relate to the production of witness statements and preparation of the document file; make practical preparations for visit (e.g., arrange cover etc.). Plan activity for assessor observation

Step 11	Send copies of written tasks, assignments and any other documentation (e.g. witness testimonies) required to the training centre to be forwarded to the assessor for examination before the visit
Step 12	Visit to setting by assessor. Timings and order of the day's activities will vary, but will typically include time for the assessor to: ● Examine the Portfolio of evidence (Document file) which must include at least three witness statements ● Undertake a tour of the setting ● Undertake an observation of practice ● Undertake an interview with the candidate ● Plus reflection and writing time at various points in the process. The visit is therefore likely to take up most of one working day.

What is the Development Review?

The Development Review is a formative assessment process undertaken by the training provider that aims to review and provide feedback on a candidate's readiness for EYPS validation. The assessor will also need to consider the extent to which the candidate fully understands the Standards, and the level at which they will be assessed with respect both to practice and leadership skills.

The government have proposed that the core attributes that identify an Early Years Professional are:

● A reflective practitioner;

● A practitioner who leads and supports colleagues in order to effect change and improve outcomes for children;

● A good listener;

● Able to tune into what colleagues know and can do;

● Sensitivity to colleagues' readiness for change;

● Able to explain the rationale for particular changes;

● Able to draw on a repertoire of strategies for inspiring, influencing and negotiating with others.

(The Teaching Agency 2012a, pp.6–7)

How do I prepare for the Development Review?

The Development Review will:

● Determine the candidate's understanding of the EYPS Standards

● Determine the candidate's progress in evidencing the EYPS Standards

● Determine the candidate's ability to communicate clearly and confidently

- Provide the candidate with an opportunity to receive interim feedback on their progress
- Review and support the candidate's progress towards achieving a successful EYPS validation outcome
- Produce an action plan for the candidate to support successful completion of EYPS.

(The Teaching Agency 2012b, p.6)

Every consortium will go about this process slightly differently, but the key supporting statements outlined above should be thoroughly covered. Training providers who belong to the same consortium will follow the same procedures in both the Development Review and the validation processes.

The early stages of preparation for validation includes a briefing on the Standards, and candidates should consider early in their pathway what is actually required to demonstrate practice and leadership against the EYPS Standards. They will be invited to complete a self-review against each of the Standards and in this, they should consider a breadth of ways in which they might be able to meet the requirements Standard. Candidates should be able to flexibly apply the Standards to the examples that they provide for the assessor in their written tasks and documentary evidence – the supporting statements and amplifications provided for each standard should be of use here (The Teaching Agency 2012c).

> **Reflection** *Consider the example of the candidate producing a safeguarding policy for a setting that we gave you in Chapter 3. How many Standards/supporting statements do you think that she would be able to apply to this if she includes this in her document file?*
>
> *Standard 3 'Safeguard and promote the welfare of children' is an obvious one to select here, but can you also see some relevance in Standard 8 'Lead practice and foster a culture of continuous improvement'?*

In preparation for the Development Review, candidates will be asked to analyse the Standards using the supporting statements and amplification in terms of which areas might be easily met from their current body of practice examples and why, and which might need further development before the assessor's visit to their setting.

Here are two examples:

Candidate A is an experienced leading practitioner on the GPP; she writes:

Standards about which I am most confident and why	I am very confident about Standard 1 'Support the healthy growth and development of children from birth to the age of five' and Standard 2: 'Work directly with children and in partnership with their families to facilitate learning and support development'. I have 15 years of experience in practice since gaining my CACHE diploma, and gaining my BA (Hons) in Early Years five years ago after managing a setting for ten years has boosted my confidence to engage in a round of continuous improvement that was rewarded by an 'excellent' Ofsted grade six months ago. Specific examples are as follows:

➡

	• I was commended by the latest Ofsted report for a series of presentations that I had given relating to the interface of theory and practice, first of all to practitioners, and then in a slightly revised version to parents. • I created a series of activities to help children understand 'keeping healthy' relating to diet and exercise, and revamped the key worker system to ensure better communication between the setting and the children's families. • I supported one of our young placement students in her creation of a 'kindness tree' where children nominate each other to have their name and kind behaviour written onto a leaf-shaped post-it by a member of staff, and stuck onto a large poster of a leafless tree that the student made at college.
Standards about which I am least confident and why	I am less confident about Standard 3: 'Safeguard and promote the welfare of children', as my setting is one of a chain of private day nurseries which deals with safeguarding at a higher level than the individual setting manager. Policies are provided, and reports have to be made to an Early Years teacher who is employed to circulate around three settings in different parts of the city. In particular, I am not sure how I am going to show leadership in this area.

Candidate B is on the GEP, he writes:

Standards about which I am most confident and why	I am generally confident that I have the knowledge and practice ability to demonstrate Standard 1 'Support the healthy growth and development of children from birth to the age of five'. My placement has given me the opportunity to lead on the provision of a number of stimulating activities for children of different age groups and of various stages of learning development once they found that I was quite innovative in this way. I think this is due to my degree in psychology, where I did all the developmental module options. I feel that I am also quite good at meeting individual needs, as I was painstakingly taught how to observe behaviour in my first degree; I also volunteered at a youth club during my entire three years at uni, and soon began to use the observations I had to carry out to inform some of my assignments to additionally inform planning for activities with particular youngsters in mind. This has been directly transferrable to my work in the Early Years setting. So I do have some confidence that I will at least be able to make a start on demonstrating Standard 5: 'Make use of observation and assessment to meet the individual needs of every child': and Standard 6: 'Plan provision taking account of the individual needs of every child'.
Standards about which I am least confident and why	To be honest I am quite worried about all the other Standards, particularly Standard 8 'Lead practice and foster a culture of continuous improvement' and Standard 7: 'Fulfil wider professional responsibilities by promoting positive partnership working to support the child'. While my placement has been very good at letting me pilot activities, and bring other practitioners in to help me with this, particularly the level 3 placement students, I don't really lead anyone, and I am not party to the conversations that they have with other professionals coming into the setting such as the health visitor and the speech therapist. It is so difficult to show leadership of all types when you are not a paid member of staff in the setting.

The completion of a Standards reflection exercise may turn out to be quite a stressful experience for some candidates. They may not have as much time to give to this as they might ideally like, and it can also make the prospect of the summative assessment extremely 'real', magnifying their concerns that they may not 'make the grade'. Early Years practitioners are also typically quite modest and conscientious individuals, hence rather inclined to be 'hard on themselves', so do seek out advice and support from your mentor or tutors if you begin to feel like you will never get there! We can already see that the GEP candidate above certainly *is* likely to have some leadership evidence to offer, from the points that he has made about his work with the level 3 placement students in the setting! Perhaps he does also need to seek further experience of this nature however, and honest self-reflection may be the catalyst to talking to his mentor and placement supervisor about how this might be accomplished in the time available. Don't forget that peers may also be useful 'sounding boards' if you are just feeling a bit low!

One of the skills that entry pathway candidates in particular may benefit from practising in 'scenario-based' simulation activities is the requirement to see beyond immediate problems that arise in practice. Leaders often have to deal with such situations 'on the hoof', but they should also use them as reflective exercises to ensure that the same situation does not arise again. Your training provider may use such scenarios in training sessions to try to build confidence and understanding of wider issues. The following is an example of such a scenario for general discussion and reflection.

Focus on practice

Kushi is the manager of a small day nursery that is located within a large converted terraced house. It has a large, enclosed garden at the back to which the children have free, supervised access during dry weather. The front door is accessed from a flight of steps that lead down to the pavement outside. The setting is located on a moderately busy road in a suburb of a large city. The front door is secured by a code-operated lock that is deliberately placed too high for the children to be able to access. Staff at the practice know that the front door is to remain closed at all times. The children's rooms are on the ground floor, the basement is used for storage, and the rooms for food preparation, staff room and office are on the top floor.

When the setting first opened, the owners had not intended to divulge the front door entry code to anyone but staff; however, as the children arrive and leave at very different times during the day, it was eventually decided that parents would be given the entry code if they would agree to ensure that the door was carefully closed after entry, and to sign a form promising not to divulge the code to others. The code is changed regularly, and Kushi carefully maintains an ongoing database of code rotation, and past/present code holders.

On this particular day, Kushi is coming down the stairs after her break when the front door opens and a very young woman who she does not recognise walks through the door. The woman then walks into the toddler room, leaving the front door and the toddler room door ajar.

Response

- What would you do?
- What underlying issues does it raise?

Kushi moves quickly to close the front door. She then walks quickly into the toddler room, closing the door behind her, to find one of the staff in conversation with the young woman. Kushi intervenes, informing the woman that she is the manager of the setting, and asking politely what she is doing here today, as she does not remember that they have previously met. The woman informs Kushi that she is Vicky, the aunt of one of the children, Nathan, and that she has arrived to pick him up early, as her sister (who is in the middle stages of pregnancy), has been unexpectedly admitted to hospital.

Response

- What would you do?
- What underlying issues does it raise?

Kushi explains that she is not able to release children to an adult who is not listed by the setting as a carer, and that before releasing the child to his aunt's care, she will have to check with the designated carers that it will be OK to do this. Vicky begins to argue that she must take Nathan now, as her sister . . . But Kushi continues to quietly but firmly insist that she must follow agreed procedure, and takes Vicky to a waiting area, asking her deputy manager to ring the designated numbers for Nathan's carers. When no answer is forthcoming, Kushi asks Vicky for the details of the hospital to which her sister has been admitted, and manages to ensure, through the hospital staff, that Vicky *has* been asked to collect Nathan by the designated carers. She then subsequently releases Nathan to Vicky's care.

Leading practice

As the leading practitioner in the setting, Kushi now needs to reflect on the situation that has occurred. She notes that:

- The divulging of the code by a parent to a non-designated adult has resulted in a situation arising that has endangered all the children in the setting; the situation has developed into a clear breach of safeguarding. If Kushi had not been coincidentally coming down the stairs when Vicky let herself in, one or more of the children could have emerged onto the street through the open door

- The situation then developed to a point where senior staff in the setting were put into a position where they were unable to avoid adding an extra problem for a family already trying to deal with a crisis situation.

She subsequently discusses the situation with her deputy manager. They decide on the following course of action:

- The owner of the setting will be asked whether the entrance can be restructured so that adults collecting children must pass through two doors, the outer one being unlocked, allowing them into a toughened glass 'porch' area, with the inner one remaining securely locked until opened by a member of staff.

- In the meantime, the entry code will be changed and parents/carers will have to ring at the existing front door. Kushi will construct the letter explaining the reasons for this (without reference to the specific incident).

- Parents will receive a completely separate communication asking them to update their 'emergency contact' record, with a specific reminder that it is particularly important to update this with the setting at times where there is some amount of change ongoing in the family, such as pregnancy, moving house etc.

- Kushi will ring Nathan's first named contact when the family emergency is over and express regret for any stress added to the event concerned, but also tactfully explain the situation that arose in the setting, and request during the conversation that the family are very careful to update Nathan's contact records during this time, so a similar situation does not arise again.

Reflection

- *How far does Kushi demonstrate the core attributes of an EYP outlined earlier?*

- *The course of action that Kushi and her deputy manager agreed to ensure that this situation would not occur again is only one set of choices – there would be other, equally useful ways to respond. Try to find an opportunity to discuss with colleagues or fellow students how you would collectively decide to deal with a situation of this nature.*

- *How should Kushi and her deputy manager respond if the owner of the setting decides that they are is not prepared to spend the necessary money for the entrance modifications?*

What must be remembered about the Development Review is that it is rare that a candidate can demonstrate a broad range of examples for every single Standard, however experienced they are, and it is equally rare for a candidate to have problems evidencing every single Standard; remember, no one is perfect! Feedback from the review should be informative and constructive, and should be discussed as soon as possible with your mentor. All feedback should make it clear whether weaknesses are significant or of minor importance, however, the vast majority of candidates who have been permitted to proceed into the Development Review by their training provider are likely to be generally working at the appropriate level. If they were not, the relevant issues will most likely have been raised before this point, most likely in interaction with a mentor.

As a result of the feedback discussion, candidates should be clear about whether they need any additional experience in order to meet the EYP Standards and what actions they need to take in order to meet all the Standards within the relevant time (for example a short placement). It is important to pay attention to this, and be guided by your Development Review assessor and your mentor because if a candidate does not have the necessary skills and practical experience by the time they arrive at the summative assessment, the thorough assessment processes undertaken will certainly find them out, and obviously a disappointing result is to be avoided at all costs.

Preparing for validation

Validation consists of the following:

- The candidate must produce a portfolio of evidence (a 'document file') which includes at least three witness statements relating to the candidate's practice against the EYPS Standards

- The candidate must produce a series of written tasks/assignments designed to assess the candidate's knowledge and understanding of the Standards, the content and construction of which will be specified by the relevant consortium

- An assessor will visit the candidate in their setting during a working day, during which they will:
  - Examine the portfolio of evidence (document file)
  - Undertake a tour of the setting, conducted by the candidate
  - Observe the candidate in a demonstration of practice against the Standards
  - Carry out an interview with the candidate.

The written assignments/tasks and the portfolio of evidence

We suggest that in order to make your evidence as thorough as possible, you consider the following:

- Produce comprehensive texts that refer to *current* policy, documentation and child development theory

- Remember the importance of showing underpinning knowledge and understanding at all times

- Make sure that you have *sufficient* evidence– each Standard has to be evidenced in at least two different sources

- Be succinct and specific

- Be clear and focused

- Make time to plan and produce the required evidence, and ensure that you have sought some time for feedback from your mentor on this point

- Explain *why* an activity or intervention took place and *how* leadership was accomplished, don't just produce 'what I did' accounts. In particular make sure you properly evaluate and reflect on the activity at the end of your account rather than making vague claims that 'it went well'!

- Consider as early as possible who might be useful witnesses, and discuss this with your mentor. If you do have work placement provided for your EYPS training needs, it would be a very good idea to aim to secure at least one witness from each placement if possible

- Think about and collect supporting evidence as you go along, don't wait until validation looms large!

- Aim to demonstrate a good balance of personal practice across your documentary and written evidence, and consider how you might plan the observation or practice to cover any gaps that might be present in the written/printed materials you are presenting.

- Make sure that you adhere to the deadlines and word counts that you are set. Successfully meeting deadlines is nearly the first test of leadership ability!

- Talk about 'I' not 'we'. Some Early Years Practitioners find this difficult as they are used to thinking about their practice as being part of a team. While this is of course vital to demonstrating EYPS competence, the assessor will be seeking to understand what you personally contribute to the processes within the setting in which you undertake your validation. In this instance, do remember that while there is no 'I' in team, there is a 'me'!

- Make sure you are very clear about age ranges (follow the EYFS here) and how you make activities age-appropriate – refer back to child development theory to support your accounts here

- Make substantial use of a reflective log, as the source material for constructing your reflections as outlined in Chapter 1.

The documentary evidence you provide should reflect your everyday professional activities. The evidence should be numbered clearly and be easily accessible to the assessor who has very limited time to scrutinise this. The portfolio of documentary evidence should be securely kept for six months after the validation visit, in the very rare possibility that some type of further check is needed.

The following is an example of what might be included in the portfolio of evidence (or 'document file') by an experienced practitioner. This includes examples of a number of policies and procedures, which it was the candidate's responsibility to evidence she had drafted and written. The Candidate's role in the production of materials used in the document file should be very clear: always remember *you* are the one being validated, *not* your setting.

D	Primary Source of Documentary Evidence
D1	Witness testimony from parent - settling a new child
D2	Witness testimony from supervisor - leading and supporting others in the use of outdoor play
D3	Witness testimony from colleague - delivery of training session on outdoor play and child development theory
D4	Outdoor play policy - explanation of the role of the adult handout in training session
D5	Example of planning sheet being piloted for wider use
D6	Example of handout on number, reasoning and problem solving developed by candidate for staff training session
D7	Investigation by candidate and colleagues into complaint (Ofsted format) copy to parents who made a complaint about a biting incident
D8	Letter to parents re: biting incident

D	Primary Source of Documentary Evidence
D9	Observation of behaviour – follow-up to biting incident
D10	Behaviour Management Policy – outline of expected behaviour – revised by candidate
D11	Inclusion Policy revised by candidate – explains roles and responsibilities of different people inside and outside the setting
D12	Quarterly Parents' Newsletter with own contribution highlighted
D13	Action plan following from audit of provision and resources by candidate
D14	Example of planning sheet for the new EYFS
D15	Admission forms – settling in procedures revised by candidate
D16	Play, Care and Learning statement – role of key worker explored and revised by candidate
D17	Planning and assessment procedures for two-year check – own contribution highlighted
D18	Example of personalised learning managed by candidate
D19	Example of language assessment records completed by candidate
D20	Anti-discriminatory practice statement originated by candidate
D21	Policy on Nutrition and Food – importance of social and nutritional aspects originated by candidate
D22	Safeguarding Children Policy updated by candidate
D23	Training session notes – led staff development session on the use of descriptive praise

Reflection *Can you see where this candidate might have opportunities for seeking additional witness statements? For example, consider D23, training session notes, and the documents relating to a biting incident.*

Most entry pathway candidates would not be expected to practise such wide-ranging evidence; some helpful suggestions for inclusion of particular documents in their portfolio of evidence could be:

- Assessment records
- Plans
- Minutes of meetings
- Reports
- Case studies
- Observation notes
- Notes from parents and carers
- Memos from staff and other professionals
- Audits of resources
- Feedback reports from mentors who may have completed direct observation of the candidate's personal practice and/or leadership and support of other practitioners.
- Always remember to highlight the candidate's own role, of course.

While it is highly unlikely that candidates will be permitted to include detailed written assignments completed for academic modules taken alongside the EYPS training pathway, it may well be useful to include documentary evidence that reflects any impact of such assignment activities on the setting (for example from an action research project – see the example of Jim's research project in Chapter 9), as this can help a GEP/UEP candidate to add depth and a wider context to their documentary evidence.

Preparing for the setting visit

The needs of the setting

Remember the visit can only take place with the consent and good will of the staff in the setting and they need to be kept informed about what is happening. The 'tour' section of the visit can only take place when the setting is in operation and the candidate needs to think ahead and ensure it is carried out with courtesy and consideration for all. This is particularly important if you are on placement in the setting in which you are undertaking your validation. If you are a paid member of staff, you must make sure you are supernumary (not counted in the numbers of adults in the setting) during the day of the validation. The date of the setting visit is set by the training provider centre from a schedule used across the relevant EYPS consortium and may be somewhat inflexible; however, again it is the candidate's responsibility to communicate any major concerns or issues that may arise with regard to dates or times, and if communicated in good time, a compromise is nearly always achievable.

The needs of the assessor

A quiet, private space is needed by the assessor to carry out the interviews and scrutiny of documents and to be able to undertake the necessary periods of reflection and recording. It is the candidate's responsibility to make the best possible arrangements within the relevant premises. This can be challenging for some small, compact settings and requires forethought, planning and liaising with management. We remember one unfortunate candidate who had not considered this until the last minute suggesting the assessor go in and out to her car for the required writing up and reflection time! Fortunately, space was eventually negotiated in an adjacent building; however, this type of mix-up can give the assessor a very poor first impression, and unnerve the candidate from the very beginning of the process. Candidates must always remember that the conduct of the day is *their* responsibility, not the responsibility of the setting management, the assessor, or the training provider. Making competent arrangements for the conduct of the validation visit is one of the very first pieces of evidence of leadership capability that the assessor will be looking for – so do make sure that you do not fall at the first hurdle in this respect!

The tour

Every tour will be as different as the settings in which they are undertaken, so it is impossible for us to give comprehensive advice here, but we offer a few 'tips' based on our previous experience:

- Make sure you are careful to explain things that you may normally take for granted. For example, the assessor may have no knowledge of the local geography, so for example, when asked if a child has travelled far to the setting saying 'Well, he comes from the Greenwood Estate' is not very helpful! Try (as Piaget describes) to 'decentre' to the assessor's position as an interested stranger to the setting environment.

- Do also give the assessor time to ask questions and to make brief notes as you are walking around.

- As far as possible, allow the assessor to move through the tour at a speed of their choice. One of us remembers a candidate getting increasingly fraught towards the end of a tour; it turned out this was because she had only arranged cover for the exact amount of time stipulated for the tour on the visit schedule!

The observation of practice

It is likely that your training provider will require you to produce a brief plan for your observed activity prior to the assessor visit; it may then be expected that you produce a more detailed plan 'on the day'. Whatever documentation you are asked for, remember to produce one copy for yourself and one copy for the assessor. Most teachers (including both the authors of this chapter) have at some point in their career found themselves having to give the one and only copy of their lesson plan in their possession to their observer, while desperately hoping that they will be able to remember what they had planned to do . . . so do make sure that this does not happen to you when it comes to your validation observation!

The concept of 'activity' can be quite widely interpreted; for example, it could relate to an adult-initiated activity with a small group of children or an interaction with children accessing an area of continuous provision that you have set up. You should discuss this with your mentor to ensure that what you have in mind will be broadly what is expected by your training provider. It is quite possible that there may be room for negotiation on this, particularly bearing in mind the moment-to-moment flexibility required of practitioners in the Early Years environment, but this presumes that you do not leave creating the plans required by your training provider until the last possible moment! It is also quite possible that your provider will allow you to structure your plans in your setting's 'house-style' – again, it is your responsibility to access the information to ensure what is required, and ask further questions if you wish for further clarification.

Whatever 'activity' you plan, it must give you the opportunity to demonstrate your direct work with children – for example, it should not be an information session for staff and parents.

The assessor should ideally be given some opportunity to observe interactions with both children and fellow practitioners beyond the formal observation of a specific activity. Remember that they will also be looking for you to demonstrate that you are aware of all the fundamental considerations; e.g., health and safety, risk assessment, inclusion, individual needs. You may be asked for 'pen portraits' of anonymised children in order to evidence standards relating to meeting individual needs. If so, demonstrate that you also understand the need for confidentiality in this respect; for example, make sure the assessor knows that any documents with the children's actual names included will not leave the setting – perhaps by referring to the children by pseudonyms such as 'child A, B, C' etc. on any documents that you submit to the training centre.

Collecting witness testimony

It is very important that the evidence provided in the witness testimonies is clear, concise and obviously relevant to the Standards. Your training provider should give you a witness testimony template that helps to ensure this; you may also have to help witnesses (non-professionals in particular) structure their accounts to fit the template provided, so do leave sufficient time for this! When selecting a witness, you do need to consider what they have to add to your body of evidence. The witnesses' roles should initially provide a clue; for example, parents may be able to provide very useful evidence in relation to Standard 2: *Work directly with children and in partnership with their families to facilitate learning and development* and Standard 6: *Plan provision taking account of the individual needs of every child.* However, you are likely to need a senior practitioner, and ideally an EYP to give evidence for Standard 3: *Safeguard and promote the welfare of children* and Standard 8: *Lead practice and foster a culture of continuous improvement.* You will generally need to work with and support the witness to draft the testimony in the format and style required, particularly those who are not senior Early Years practitioners or teaching staff. If you have any problems with this do seek advice from your mentor at the earliest possible opportunity.

An assessor's perspective

'Verity' has assessed candidates in every assessment period since the national EYPS programme began in 2007. Here are some of her reflections on her experiences

It's a serious occupation, but one that is usually full of the delights and surprises that working with young children can bring. There are occasional moments when you wish it was possible to comment on a particular practice, wanting to extend what is good practice into something excellent. Very occasionally it has been the obverse when certain activities or experiences have been entirely inappropriate or the kind of lazy or bad practice you wish never happened in the care and education of young children. Usually, those occasions are not the fault of the potential EYP, who sometimes has to work in less than ideal situations. The government's hope in establishing the EYPS is to eliminate bad practice and raise the practice of all those responsible for the care and education of young children to the highest levels possible. An aim I'm sure the majority of us involved in Early Years provision all share. The new EYFS statutory framework and practice guidance are evidence of this intent, putting, as it does, the child at its centre. Many settings have now embraced it, and I have seen some laudable attempts to present its principles in a jargon-free way to parents and carers, through the use of colourful displays of children photographed in exciting and challenging experiences, or through the magic of ICT, a video running on a loop, of children 'playing', in the fullest sense of that word.

The best practice has looked with fresh eyes at previous methods of planning, observations and assessments and developed new, user friendly proforma and

➡

---

techniques that reflect the emphasis on the use of formative observations and assessment that track and describe the unique learning journeys of individual children from birth to five years. The children's profiles have been a joy to read with much evidence of shared thinking, open-ended questioning and the children's own words recorded and valued, so accurately demonstrating the stage a particular child has reached in their communication skills. Lesser practice has struggled to move from the previous frameworks and as a result is still fragmented and compartmentalised in its recording procedures and practice.

Over the period of the first EYPS project, 2007–2011, all settings have been faced with the issue of providing more effective outdoor provision, and I have witnessed some outstanding practice where EYP candidates have been at the forefront of inventive and creative uses of outdoor spaces. They have also pushed for changes, some quite radical, in established routines for set 'playtimes', which favour staffing needs rather than the needs of children, or what I call 'weather resistant' attitudes on the part of staff who fail to see the pleasure rain, puddles, wind and snow can have for children, if appropriately dressed.

EYPS candidates, on the whole, have clearly demonstrated a child-centred approach, understanding that children being 'creative' doesn't mean the formation of a production line of the same greetings card, or miles of scrunched up tissue paper pasted onto card cut outs, so 'adulterated' a child doesn't recognise his or her own handiwork. Praise and encouragement given for that first tentative attempt at marks on a paper or in the sand or chalked on the ground outside, has demonstrated some real understanding of how children develop and learn. In the best practice, EYPS candidates have achieved all this, through diplomacy and a real wish to be part of a team of practitioners who strive for excellence. Some settings providing placement experience have welcomed a knowledgeable and informed extra pair of hands, giving the EYPS candidate space and encouragement to trial new ideas. Other settings have stood back and waited, unsure what to expect, while a few have been resistant to the changes the government has initiated. Correspondingly, settings have had varied approaches to my visits. In some, the EYP has been handsomely supported, a room put aside for the assessor to work in quiet, with a table on which to spread considerable amounts of paperwork (there is quite a lot of documentation to consider!). A recent 'room' doubled up as a 'themed' room for parties with piped music accompanying my every thought, another 'space' was found in a 'family room' at a children's centre, with very young curious faces appearing and giggling at intervals. In summer an outside area was found, quiet and secluded until a wind sprung up and the adjoining primary school had its playtime!

Some settings have shown clear evidence of such hard work and effort on the part of staff, not simply for my visit, I hasten to add, and I know any EYP would be supported and be surrounded by good practice. I find it amazing still, after many years in Early Years, that some very unpromising buildings can be transformed with a team will and determination into wonderful 'enabling environments' for children, It obvious from the moment you enter that here young children are trusted and their ideas respected – often the EYPS candidate will have been a longstanding member of staff who had naturally been following the ethos and principles underpinning the EYPS. There are so many examples: A 'kindness tree' where children decided as a group themselves who had done a 'kind' act that day, and deserved a place on the special tree; an EYP's very effective behaviour management strategy; a setting where difference and diversity were totally accepted, in this particular instance, the setting had a young amputee who was quite forgetful. During the tour, I heard several children call out 'Everybody – look for Peter's leg – he's lost it again.' In another setting, children sat down to lunch still in 'role' as a fairy, a doctor and a fireman, showing how flexible rules allow for growth and continuity of play.

I have also witnessed less flexible routines where several energetic 3-year-old boys ran round a room, being constantly told to 'stop it' and it 'wasn't time for play' when a perfectly adequate (and well-resourced) outdoor area was available. Thankfully, the EYPS candidate spoke with the room leader and the children were 'released' into the fresh air. I know from later discussions that the EYP discussed changing the indoor/outdoor access of the room in question. I feel that this example perhaps captures why I feel very hopeful about the future of the EYPS and its impact on Early Years practice and provision. It's about changing attitudes and practices that needed to be reappraised in the light of what we now know about children's learning and development, and it is EYPs who will be the catalysts for such change.

References

The Teaching Agency (2012a) *Updates to assessments, outcomes and moderation*. London: DFE.

The Teaching Agency (2012b) *Handbook for Early Years Professional Status (EYPS) Prime Organisations and Delivery Partners*. London: DFE

The Teaching Agency (2012c) *Guidance to the Standards for the Award of Early Years Professional Status*. London: DFE.

11

Early Years Professionals: in their own words

Pam Jarvis

Introduction

Over the past five years, I have carried out two sets of interviews with Early Years Professionals we have trained, some in the autumn of 2008, nearly two years into the New Labour EYPS programme, and some in the spring of 2012, four months after the commencement of the Coalition Government EYPS programme. The views that they expressed were quite surprisingly similar across the two time periods, and all were broadly positive about their ability to contribute a valuable set of skills to the society that they inhabited. The ideas outlined by the 2008 interviewees made such a deep impression upon me that when Wendy Holland and I were asked to write a chapter on the future of EYPS in the period between the New Labour and Coalition programmes (at a time of concern that EYPS may be lost to deep cuts in public funding) I tried to do justice to such conversations by writing the following:

> It is very easy to make a quick saving on early years when national resources are stretched by leaving families in difficulty to fend for themselves, but several years hence, even greater expenditure is needed to deal with the problems that condemning small children to poverty, poor parenting and broken communities create . . . If we can show children that their community cares for them, then they will be far more likely to grow up to care for their community; to truly embrace David Cameron's concept of 'the Big Society'. The EYP role has been designed to sit at the hub of such communities, and as such, we would urge those with the power to allocate funds to keep faith with the project, particularly within disadvantaged areas, allowing EYPs to blossom into the pivotal task that awaits them in the troubled local communities of post-Thatcherist, post-credit crunch Britain.

> (Jarvis and Holland 2011, p.92)

While it is highly unlikely that the Prime Minister actually read our plea (as much as we might like to flatter ourselves) the Early Years programme that eventually emerged from the Coalition Government was very much aimed in this general direction, with Cameron proposing that early intervention initiatives led by graduates was to be a key plank of this government's policy for children and families, including the offer of 15 free hours of childcare and education for the nation's most disadvantaged 2-year-olds through the Early Years Intervention Grant (DFE 2012, online).

One of my 2008 interviewees also correctly predicted this trajectory:

(We) need the right people in place (working with) the under 5s, who understand we need self-confident self-starters, children with a good self-esteem . . . (it's) not just the transition to school . . . Hopefully they'll stand up in the gun cultures that they then might be living in, and hopefully they'll have the confidence to say 'I know what the right path is'. You see a lot of young people that, they're led into these things; if we can give them a bit more freedom to speak up, have that confidence, have that self-esteem, foster that independence. [Children] need a good set of ethics and that doesn't come about from sitting down and doing worksheets, it comes about from fostering independence, improving self-esteem, self-worth [and] problem solving.

The interviews generated several generic themes across the set as a whole (undertaken with four participants in 2008 and three participants in 2012), some of which had a clear 'flavour' from the particular time period, and others which were very similar overall.

What benefits did EYPs feel they got from achieving Early Years Professional Status?

The ability to reflect

2008: I do think that it does help you to properly examine your own skills . . . that . . . doesn't come up earlier on in your education in childcare, so I think it was a really valuable skill to take back, and I think having done the EYP process now, I do engage in reflective practice a lot more; from the business perspective I think the nursery went through some period of improvement, so that was good.

2008: By having that theory of development behind you, and the knowledge, I think you understand more and you appreciate things, why things happen . . . The EYP and BA help build that knowledge for you.

2008: It really made you look at what you were doing and see why you were doing it . . . you do need the theory to back up the practical; I mean you need to be able to know and to justify, to explain why you're doing.

2008: I think the thing is that as an Early Years Practitioner, you look very holistically at children and then the development is a huge part of that, it's a massive part of that, but you're looking very holistically at the whole picture.

2012: I got greater insight; EYPS and the BA changed my practice. But I am still in the same job for the same money!

A confidence boost

2008: (Achieving EYPS) is a confidence boost . . . [Also] there's been a business impact, in that every prospective customer who has come to us since I've got EYPS has signed up with us, so it's quite a marketing tool if you like. You feel like you've got more authority to say the sort of thing that you're saying; it gives you that bit more credence; it gives you that level of authority.

2012: It gave me a formal status, and that gave me the confidence to lead – to show people how to improve their practice and reflection; I think I got better at 'opening people's minds'!

Career development

2008: I've benefited because I have been able to become a mentor and to work with a lot of candidates, which is really stimulating.

2012: There's a job opportunity opening up at work in the near future – I wouldn't have been eligible for it without EYPS. But I am worried that they will give me the role, but not anything like the pay that the person who is leaving got.

2012: I'm not sure. I do get concerned about being a 'cheap alternative' (to QTS). I did it because it is the next step, help with getting my first job. But I might use it as a route into teaching in the end.

What impact do you think EYPs might have upon society?

2008: We've got to get children's centres established; we've got to get multi-agency working, really working; you know we've really got to be working to-gether. I do think hopefully all the edges will be blurred; there will be crossover and you will get people, for example, who might be on such as a health support team who could perhaps go and do some stuff down at the nursery . . . which has got to benefit the children if [we] have got more knowledge in different aspects.

2008: My children's centre – we're supposed to support a specific demographic area. The people who know about the children's centre services are actually coming forward but those people who don't, and the outreach workers . . . if they're not getting the statistics of who's being born into which area, who's moving to this area, what's changing, if we don't get that information and work in partnership with everyone, with each other, then those people are going to fall deeper and deeper into [poverty].

2008: The working with parents would be essential wouldn't it, in children's centres, 'cause that's the main thing. This whole idea of the parents' voices being heard and shaping services so as children's centres become established if they're really doing that well, then the working with parents will be an absolutely key part of it. Recently we've had more and more mums, young mums funnily enough, 17-year-olds 18-year-olds wanting to do the baby massage and the baby yoga. What is happening slowly is the conversations are not about who's fallen out on the estate, although you do get a little bit of that. Conversations are about the children when the children are playing, parents are saying 'Oh well I've never noticed he did that before' and, you know, just this idea of talking about the children, the children are what we're here for. We are [also] here for the parents and support how they make their social network . . . We give the community a chance to be a community instead of just a word. So they know each other, know your neighbours; in the local community outside those doors there.

2008: [The government] need to put more money into outreach and family support; there's a lot of funding posts out there that'll end in 2010. The other day this lady . . . she's in floods of tears because she couldn't thank me enough for the support I'd given her and for her children being in the children's centre. Her partner had left her, she was just completely all alone. You know it's a wonderful place to be in a children's centre [but] the money does need to continue . . . Children's centres are heavily subsidised; if they're not subsidised, the children's centre is not going to be sustainable.

2012: Children's centres – I love them. But I think the current cuts and privatisation are a huge problem.

2012: I worked in a children's centre on placement (*this interviewee had paid employment in a nursery attached to a private school*). It opened up new ideas for me with respect to working with the full range of age groups and working more closely with families.

2012: I am increasingly concerned with the narrowing of focus on to disadvantaged families and younger and younger children. I understand the reasons for the 2-year-old offer, but is this going to end up with the expectation that practitioners do the parenting? We have to consider what we actually *want*, given the way that practice is being structured here.

Possible futures for EYPs

2008: Some children's centres have put out ads specifically looking for EYPs . . . And I thought to myself, you know, fantastic, and people are recognising that EYPs have got something good to offer. On top of that I know that there is a union set up now as well (ASPECT, see http://www.aspect.org.uk/about/eyp/) and there's lobbying that will proactively look at pay and conditions and terms for EYPs.

2012: I'm very disappointed that both governments that have offered EYPS training have failed to 'write in' EYPS when it comes to Early Years planning and policy documents that do not specifically relate to EYPS training. For example, now as the CWDC closes and the Teaching Agency takes up responsibility for EYPS, it is almost impossible to find reference to EYPS on their website at the moment; and the Nutbrown Review (2012) was very discouraging.

Conclusion

The message from this small group of EYPs is generally positive, despite some understandable misgivings, which seem to have increased alongside the growing emphasis upon national (and international) austerity over the period in which these interviews were undertaken. As a researcher with a keen interest in the developmental processes of children of all ages, and the policies that underpin societies' support of children and families, I was particularly interested in the key societal role that these EYPs envisioned for children's centres, not only in caring for children in the present, but playing a major role in the development of whole local communities for the future. This again seemed rather more muted in 2012, with some misgivings about possibly divisive policies that might put EYPs into a 'professionalised parenting' role, possibly in competition with parents, which did not match the 'potential agent of community cohesion' vividly described by two of those who were interviewed in 2008.

I was also very interested in an expressed frustration that again seemed to increase between the two time periods, relating to a concern that EYP expertise was being sidelined by a lack of recognition of the unique specialist training for practice with babies and very young children that underpins the status. This aspect, I felt, led to the suggestion from one 2012 interviewee that she might simply use EYPS as a stepping stone into teacher training if she failed to get the commensurate recognition for her professional status. This issue was raised, although not particularly helpfully, in the 2012 Nutbrown Interim Review of Early Education and Childcare Qualifications:

The Early Years Professional Status (EYPS) is acknowledged to equip people to make a positive difference to babies and young children. But there are also concerns as to whether all those with EYPS are being effectively deployed, that often they move away from working with the youngest children, and some seek employment opportunities outside of settings or even the early years sector. Issues of parity with Qualified Teacher Status (QTS) have also been raised, both in terms of rigour of status, and in terms of job opportunities and responsibilities. Alongside this, positive comments have been made about the impact those with QTS can have, along with a call by some to introduce some form of Initial

Teacher Education (ITE) route for working in the early years, building on the successes of EYPS, to sit alongside or replace it.

(Nutbrown 2012, pp.9–10)

This really raises even more difficult questions, without providing any satisfactory answers. At time of writing (spring 2012) we await the final report on this review.

However, the same point was previously explored by UNICEF, but this time with an international perspective:

[UNICEF] Benchmark 6 reinforces the training dimension of 'high quality care' by stipulating that a minimum of 50 percent of staff in early education centres . . . should have a minimum of three years tertiary education, with specialist qualifications in early childhood studies or a related field. This benchmark has had to be interpreted somewhat liberally in order to admit countries such as France, Ireland, and the United Kingdom, where a primary school teaching qualification, with no special training in the developmental needs of pre-school children, is all that is required.

(UNICEF Child Care Transition report 2008, pp.25–6)

In this forum at least then, the specific expertise of the EYP should have a clear potential to get the professional recognition that it deserves.

While conditions in the national environment may remain challenging for the foreseeable future, it is clear that EYPs potentially have a crucial role to play, not only in improving the immediate lives of young children and their families, but in optimising children's opportunities across the whole developmental period, and to regenerate the communities in which they live – whether or not the current government in power is able to recognise and/or fully capitalise upon such promise.

It cannot be stressed too strongly that government funding spent on training and wages for Early Years practitioners is likely to result in a net *saving* for society. The High/Scope Perry Pre-School study estimated that the saving to society from a similar project undertaken in the US (Headstart) involving the establishment of children's centres with the brief to offer non-judgemental support to disadvantaged families and young children during the early 1960s was, by the early 2000s: '$258,888 per participant, on an investment of $15,166 per participant – $17.07 per dollar invested' (Schweinhart *et al.* 2005, pp.xvi–xvii).

The programme in question was initially labelled a failure when it failed to significantly raise childrens' IQs at school entry, but from the point at which the children became adolescent the positive results began to emerge, and kept on going. In mid-adolescence, the project children were significantly less likely to be in trouble with the law, and the girls were significantly less likely to experience teenage pregnancy. As the project participants emerged into early adulthood, it was found that they were significantly more likely to form stable families, and to be in regular employment. The study continues, and it will be interesting to find out whether the effects continue into subsequent generations of these families. It seemed that these children were shown in infancy that their society placed some value upon them, so they grew up to respect the conventions of society: a Bronfenbrennerian take on Bowlby's 'Internal Working Model'.

If, in the light of this information, you return to the EYP's reflection which opens this chapter, you will see what an important profession you are seeking to join, not only in its potential benefits for young children and their families, but for the nation as a whole. We wish you well as you complete your Early Years Professional Status and emerge into a world which, regardless of the recognition (or not) of transient governments with limited five-year agendas, will always need your skills, vocational dedication and enthusiasm.

Further reading

Schweinhart, L., Montie, J., Xiang, Z., Barnett, W.S., Belfield, C. and Nores, M. (2005) *Lifetime Effects: The High/Scope Perry Preschool Study Through Age 40.* Yipsilanti, MI: High/Scope Press.

Shonkoff, J. and Phillips, D. (2000) *From Neurons to Neighborhoods.* Washington, DC: National Academy Press.

UNICEF (2008) *The Child Care Transition: A league table of early childhood education and care in economically advanced countries. Available at:* http://www.unicef-irc.org/publications/pdf/rc8_eng.pdf.

References

CWDC (2011) *Handbook for Early Years Professional Status (EYPS) Prime Organisations and their Delivery Partners.* Leeds: CWDC.

DFE (2012) *Early intervention grant and free early education places for disadvantaged two-year-olds FAQs.* Available at: http://www.education.gov.uk/childrenandyoungpeople/ earlylearningandchildcare/delivery/free%20entitlement%20to%20early%20education/ a0070230/eigel. Accessed on 18 April 2012.

Jarvis, P. and Holland, W. (2011) 'The Early Years Professional and the children's centre: At the hub of the "Big Society"?', in A. Book and C. Rankin (eds) *Making it Work for the Child: Professionalism for the Early Years Interdisciplinary Team.* London: Continuum, pp.79–92.

Nutbrown, C. (2012) *Review of Early Education and Childcare Qualifications: Interim report.* Available at: https://www.education.gov.uk/publications/eOrderingDownload/Review%20of%20 early%20education%20and%20childcare%20qualifications%20-%20Interim%20report.pdf. Accessed 18 April 2012.

Schweinhart, L., Montie, J., Xiang, Z., Barnett, W.S., Belfield, C. and Nores, M. (2005) *Lifetime Effects: The High/Scope Perry Preschool Study Through Age 40.* Yipsilanti MI: High/Scope Press.

UNICEF (2008) *The Child Care Transition: A league table of early childhood education and care in economically advanced countries.* Available at: http://www.unicef-irc.org/publications/pdf/ rc8_eng.pdf. Accessed 18 April 2012.

Index